MILL'S *ON LIBERTY*

John Stuart Mill's essay *On Liberty*, published in 1859, has had a powerful impact on philosophical and political debates ever since its first appearance. This volume of newly commissioned essays covers the whole range of problems raised in and by the essay, including the concept of liberty, the toleration of diversity, freedom of expression, the value of allowing "experiments in living," the basis of individual liberty, multiculturalism, and the claims of minority cultural groups. Mill's views have been fiercely contested, and they are at the center of many contemporary debates. The essays are by leading scholars, who systematically and eloquently explore Mill's views from various perspectives. The volume will appeal to a wide range of readers including those interested in political philosophy and the history of ideas.

C. L. TEN is Professor of Philosophy at the National University of Singapore. His publications include *Was Mill a Liberal?* (2004) and *Multiculturalism and the Value of Diversity* (2004).

CAMBRIDGE CRITICAL GUIDES

Volumes published in the series thus far:

Hegel's *Phenomenology of Spirit*
EDITED BY DEAN MOYAR AND MICHAEL QUANTE

Mill's *On Liberty*
EDITED BY C. L. TEN

MILL'S
On Liberty
A Critical Guide

EDITED BY

C. L. TEN
National University of Singapore

CAMBRIDGE UNIVERSITY PRESS
Cambridge, New York, Melbourne, Madrid, Cape Town, Singapore, São Paulo, Delhi

Cambridge University Press
The Edinburgh Building, Cambridge CB2 8RU, UK

Published in the United States of America by Cambridge University Press, New York

www.cambridge.org
Information on this title: www.cambridge.org/9780521873567

First published 2008

Printed in the United Kingdom at the University Press, Cambridge

A catalogue record for this publication is available from the British Library

Library of Congress Cataloguing in Publication data
Mill's On liberty : a critical guide / edited by C. L. Ten.
p.   cm. – (Cambridge critical guides)
Includes bibliographical references.
ISBN 978-0-521-87356-7
1. Mill, John Stuart, 1806–1873. On liberty. 2. Liberty. I. Ten, C. L. II. Title. III. Series.
JC585.M75M55   2008
323.44–dc22
2008040780

ISBN 978-0-521-87356-7 hardback

Contents

Contributors

ROBERT AMDUR teaches in the Department of Political Science and the American Studies Program at Columbia University. His main areas of interest are political philosophy and American constitutional law. He is the author of articles about Rawls, compensatory justice, and freedom of speech.

DAVID O. BRINK is Professor of Philosophy at the University of California, San Diego, and Co-Director of the Institute of Law and Philosophy at the University of San Diego Law School. He is the author of *Moral Realism and the Foundations of Ethics* (1989) and *Perfectionism and the Common Good: Themes in the Philosophy of T. H. Green* (2003), as well as articles in ethical theory, history of ethics, political philosophy, and jurisprudence.

JUSTINE BURLEY is Associate Professor in the Department of Philosophy at the National University of Singapore (NUS), and Deputy Executive Director of the Graduate School for Integrative Sciences and Engineering. She has published in both science and philosophy journals, and has edited several volumes, including *Ronald Dworkin and His Critics* (2004).

WENDY DONNER is Professor of Philosophy at Carleton University, Ottawa, Canada. She is the author of *The Liberal Self: John Stuart Mill's Moral and Political Philosophy* (1991), as well as articles and chapters of books on Mill, including "John Stuart Mill's Liberal Feminism" in *Philosophical Studies* (1993), "Mill's Utilitarianism" in *The Cambridge Companion to Mill* (1997), "Mill's Theory of Value" in *The Blackwell Guide to Mill's Utilitarianism* (2006), and "John Stuart Mill on Education and Democracy" in *J. S. Mill's Political Thought: A Bicentennial Reassessment* (2007). She is currently writing a book on Mill (co-authored with Richard Fumerton) for the Blackwell *Great Minds* series. She has also published articles on environmental ethics, feminist ethics, and Buddhist ethics.

GERALD F. GAUS is James E. Rogers Professor of Philosophy at the University of Arizona. Among his books are *Value and Justification* (1990), *Justificatory Liberalism* (1996), and *Contemporary Theories of Liberalism* (2003). Along with Jonathan Riley, he is a founding editor of *Politics, Philosophy and Economics*. He is currently writing books on *The Order of Public Reason*, and, with Julian Lamont, *Economic Justice*.

FRANK LOVETT is an Assistant Professor of Political Science at Washington University in St. Louis. His primary research concerns the role of freedom and domination in developing theories of justice, equality, and the rule of law.

JONATHAN RILEY is Professor of Philosophy and Political Economy, Tulane University. He has published extensively on various topics in philosophy, politics, and economics, including John Stuart Mill's utilitarian liberalism. He is a founding editor of the journal *Politics, Philosophy and Economics*. His most recent book is *Radical Liberalism* (forthcoming).

C. L. TEN is Professor of Philosophy at the National University of Singapore. He is the author of *Mill on Liberty* (1980), *Crime, Guilt, and Punishment* (1987), and four volumes of essays, *A Conception of Toleration, The Soundest Theory of Law, Was Mill a Liberal?*, and *Multiculturalism and the Value of Diversity*, which appeared in 2004.

JEREMY WALDRON is University Professor in the New York University Law School. He gave the Seeley Lectures which were published as *The Dignity of Legislation* (1999). He is the author of many other books and papers, including *God, Locke, and Equality* (2002), *Law and Disagreement* (1999), and *Liberal Rights: Collected Papers 1981–1991* (1993).

HENRY R. WEST is Professor of Philosophy at Macalester College, USA. He is the author of *An Introduction to Mill's Utilitarian Ethics* (2004), and *Mill's Utilitarianism: A Reader's Guide* (forthcoming), and the editor of *The Blackwell Guide to Mill's Utilitarianism* (2006).

ROBERT YOUNG is affiliated with the Programme in Philosophy at La Trobe University, Australia. His most recent book, *Medically Assisted Death*, was published in 2007.

Mill's On Liberty: *Introduction*

C. L. Ten

FREE EXPRESSION AND INDIVIDUALITY

In a letter to his wife, Harriet, of January 15, 1855, Mill discussed the urgency of writing an essay on liberty. He claims that "opinion tends to encroach more and more on liberty, and almost all projects of social reformers are really *liberticide* – Comte, particularly so."[1] *On Liberty* was published in 1859, the year after Harriet's death, and it carried a lavish dedication to her. Mill believed that the essay was "likely to survive longer than anything else that I have written (with the possible exception of the *Logic*)."[2] *On Liberty* has not only survived, but it has also been the center of much discussion, most of it rather hostile. It has done so precisely because the tendency towards *liberticide*, to which Mill had alluded, remains a constant threat to individual liberty, as Mill conceived and cherished it.

But what is the nature of the liberty that Mill wanted to defend, and what are the sources of danger to it? First, Mill is very clear that the real danger to liberty comes from "a social tyranny," which is greater than any kind of political oppression because "it leaves fewer means of escape, penetrating more deeply into the details of life, and enslaving the soul itself" (*CW* XVIII, 220 [1, 5]).[3] He sees this tyranny as encroaching on both opinions and

---

[1] *The Later Letters of John Stuart Mill (1849–1873)*, vols. XIV–XVII of *The Collected Works of John Stuart Mill*, ed. Francis E. Mineka and Dwight N. Lindley (Toronto: University of Toronto Press; London: Routledge & Kegan Paul, 1972), vol. XIV, 294, Mill's emphasis.

    Throughout the present volume, references to Mill's works are given by volume and page(s) to *The Collected Works of John Stuart Mill*, 33 vols., gen. ed. John M. Robson (Toronto: University of Toronto Press; London: Routledge & Kegan Paul, 1963–91), abbreviated as *CW*; and, where appropriate, to the chapter and paragraph number(s) of the relevant work.

[2] John Stuart Mill, *Autobiography* (1873), in *The Collected Works of John Stuart Mill*, vol. I: *Autobiography and Literary Essays*, ed. John M. Robson and Jack Stillinger, introduction by Lord Robbins (Toronto: University of Toronto Press; London: Routledge & Kegan Paul, 1981), 259.

[3] Throughout this volume, references to *On Liberty* are to *The Collected Works of John Stuart Mill*, vol. XVIII: *Essays on Politics and Society*, Part I, ed. John M. Robson, introduction by Alexander Brady (Toronto: University of Toronto Press; London: Routledge & Kegan Paul, 1977), 213–310, giving the page number(s) and the chapter and paragraph number(s).

conduct, and thereby preventing the development of genuine individuality. The liberty he values therefore includes liberty of thought and discussion, and liberty of conduct. Both are required for the flourishing of individuality. As he notes, "there needs protection also against the tyranny of the prevailing opinion and feeling; against the tendency of society to impose, by means other than civil penalties, its own ideas and practices as rules of conduct on those who dissent from them" (*CW* XVIII, 220 [I, 5]).

But Mill realizes that, as important as it is to nurture and protect individuality against the tyranny of ideas and practices, no form of civilized life is possible without the enforcement of some restraints on conduct. Thus if people could freely harm one another, then there would be no security, without which, as Mill points out in *Utilitarianism*, we would not be able to achieve anything of value, apart from instant gratification (*CW* X, 251 [v, 25]). So the problem is to establish a proper balance between "individual independence and social control" (*CW* XVIII, 220 [I, 6]).

Mill identifies three areas which constitute "the appropriate region of individual liberty":

It comprises, first, the inward domain of consciousness; demanding liberty of conscience in the most comprehensive sense; liberty of thought and feeling; absolute freedom of opinion and sentiment on all subjects, practical or speculative, scientific, moral, or theological. The liberty of expressing and publishing opinions may seem to fall under a different principle, since it belongs to that part of the conduct of an individual which concerns other people, but, being almost of as much importance as the liberty of thought itself, and resting in great part on the same reasons, is practically inseparable from it. Secondly, the principle requires liberty of tastes of pursuits; of framing the plan of our life to suit our own character; of doing as we like, subject to such consequences as may follow: without impediment from our fellow-creatures, so long as what we do does not harm them, even though they should think our conduct foolish, perverse, or wrong. Thirdly, from this liberty of each individual, follows the liberty, within the same limits, of combination among individuals; freedom to unite, for any purpose not involving harm to others: the persons combining being supposed to be of full age, and not forced or deceived. (*CW* XVIII, 225–6 [I, 12])

He then summarizes his view: "The only freedom which deserves the name, is that of pursuing our own good in our own way, so long as we do not deprive others of theirs, or impede their efforts to obtain it" (*CW* XVIII, 226 [I, 13]). This shows how closely he sees the connection between liberty and individuality. Without securing "the appropriate region of individual liberty," persons will lack individuality in that they are unable to form independent beliefs about the shape they want their own lives to take, nor are they able to lead their lives in accordance with their own conception of what a good life for them should be. Mill then proceeds to give a detailed defense of liberty of thought and discussion, and of the ideal of individuality that such liberty ultimately serves. But as the defense is intended to persuade the general public, many of whom do not as yet share his deep convictions about the value of individuality, the defense has to be broad-based. It has to show not just the intrinsic value of individuality, but also its various instrumental values.

Thus Mill first defends the freedom to express opinions, all opinions no matter what their content or intrinsic nature, on the ground that we would all be losers by their being silenced. The argument rests on the value of truth. He points out that if the suppressed opinion is true, then we would have lost the opportunity of replacing the error of our received opinion with the truth of the silenced opinion. On the other hand, if the suppressed opinion is false, we would lose the benefit of having "the clearer perception and livelier impression of truth, produced by its collision with error" (*CW* xviii, 229 [ii, 1]). But in the end what is really at stake is a certain relationship between individuals and the opinions which they hold, whether or not these opinions are true in some impersonal sense. Thus Mill elaborates on the possibility that the suppressed opinion may be true by maintaining that those who seek to suppress an opinion they believe to be false "have no authority to decide the question for all mankind, and exclude every other person from the means of judging" (*CW* xviii, 229 [ii, 3]). Here the argument has shifted from the likelihood of the opinion being true or false, to the claim that every person should be able to judge for himself or herself the truth or falsity of an opinion. However, this claim is not accurately put, as Mill does, by asserting that "All silencing of discussion is an assumption of infallibility" (*CW* xviii, 229 [ii, 3]). For those who suppress an opinion need not even claim that the opinion is false. Opinions may be suppressed because it is feared, but not known, that it might be true, or partly true, or because, true or false, it is deemed to be offensive, or politically or socially incorrect, or just inappropriate for the occasion. When Mill explains further what he means by "an assumption of infallibility," his emphasis is not on the truth as such of a suppressed opinion, but on the importance of allowing each person to decide for himself or herself what opinions to hold. He asserts, "It is the undertaking to decide that question *for others*, without allowing them to hear what can be said on the contrary side" (*CW* xviii, 234 [ii, 11], Mill's emphasis).

In fact Mill is not only claiming that each person should be allowed to form his or her own opinions, rather than have them imposed by others. He also wants to depict the basis on which we should or should not make our own judgments, or form our own opinions. We should be open to "facts and arguments." Our minds should be open to criticisms of our opinions and conduct, and we should "listen to all that could be said against" us (*CW* xviii, 232 [ii, 7]). He does not clearly distinguish between the conditions which in fact make us confident of the truth or reliability of our opinions, and the conditions which justify us in having such confidence. But it is the latter normative claim that he is most concerned to defend. He believes that we should not be confident about the truth of our opinions unless there is complete freedom to challenge it, and it remains unrefuted. As he puts it,

The beliefs which we have most warrant for, have no safeguard to rest on, but a standing invitation to the whole world to prove them unfounded ... if the lists are kept open, we may hope that if there is a better truth, it will be found when the human mind is capable of receiving it; and in the meantime we may rely on having attained such approach to truth as is possible in our day. This is the amount of certainty attainable by a fallible being, and this is the sole way of attaining it. (*CW* xviii, 232 [ii, 8])

If his argument has anything to do with the truth, it is evident that he is not so much concerned about whether freedom of expression will lead to the discovery of true beliefs, and all the individual and social benefits which such discoveries would bring. Rather, he is more interested in the manner in which people hold their beliefs, whether true or false. For him there is no great value in merely having a true opinion, if one does not know the meaning and the grounds of that opinion. A person can acquire a true opinion by simply relying on authority, without having any ability to "make a tenable defence of it against the most superficial objections." A true belief could be held like "a prejudice, a belief independent of, and proof against, argument." Mill rejects such an approach to the acquisition of true beliefs: "this is not the way in which truth ought to be held by a rational being. This is not knowing the truth. Truth, thus held, is but one superstition the more, accidentally clinging to the words which enunciate a truth" (*CW* xviii, 244 [ii, 22]).

Mill spends much time in explaining his notion of "knowing the truth." First, he advises us to follow the example of Cicero, whose "forensic success" depends on his studying with great intensity his adversary's case. It is not enough that we should learn about an opposing view, and the arguments and evidence for it, from well-informed people who do not, however, believe in it. We must hear the case against our own beliefs, and in favor of the opposing view, from those who really accept the opposing belief, and who would expound it in its most plausible and persuasive form, and who would raise the greatest difficulties for our views. Without allowing those who wish to challenge our beliefs to speak their minds, we can have no "rational assurance" that all objections to those beliefs can be adequately answered.

For Mill, therefore, the connection between freedom of expression and knowing the truth is not one of means to end. Those who seek to know the truth will not only want to judge for themselves which opinions are true or false, but they will also seek to understand the meaning and grounds for these opinions. They will seek a rational assurance for their beliefs, and this requires them to be open to all arguments and evidence for and against these beliefs, especially as these are presented by those committed to the relevant beliefs. Those aspiring to knowledge of the truth would therefore require freedom not only for themselves, but also for all others who may wish to challenge prevailing views, and who wish to decide for themselves the truth or otherwise of an opinion. Mill would concede that even with extensive censorship, it is possible for people to have true opinions, perhaps because they are lucky, or can rely on authority. But they would not know the truth. "Their conclusion may be true, but it might be false for anything they know: they have never thrown themselves into the mental position of those who think differently from them, and consider what such persons may have to say; and consequently they do not, in any proper sense of the word, know the doctrine which they themselves profess" (*CW* xviii, 245 [ii, 23]).

In a footnote to the chapter on liberty of thought and discussion, Mill asserts, "If the arguments of the present chapter are of any validity, there ought to exist the fullest liberty of professing and discussing, as a matter of ethical conviction, any doctrine, however immoral it may be considered" (*CW* xviii, 228 [ii, 1n.]). Mill therefore condemns the imposition of sanctions against those who profess views which society regards as impious and immoral, as Socrates was supposed to have done, or blasphemous, as in the case of Christ (*CW* xviii, 235 [ii, 12–13]). It is only when "the fullest liberty of professing and discussing" any doctrine has been secured that you can have "an intellectually active people." It is in such an atmosphere of freedom that "even persons of the most ordinary intellect" can be raised "to something of the dignity of thinking beings" (*CW* xviii, 243 [ii, 20]). For Mill, intellectual progress cannot be achieved simply by the replacement of false beliefs by true beliefs. The atmosphere of freedom is a crucial part of intellectual progress. Individuals, who have "the dignity of thinking beings," will accept as true only a belief that survives the challenges thrown at it in a free and open society where those holding diverse and conflicting views are encouraged to assert their opinions and debate with one another.

Whatever Mill's personal views may be about the truth of various opinions, such as controversial religious doctrines, his overriding commitment is to free and open discussion. He makes this clear in his example of Christianity, which he treats as the received opinion in his society. Many who regard themselves as Christians do not treat the doctrines of Christianity as living beliefs. Instead, "The sayings of Christ coexist passively in their minds, producing hardly any effect beyond what is caused by mere listening to words so amiable and bland" (*CW* xviii, 249 [ii, 29]).

Freedom of thought and discussion is part of the liberty which Mill sees as necessary for his defense of the right of individuals to form opinions in a rational manner, sensitive to argument and evidence, in pursuit of knowledge of the truth. But individuals also need the liberty to act in accordance with the opinions they have adopted, and Mill takes up the case for liberty of conduct in the chapter on individuality, which immediately follows that on liberty of thought and discussion.

He begins by pointing out that liberty of conduct should not enjoy the absolute non-interference of liberty of thought and discussion. He adds, "even opinions lose their immunity, when the circumstances in which they are expressed are such as to constitute their expression a positive instigation to some mischievous act" (*CW* xviii, 260 [iii, 1]). He gives an illustration with the opinion that corn-dealers are starvers of the poor, or that private property is theft. The opinion may be freely circulated through the press. But the verbal expression of the opinion before an excited mob gathered outside the corn-dealer's house, or the circulation of the opinion on a placard to the angry mob, may be punishable. So it is not the content of the opinion as such, but rather the circumstances of its expression, which determine whether interference is justified. Where the clear intention of the speaker or writer, or the obvious immediate effect of the expression of an opinion, is to instigate people to engage in harmful, illegal acts against others, there would be no hindrance to the quest for knowledge of the truth in prohibiting the expression. Earlier, Mill had imposed even more stringent conditions on the punishment of instigation. In a footnote at the beginning of the chapter on liberty of thought and discussion, he discusses whether it should be permissible to advocate the lawfulness of tyrannicide. He concludes that "the instigation to it, in a specific case, may be a proper subject of punishment, but only if an overt act has followed, and at least a probable connection can be established between the act and the instigation" (*CW* xviii, 228 [ii, 1n.]). Here the requirement is that a harmful, illegal act should have taken place, which can be causally related to the act of instigation, whereas in the corn-dealer example, it is enough that the harm is very likely to result from the instigation. What remains common is Mill's view that no punishment is to be directed at the expression of "any doctrine, however immoral it may be considered." The intrinsic nature and offensiveness of the opinion expressed are not in themselves the reason for punishment.

At the very beginning of the chapter on individuality, Mill asks whether the same reasons for giving freedom to individuals "to form opinions, and to express their opinions without reserve," would also apply to giving them freedom "to act upon their opinions – to carry these out in their lives, without hindrance, either physical or moral, from their fellow-men, so long as it is at their own risk and peril" (*CW* xviii, 260 [iii, i]). Mill's answer is in the affirmative. So we have to see how the central argument in the earlier chapter is duplicated in the case of conduct. We have identified that central argument as the quest for knowledge of the truth, the manner in which one holds on to one's opinions, rather than the mere discovery or holding of true opinions. In the case of conduct, freedom to engage in "experiments in living" can lead to useful discoveries of new and better ways of life. But imposing these superior ways of life on individuals who do not endorse them is not conducive to the development of individuality. Just as individuals must make their own judgments about an opinion, so too they must choose for themselves their plans of life, the kind of life they regard as worthwhile and to which they want to be committed. Part of the reason for this is that it is through the exercise of choice that the human faculties can develop.

The human faculties of perception, judgment, discriminative feeling, mental activity, and even moral preference, are exercised only in making a choice. He who does anything because it is the custom, makes no choice. He gains no practice either in discerning or in desiring what is best. The mental and moral, like the muscular powers, are improved only by being used. The faculties are called into no exercise by doing a thing merely because others do it, no more than by believing a thing only because others believe it. (*CW* xviii, 262 [iii, 3])

This suggests that unreflective dependence on custom, without the exercise of choice, will not serve us well, as it will leave us mired in ways of doing things which have outlived their usefulness when the circumstances of social and individual lives change. Only the regular exercise of choice will give us the capacity to adapt to these circumstances. But while this is certainly a part of what Mill regards as valuable when individuals have freedom to choose, it is not the most crucial part of his defense of choice. He believes that without choice there is a reduction in a person's "comparative worth as a human being."

It really is of importance, not only what men do, but also what manner of men they are that do it. Among the works of man, which human life is rightly employed in perfecting and beautifying, the first in importance surely is man himself. Supposing it were possible to get houses built, corn grown, battles fought, causes tried, and even churches erected and prayers said, by machinery – by automatons in human form – it would be a considerable loss to exchange for these automatons even the men and women who at present inhabit the more civilized parts of the world, and who assuredly are but starved specimens of what nature can and will produce. Human nature is not a machine to be built after a model, and set to do exactly the work prescribed for it, but a tree, which requires to grow and develop itself on all sides, according to the tendency of the inward forces which make it a living thing. (*CW* xviii, 263 [iii, 4])

The passage exactly parallels Mill's emphasis on the importance of not merely having true opinions but also arriving at and holding them in the proper manner, captured in the requirement of knowing the truth. Now, he is arguing that even if it is possible to discover ways of life that are otherwise ideal without exercising choice in accepting them, something of great value would be missing. For choice itself is a vital constitutive element of a worthwhile or valuable human life.

Individuality is a value that can be realized only when each person freely chooses her own plan of life for herself. So while the "highly gifted One or Few" could initiate "wise and noble things," it is not "only persons of decided mental superiority who have a just claim to carry on their lives in their own way." Mill goes on to claim, "If a person possesses any tolerable amount of common sense and experience, his own mode of laying out his existence is the best, not because it is the best in itself, but because it is his own mode" (*CW* xviii, 270 [iii, 14]). Individuality cannot be imposed, and all that "the strong man of genius" can do is to exercise "freedom to point out the way": "The power of compelling others into it is not only inconsistent with the freedom and development of all the rest, but corrupting to the strong man himself" (*CW* xviii, 269 [iii, 13]).

In a footnote, Mill refers to individuality as "the right of each individual to act, in things indifferent, as seems good to his own judgment and inclinations" (*CW* xviii, 271 [iii, 14n.]). This same idea, that the right to individuality is an equal right of all who have "any tolerable amount of common sense and experience," is pervasive in the chapter. There is no conception of individuality as an aggregative goal whose maximum realization can, in appropriate circumstances, require the trading off of the individualities of some for the greater individualities of others. In declaring the nature of his defense of liberty, Mill asserts, "I forgo any advantage which could be derived to my argument from the idea of abstract right, as a thing independent of utility. I regard utility as the ultimate appeal on all ethical questions; but it must be utility in the largest sense, grounded on the permanent interests of man as a progressive being" (*CW* xviii, 224 [i, 11]). It is clear that Mill identifies "utility in the largest sense" with individuality, and individuality is not an ethical ideal that is separate from Mill's rich conception of happiness or pleasure. The highest pleasures are those acquired in the attainment of individuality, involving the exercise of the distinctive human faculties in making a choice for oneself about one's own plan of life. Sometimes Mill refers to these pleasures as the "native pleasures," and the opinions and feelings associated with them as those of "home growth" (*CW* xviii, 265 [iii, 6]). But the right to individuality is the right that *each person* has, and it is an equal right to individuality, which the greater wisdom and competence of others cannot forcibly overrule, although they can, and should, guide and persuade.

Although this right to individuality is central to Mill's defense of individual liberty, his formulation of the object of his essay does not directly invoke the notion of individuality. Instead, it identifies different types of reasons for coercive interference with individual conduct, and declares some of them as absolutely ruled out:

the sole end for which mankind are warranted, individually or collectively, in interfering with the liberty of action of any of their number, is self-protection. That the only purpose for which power can be rightfully exercised over any member of a civilized community, against his will, is to prevent harm to others. His own good, either physical or moral, is not a sufficient warrant. He cannot rightfully be compelled to do or forbear because it will be better for him to do so, because it will make him happier, because, in the opinions of others, to do so would be wise, or even right. (*CW* xviii, 223–4 [i, 9])

The reasons explicitly excluded are of two types – paternalistic and moralistic. The former rules out interference on the grounds that it will be better for the person, or that "it will make him happier." Mill's anti-paternalism is opposed to intervention which overrides the person's own judgment about how he wants his life to run, for such intervention would be a violation of individuality. But Mill does not object to interventions which give effect to, or are at least consistent with, a person's considered judgments, even though they go against his or her current wishes which are encumbered in some way. Thus he thinks it permissible for a public officer, or any other person, who has insufficient time to issue a warning, forcibly to prevent a person from crossing an unsafe bridge. The assumption is that the person "does not desire to fall into the river" (*CW* xviii, 294 [v, 5]). This is of course different from those interventions which are never going to be acknowledged as proper by the intended beneficiary.

The moralistic reasons, that intervention is judged to be "wise, or even right," would also violate the right to individuality because they give overriding effect to the opinions of the intervening party against the views of the person whose conduct is restricted. Consider the case of the legal prohibition of voluntary euthanasia by persons who are suffering from painful terminal illnesses. The prohibition is paternalistic if it is based on the claim that it is not in these people's best interests because cures for their conditions would soon be found. It is moralistic if the reason is, for example, that it is morally wrong to take our own lives because God alone should determine the time of death. On the other hand, if the prohibition is based on a well-established "slippery slope" empirical claim that legally permitting voluntary euthanasia would unleash psychological or sociological forces which would lead to involuntary euthanasia, then this is a non-paternalistic and non-moralistic reason, appealing to harm to others. The prohibition is not then a violation of the right to individuality.

Indeed Mill identifies the prevention of harm to others as the only legitimate ground for coercive interference with the conduct of a person. Obviously, for him an individual's conduct does not harm others simply because it is self-harming, or because it violates what they regard as correct moral standards. So a crucial part of what counts as harm is directly based on his account of the right to individuality. But not all of it is. Thus the right to individuality is the basis of Mill's anti-moralism, and he would not therefore treat the unpleasant feelings or moral distress, as such, elicited by the knowledge that others are acting perversely or wrongly by our moral standards as harm to us. In defending "liberty of tastes and pursuits," he asserts that "our fellow-creatures" should not interfere "so long as what we do does not harm them, even though they should think our conduct foolish, perverse, or wrong." Here harm is clearly contrasted with any unpleasant feelings associated with the thought that the conduct is "foolish, perverse, or wrong." This is one area where he disagrees with the more straightforward hedonism of Bentham, in which every form of pleasure, as such, is intrinsically good, and every form of pain, as such, is intrinsically bad in the calculation of what will maximize overall happiness.

Mill underlines his anti-Benthamite view when he rejects the claim that the outrage to the religious or other feelings of others can be treated as a kind of injury or harm to them:

There are many who consider as an injury to themselves any conduct which they have a distaste for, and resent it as an outrage to their feelings; as a religious bigot, when charged with disregarding the religious feelings of others, has been known to retort that they disregard his feelings, by persisting in their abominable worship or creed. But there is no parity between the feeling of a person for his own opinion, and the feeling of another who is offended at his holding it; no more than between the desire of a thief to take a purse, and the desire of the right owner to keep it. And a person's taste is as much his own peculiar concern as his opinion or his purse. (*CW* xviii, 283 [iv, 12])

Again, Mill argues that the strong disgust, "resembling an instinctive antipathy," which Muslims have toward the eating of pork by Christians, does not count as a reason for prohibiting the practice, even when Muslims are in the majority (*CW* xviii, 284–5 [iv, 14]). The implication is that eating pork does not harm Muslims, even if it arouses in them strong and unpleasant feelings of disgust and hatred.

Some of Mill's other comments indicate that his notion of harm includes elements which have bases independent of his account of individuality. For example, he argues that "A person may cause evil to others not only by his actions but by his inaction, and in either case he is justly accountable to them for the injury" (*CW* xviii, 225 [i, 11]). We may legitimately be compelled to perform "many positive acts for the benefit of others." He gives as an example the bearing of our fair share in the common defense, or in any joint work necessary to the interest of the society from which we have received protection. Although no detailed justification of these "social obligations" is given, they seem to rest on notions of reciprocity and mutual benefit. He refers to bearing our share of labor and sacrifice as being fixed on "some equitable principle" (*CW* xviii, 276 [iv, 3]). There are also other obligations which rest on a different basis, "certain acts of individual beneficence, such as saving a fellow-creature's life, or interposing to protect the defenceless against ill-usage" (*CW* xviii, 225 [i, 11]). The exact bases and limits of the various social obligations to others are matters open to further discussion and disagreement among, for example, those who adopt a contractarian approach, on the one hand, and those who appeal to straightforward utilitarian or consequentialist considerations of maximizing welfare, on the other hand.

Mill also maintains that "trade is a social act" and "the principle of individual liberty is not involved in the doctrine of Free Trade" (*CW* xviii, 293 [v, 4]). Whenever individuals seek to sell any goods to the public, their conduct affects the interests of others and may legitimately be regulated, even coercively, by the state. He generalizes this point with the comment that "In all things which regard the external relations of the individual, he is *de jure* amenable to those whose interests are concerned, and, if need be, to society as their protector" (*CW* xviii, 225 [i, 11]). Presumably, among the regulations on social conduct would be principles of distributive justice which determine the appropriate share each person may use or keep of the external resources available in society.

In all these cases, what counts as conduct harming the interests of others, whether by positive acts, or by omissions, does not involve an appeal to individuality. The three areas of liberty needed for the promotion of individuality are, as we have seen: first, liberty of thought and feeling, and liberty of expression; second, liberty of tastes and pursuits; and third, freedom to associate with others for purposes not involving harm to others. These areas are not undermined by restrictions in our general "external relations" with others. For example, the requirement that I should spend some time and resources discharging certain social obligations to others does not in itself prevent me from forming and pursuing my own plan of life, in the way that restrictions on freedom of expression and paternalistic and moralistic prohibitions on carrying out my plan of life would.

There is therefore some scope for disagreement among those who accept Millian liberalism, as it is explicated in his account of individuality and in the defense of the associated areas of human freedom. Some of the disagreement will focus on the principles of efficiency, fairness, and productivity, which will determine each person's entitlement to the existing and future resources of the community.

Mill seeks to provide a principled defense of liberty in the areas of thought, expression, and action. He notes that it is only in the case of religious belief that there has been something like such a principled defense of liberty. Everywhere else the coercive instruments of law and public opinion have been based on the "likings and dislikings of society, or of some powerful portion of it" (*CW* xviii, 222 [I, 7]).

Even today, the principle of religious toleration seems to be much more widely accepted than is the case with individual liberty generally. Thus it is widely acknowledged that with respect to religious practices which cause no harm to others, the mere "dislikings," disapproval, or disgust of others are not good reasons for restricting religious freedom. And yet many religious people refuse to extend toleration to, for example, sodomy among consenting adults, even though much of the opposition to it is religiously based. Mill's plea for individuality is an attempt to give "much wider application" to the proper foundations of individual liberty (*CW* xviii, 227 [I, 16]). If religious people acknowledged that religious toleration applies to atheists and agnostics, then on what grounds could they not extend toleration to homosexuals acting on their moral convictions that homosexual acts or same-sex marriages are desirable, or to patients suffering from painful terminal illnesses, who seek to end their lives earlier?

Mill's society was culturally more homogenous than many societies today. The application of his plea for individuality to our contemporary society would also lead to freedom for members of minority cultural groups to participate voluntarily in the cultural practices of their groups, even when these are regarded as undesirable by the majority. Mill himself strongly disapproves of Mormon polygamy, and yet he argues for its toleration, on the assumption that the women involved voluntarily accepted the relationship. On the other hand, Mill would not regard cultural diversity as intrinsically good if it is the product of enforcement and internal oppression by the leaders of a cultural group, or a powerful section of it. The dissidents in a cultural group should be free to leave it, and to associate themselves with other groups. The result of the exercise of such freedom by dissidents may well be the disintegration of a minority cultural group through a failure in critical mass. But whatever the intrinsic value of preserving a rare species of fauna or flora, there is no similar value in the survival of a cultural group through oppression and forced membership.

Similar issues arise with the treatment of children. Some cultural groups may seek to hold back the education of their female children, or deprive their children generally of any education or social intercourse that would make them more likely to leave the group. Mill has strong views about the obligations of parents to their children. He thinks that here "misplaced notions of liberty prevent moral obligation on the part of parents from being recognized, and legal obligations from being imposed" (*CW* XVIII, 304 [v, 15]). He does not believe that parents have "absolute and exclusive control" over their children, and argues for the right of the state to "require and compel the education, up to a certain standard, of every human being who is born its citizen" (*CW* XVIII, 301 [v, 12]). Although Mill also argues against state monopoly of education, the basis of children's education should not be the interests of their parents. So it might well be in the interests of parents or of other members of a cultural group that the lives of children should be shaped solely in order that they may fit into social roles they themselves have not chosen, but which are conducive to the smooth running of the cultural community along traditional lines. But it would not be in the interests of the children themselves that they be so treated. Paternalism directed to children has a place, but it must be paternalism that develops their capacities for genuine choice, and makes possible a life of individuality.

Mill's views are controversial, and require further analysis, clarification, and debate. This is as he would have wished. For him, no opinion is worthy of acceptance by thinking beings unless it can stand up to free and critical scrutiny from all sides.

OUTLINE OF THE VOLUME

Some of the issues raised in the first section of this Introduction, as well as other related themes raised in *On Liberty*, are further discussed below.

Several essays in this volume explore from various perspectives the character and implications of Mill's defense of freedom of expression and freedom of action. Mill's views are compared and contrasted with those embodied in other versions of liberalism, such as Rawls's "political liberalism." The limitations of a purely negative conception of liberty, which is sometimes attributed to Mill, and which equates liberty with non-interference with a person's choices, are explored.

In "Mill's case for liberty," Henry R. West discusses the basis of Mill's defense of his "very simple" principle of liberty, that the prevention of harm to others is the only purpose for which the liberty of any member of a civilized community may be forcibly restricted. A person may be punished if his conduct violates the rights of others. He can violate such rights both by his action as well as by his omission. Thus a person may be compelled to give evidence in a court of justice, or to bear his fair share in the common defense of the society from which he has received protection. He may also, without violating the rights of others, adversely affect their interests, such as when he sells goods to the public, or succeeds in an overcrowded profession. Finally, there is conduct that does not harm others, even though it causes them displeasure through their dislikings and moral disapproval. Such non-harmful conduct should not be interfered with. According to West, Mill's conception of liberty is not entirely negative. Mill also advocates a positive atmosphere, requiring freedom of thought and expression, and liberty of action in choosing and exploring ways of living. West maintains that Mill is an indirect utilitarian. His version of utilitarianism does not require applying the principle of utility case by case in order to ensure that utility is maximized in each case. Instead, the principle of utility is used to identify secondary principles, or general rules, conformity to which would have the best consequences. Mill's principle of liberty is one such secondary principle. His utilitarianism recognizes qualitative differences between pleasures. The higher pleasures are more valuable than others. The preferences of competent judges provide evidence of the higher pleasures, which are obtained by the exercise of the distinctively human faculties. Mill believes in the possibility of individual and social progress or development. Happiness is not maximized by simply satisfying people's existing desires. Individuals develop themselves by freely choosing their own values and modes of life. Individual choice fulfills human capacities, and is an essential ingredient of human happiness. As individuals and society improve, there will be social progress. Liberty is valuable because it promotes individual and social progress.

In "Mill's liberal principles and freedom of expression," David O. Brink argues that Mill's defense of freedom of expression plays a role in his more

general defense of individual liberties. He considers Mill's account of freedom of expression in the broader context of his liberalism. Mill has two
types of arguments for freedom of expression. The first regards freedom of
expression as instrumental to the production of true belief. There is a
parallel between Mill's instrumental argument for freedom of expression
and his instrumental opposition to paternalism, which applies only to
unsuccessful paternalism. The instrumental arguments against freedom of
expression do not condemn successful and competent censorship. There is,
however, another type of argument in Mill, which sees freedom of expression as necessary for fulfilling our natures as progressive beings. Progressive
beings have deliberative capacities, and the exercise of these capacities is
important to human happiness. They include the capacities "to form,
revise, assess, select and implement" one's views and plan of life. The
deliberative capacities are necessary for moral responsibility as responsible
moral agents must be able "to deliberate about the appropriateness of their
desires and regulate their actions according to these deliberations."
Progressive beings seek knowledge rather than mere true beliefs.
Knowledge requires the justification of one's beliefs and actions, and this
involves deliberation among alternatives. Content-specific restrictions make
it harder for certain messages to be heard and evaluated, and they thereby
adversely affect public and private deliberations. But not all content-specific
restrictions affect fundamental beliefs, or beliefs which engage or promote
the values of deliberation. Just as there are autonomy-enhancing forms of
paternalism, there could also be deliberation-enhancing forms of restrictions on free speech.

In "Racism, blasphemy, and free speech," Jonathan Riley points out that
Mill admits that freedom of expression can harm others without their
consent, and is therefore not purely self-regarding conduct. Nonetheless,
expressive conduct could still be treated differently from non-expressive
social conduct, and given special protection, if in fact it produces extraordinary benefits. According to Riley, Mill endorses a general policy of
laissez-faire, of not interfering with expression except in situations where it
directly and immediately inflicts grievous harm on others without their
consent. Racist and blasphemous opinions produce disagreeable feelings,
such as offense and disgust, in others, but these feelings do not amount to
perceptible harm, and are not the basis for restricting speech. There is to be
complete liberty of thought and discussion, but coercive measures may be
adopted against types of expression which inflict grievous harm on others,
and which do not count as discussion. Speech may be regulated with respect
to the time, place, and manner, as well as the content of expression, in order

to protect others from such harm. When individuals are left free to engage in self-regarding conduct, the benefits of self-development and individuality achieved through their choices and experimentations always outweigh the mere disagreeable feelings and emotional distress experienced by others. Others are not prevented from pursuing their own good in their own way, and they are free to avoid the agents of the offending self-regarding acts. However, they should not parade their avoidance. Where no one suffers any perceptible harm, the audience should be free to receive any message it pleases in order that it can form its own opinions. Utilitarian rules of justice will distribute rights and correlative duties in a manner that is reasonably expected to promote the general good. These rules will not confer an absolute right to free speech. While self-regarding conduct should be absolutely free, individual liberty is not confined to such conduct. The general welfare is sometimes achieved by not interfering with other-regarding conduct. Thus those engaging in public discussion may distort and misrepresent their opponent's views, or they may make honest mistakes. The audience may express disagreement, or avoid the speakers' company, but would not be justified in coercively interfering. However, types of speech which involve credible threats and incitements to serious harm against others may legitimately be prohibited and punished by law. But the pros and cons of such unjust speech should be freely debated.

In "State Neutrality and controversial values in *On Liberty*," Gerald F. Gaus maintains that Mill defended what Gaus calls "first-level neutrality." Neutrality is between persons, and not necessarily between conceptions of the good, which they may share. A neutral law can also appeal to controversial conceptions of the good which converge on the relevant issue. A neutral law is neutral in all three ways: it is neutral on its face in that the disputed position, which divides the relevant citizens, is not the ground for differential rights and duties; it is neutral in its intent in that the goal of legislation is not to favor either side in the dispute; and it is neutral in its interpretation in that the interpretation of the law does not draw on controversial conceptions of the good, which would treat the relevant parties differently on the basis of their different conceptions. Neutrality is with respect to a range of disputes, and does not extend to all issues, and it covers a group of persons, which need not include everyone. Mill's liberalism is expounded in three principles: (1) the presumption in favor of liberty; (2) the principle that only harm to others can defeat the presumption; and (3) the principle that harm to others is necessary, but not sufficient, to justify a coercive limitation of liberty. Gaus believes that these principles are strongly, but not perfectly, neutralist at the first level. But does Mill also support second-level neutrality, which provides a neutral justification of first-level neutrality? Gaus points out that the broader the range of disputes, and the broader the class of citizens among whom the justification is neutral, the broader is the second-level neutrality. He believes that Mill's justification of the three principles is very broadly neutral. Mill's neutral justification appeals to ordinary members of the public, and it does not require them to accept the value of individuality. Mill believes that governments are often mistaken in meeting their goals when they interfere with the non-harmful conduct of individuals. Secondly, he appeals to an ideal of reciprocity that is basic to social life, namely that all who receive the protection of society should in return observe a line of conduct which does not harm the essential interests of others.

In "Rawls's critique of *On Liberty*," Robert Amdur discusses Rawls's defense of liberty and his criticisms of Mill. Rawls claims that Mill's arguments for liberty are flawed, and that Mill's liberalism cannot be the basis for a stable society. Mill's utilitarian arguments do not justify equal liberty for all without bringing in additional assumptions. Even Mill's argument that freedom is intrinsically valuable as an essential element of well-being does not rule out the restriction of some people's freedom in order to increase the well-being of others. So long as the end is the utilitarian one of maximizing the sum of intrinsic value, Rawls's argument holds good. But Amdur points out that Rawls's objections do not apply to Mill's main Kantian argument in his chapter on individuality, which treats each person as inviolable. Rawls's own view gives absolute priority to the basic liberties, including freedom of thought and liberty of conscience, political liberties, freedom of association, and the liberty and integrity of the person. Amdur considers various arguments given by Rawls for the priority of liberty, especially the argument that the priority of liberty protects the fundamental interests embodied in the two moral powers, the capacity for a sense of justice, and the capacity for a conception of the good. Amdur suggests that the capacity for a conception of the good, i.e. the interest in forming, revising, and pursuing a conception of the good, resembles Mill's account of the importance of choosing and reexamining one's own plan of life. Rawls rejects Mill's version of liberalism, which he claims rests on a comprehensive doctrine about values. He believes that the stability of a free society cannot depend on agreement about any single comprehensive doctrine because it is a fact about such a society that citizens will hold a diversity of conflicting, yet reasonable, comprehensive doctrines. A shared adherence to a comprehensive doctrine can be maintained only by the oppressive use of state power. On the other hand, Rawls believes that his political liberalism requires a much more limited agreement on the design of society's basic structure. The agreement can rest on an overlapping consensus of reasonable views implicit in society's public political culture. However, Amdur argues that Mill's ideal of individuality, which emphasizes individual development, choice, diversity, and toleration, cannot be achieved by the use of state oppression. He discusses the implications of Mill's liberalism for the education of children, especially those whose parents reject the culture of the modern world. Amdur concludes that the groups which would reject Mill's liberal society are likely to be the same as these which fall outside Rawls's overlapping consensus.

In "Mill on consensual domination," Frank Lovett maintains that Mill subscribes to a negative conception of liberty, that liberty consists in the absence of interference by others with a person's choices. Lovett argues that this conception does not serve Mill well in his opposition to voluntary slavery. According to Mill's harm principle, the only legitimate reason for coercive social regulation is the prevention of harm. The harm here is harm to others without their consent. But where the individual who is harmed by another has consented to the harm, social regulation is not permissible. Yet Mill would not permit a person to sell himself voluntarily into slavery, on the ground that in so doing he ceases to be free, and, as Mill puts it, "The principle of freedom cannot require that he should be free not to be free." But Lovett believes that, on the negative conception of liberty, it is a contingent truth that slavery entails a severe loss of freedom. To a person confronted with dismal alternatives, being a slave to a benevolent master might increase his negative freedom. But even if it is true that slavery always involves a severe reduction of the slave's freedom, there are many ordinary choices, that Mill would not subject to social regulation, which reduce a person's negative liberty. The mere quantitative loss of freedom as non-interference does not explain the special wrongness of slavery, or the consensual domination of women by their husbands. A kindly husband would leave his wife largely free from unwanted interference, but this, Lovett suggests, does not make the legal subordination of women just. A different conception of liberty, as the absence of domination, would better explain the wrongness of voluntary slavery and the unjust subordination of women, even with their consent.

The issue of consensual domination is also taken up by Wendy Donner in "Autonomy, tradition, and the enforcement of morality." She maintains that autonomy and individuality are central to Mill's conception of human excellence. She applies his views to his discussion of the practice of autonomy among Mormon communities, and shows weaknesses in the application of his theory, rather than in the theory itself. She believes that Mill is mistaken in thinking that women's choices of polygamy are voluntary. Some forms of belonging and attachment can threaten autonomy and individuality. Children have a right to an education that would enable them to exercise autonomy as adults. Very few women whose education gives them a vivid sense of the range of family and partnership options, and who grow up to be autonomous and equal persons, would choose polygamy.

Donner also discusses the application of Mill's view to the enforcement of a society's shared morality, the subject of the famous Devlin–Hart debate. Devlin believes that a democratic society like England is under threat of disintegration if its shared Christian morality is not legally enforced. But Mill conceives of the realm of morality, which is enforceable by sanctions, much more narrowly than does Devlin. For Mill, morality is only part of what he calls the Art of Life. Other areas, such as virtue, are best promoted, not by coercion, but by encouragement. People's feelings of disgust and offense at the conduct of others should not be protected by coercive interference with such conduct if they are not harmful.

The application of Mill's defense of individuality and individual lifestyles to cultural choices is examined in detail by Jeremy Waldron in "Mill and multiculturalism." He suggests that one might begin with the impression that Mill, as the great defender of individuality, would also be friendly to cultural diversity and to the ethics and politics of cultural identity. However, there are strands in Mill's social and political thought which are not supportive of certain expressions of cultural identity. In *Representative Government*, Mill seems to reject the idea of a multicultural society when he claims that "it is in general a necessary condition of free institutions that the boundaries of governments should coincide in the main with those of nationalities." However, Mill does not equate culture with nationality. Sometimes he uses the notion of nationality in a thin sense to refer to whatever sentiments make people sympathetic to one another and desire to live together in one society. These sentiments may be associated with culture and ethnicity, but they could also be associated with other things, such as a common language or religion, and a shared history. It is therefore possible that a single nationality could be built on a diversity of cultures. But Mill also thinks that language differences make it difficult to sustain common sympathies and identities. He believes that where there is more than one nation in a state, the backward nation would benefit from assimilation to the superior nationality, or there would be a gradual and beneficial blending of the attributes of the various nationalities. Waldron suggests that some of Mill's concerns provide a basis for evaluating aspects of identity politics in contemporary multicultural societies. Mill does not celebrate mere diversity of beliefs, cultures, and creeds. He values interaction and confrontation of rival beliefs. Without such confrontation and intellectual engagement, the beliefs of each group would stagnate.

Within a cultural group there are minorities and dissidents who disagree with the majority about aspects of the cultural values and practices of the group. Mill's general support for cultural and ethical diversity would lead him to side with the dissidents and internal minorities. His views are less clear when we discuss cases in which people choose to identify with a culture that oppresses them. On the one hand, he maintains that the principle of liberty does not permit persons to sell themselves voluntarily into slavery. But on the other hand, he opposes forcibly preventing Mormons from practicing polygamy on the ground that the women who suffer under it do not seek external assistance.

In putting his case for individuality, Mill argues for the freedom to conduct "experiments in living." Recent developments in biotechnology have extended the range of such experiments. In "Mill, liberty, and (genetic) 'experiments in living,'" Justine Burley asks whether Mill would extend freedom to individuals to conduct reproductive cloning as expressions of their individualities. She discusses this issue in the broader context of how to evaluate the good and bad, or the right and wrong, of bringing children into existence. She argues that a person's existence is of positive value if the pleasure in his life outweighs the pain. She notes that Mill believes that we are capable of an "enviable existence" if we are not prevented from using the sources of happiness within our reach, and if further we can escape from such "evils of life" as "indigence, disease, and the unkindness, worthlessness, or premature loss of objects of affection." But he also argues that bringing someone into existence would be a crime if this is done without giving her "at least the ordinary chances of a desirable outcome." Burley maintains that at present the process of reproductive cloning involves a much higher loss of early human lives and a higher incidence of genetic abnormalities than is the case with natural reproduction. This fact justifies the restriction of the parent's right to reproductive freedom. She then considers the case against reproductive cloning even when the technology is safe. Some parents might prevent the autonomous development of their children to an unacceptable degree, but this would not justify a general prohibition of reproductive cloning. She also argues that Mill would not be troubled by the claim that cloning would undermine some shared human values and threaten customary morality. Instead, he would welcome challenges to existing morality and practices so long as the vital interests of individuals are not violated.

Finally, Robert Young discusses Mill's anti-paternalism in "John Stuart Mill, Ronald Dworkin, and paternalism." Young identifies and rejects four arguments Mill uses against paternalism: competent persons know their own interests better than others; paternalistic interferences are likely to be mistaken; paternalism shows disrespect for the equal standing of competent individuals within society; and there is value in allowing individuals to develop their individualities by deciding things for themselves, even when they make mistakes. Some of Mill's supporters have argued that for him a competent individual's good consists in her ability to choose her own way of life, and to live accordingly. But Young argues that being free cannot be exhaustive of the good, and some of a person's liberty can be legitimately traded off for other goods, or in order to enhance her future options.

Young then considers Ronald Dworkin's view that a person's life cannot be made better by forcing him to do something he does not value. Dworkin distinguishes between a person's volitional well-being, which is improved whenever she gets what she wants, and her critical well-being, which is improved only when she achieves what she should want. Dworkin further distinguishes between two views of what makes a life a good life. On the additive view, the components of someone's critical interests which make her life good are independent of whether she endorses them. But on the constitutive view, a component that is not endorsed by the individual cannot contribute to making her life valuable to her. Critical paternalism is ruled out on the constitutive view because a person's life can be improved only with her endorsement. But Young argues that, contrary to Dworkin, endorsement can admit of degrees. So a person might endorse, to varying degrees, various options, and forcing her to adopt the critically most valuable of these options would still give her an option that is of value to her, even when this is not the option that she prefers.

Dworkin's arguments against critical paternalism depend on a link between endorsement and integrity. According to him, a person achieves ethical integrity "when he lives out of the conviction that his life, in its central features, is an appropriate one, that no other life he might live would be a plainly better response to the parameters of his ethical situation rightly judged." Critical paternalism undermines integrity by forcing people to live in a way they never endorsed. However, Young argues that it is not necessarily the case that a person fails to act with integrity when he is compelled to act in a way that he does not endorse. More generally, Young believes that a competent individual may, in a particular instance, make an autonomous choice that seriously undermines his capacities in future to make autonomous choices. Paternalistic intervention in such a case may be justified.

Mill's case for liberty

Henry R. West

Mill says in chapter I of *On Liberty* that the object of the essay is to assert one very simple principle: "that the sole end for which mankind are warranted, individually or collectively, in interfering with the liberty of action of any of their number, is self-protection. That the only purpose for which power can be rightfully exercised over any member of a civilized community, against his will, is to prevent harm to others" (*CW* XVIII, 223 [I, 9]). A person's own good, if of adult age and in a civilized community, "is not a sufficient warrant. He cannot rightfully be compelled to do or forbear because it will be better for him to do so, because it will make him happier, because, in the opinions of others, to do so would be wise or even right" (*CW* XVIII, 223–4 [I, 9]).

Mill says that the basis for his argument for this principle is utility: "I forgo any advantage which could be derived to my argument from the idea of abstract right, as a thing independent of utility. I regard utility as the ultimate appeal on all ethical questions; but it must be utility in the largest sense, grounded on the permanent interests of man as a progressive being" (*CW* XVIII, 224 [I, 11]).

This essay is addressed to the way in which Mill makes his case for liberty on the basis of utility "in the largest sense, grounded on the permanent interests of man as a progressive being." The stages of the discussion are as follows. First, it is necessary to say something about Mill's conception of liberty. Liberty is the topic of other chapters in this critical guide, and Mill's conception of it is a matter of great controversy. I shall not attempt to settle the controversies but only to present a sketch of a possible interpretation for purposes of presenting the utilitarian case for liberty. Second, Mill is primarily an "indirect" utilitarian. He believes that the principle of utility should be used to develop what he calls "secondary principles" for the application of the first principle. He recognizes that these secondary principles admit of exceptions. "There is no ethical creed," he says, "which does not temper the rigidity of its laws, by giving a certain latitude, under the moral responsibility of the agent, for accommodation to peculiarities of circumstances."[1] But, in general, he attempts to frame principles of application based on the principle of utility such that the principle of utility does not need to be applied case by case. The "simple" principle of *On Liberty* would be of this nature. Utility is not to be appealed to on every occasion on which there is a conflict between liberty and other values. The principle of liberty is to be argued for as the best general rule for dealing with such conflicts. Third, Mill's theory of utility recognizes qualitative differences in pleasures, and he incorporates many descriptions of experience, such as music, virtue, and so on, as "parts" of happiness. Mill's hedonism is not one of maximizing some homogeneous quality of experience. It is one of promoting pleasures that require use of distinctively human capabilities on grounds that these are higher pleasures. Fourth, Mill does not take the highest happiness to be the satisfaction of existing desires. It is the desires of competent judges that provide evidence of higher and lower pleasures. Competence is based on a theory of development. Individuals can develop capacities for action and for feeling that they did not previously have, and one of the ingredients of this development is self-development – freely choosing one's own values and mode of existence. Furthermore, he believes that society progresses. He makes a distinction between obligatory and meritorious actions. Meritorious actions are those that are admirable when performed, but the agent is not blameworthy if they are not performed. He believes, however, that as society progresses, some actions previously only meritorious will become obligatory. These complications in Mill's version of utilitarianism are important in understanding his case for liberty.

MILL'S CONCEPTION OF LIBERTY

The liberty that Mill advocates in *On Liberty* is expressed primarily as an absence of compulsion, but it is more than that. It is also an atmosphere of openness to new directions of personal and social growth. He is concerned with the "nature and limits of the power which can be legitimately exercised by society over the individual" (*CW* XVIII, 217 [1, 1]). This power can be tyrannical not only in the hands of government but also by means of custom and the likings and dislikings of other individuals in the society. At the same time that Mill is concerned with deliberate compulsion, he is also concerned

---

[1] *Utilitarianism* (1861), in *The Collected Works of John Stuart Mill*, ed. John M. Robson, vol. X: *Essays on Ethics, Religion and Society* (Toronto: University of Toronto Press; London: Routledge & Kegan Paul, 1969), 225 (II, 25).

about a culture of mediocrity, and this is more than freedom from compulsion. "Genius," he says, "can only breathe freely in an *atmosphere* of freedom" (*CW* xviii, 267 [iii, 1]). He believes that liberty requires diversity; so, he says: "In this age, the mere example of non-conformity, the mere refusal to bend the knee to custom, is itself a service" (*CW* xviii, 269 [iii, 13]). "If it were only that people have diversities of taste, that is reason enough for not attempting to shape them all after one model. But different persons also require different conditions for their spiritual development; and can no more exist healthily in the same moral, than all the variety of plants can in the same physical, atmosphere and climate" (*CW* xviii, 270 [iii, 14]). Thus, Mill's conception of liberty is not merely negative. It is not merely restraint on government and public opinion in coercing people. It is also the promotion of the positive value of what he calls "individuality."

If it were felt that the free development of individuality is one of the leading essentials of well-being; that it is not only a co-ordinate element with all that is designated by the terms civilization, instruction, education, culture, but is itself a necessary part and condition of all those things; there would be no danger that liberty should be undervalued, and the adjustment of the boundaries between it and social control would present no extraordinary difficulty. But the evil is, that individual spontaneity is hardly recognized by the common modes of thinking, as having any intrinsic worth, or deserving any regard on its own account. (*CW* xviii, 261 [iii, 2])

Individuality can stand its ground only if "the intelligent part of the public can be made to feel its value" (*CW* xviii, 275 [iii, 19]).

Mill says that the appropriate region of liberty comprises

first, the inward domain of consciousness; demanding liberty of conscience, in the more comprehensive sense; liberty of thought and feeling; absolute freedom of opinion and sentiment on all subjects, practical or speculative, scientific, moral, or theological ... Secondly, the principle requires liberty of tastes and pursuits; of framing the plan of our life to suit our character; of doing as we like, subject to such consequences as may follow; without impediment from our fellow-creatures, so long as what we do does not harm them, even though they should think our conduct foolish, perverse, or wrong. Thirdly ... freedom to unite, for any purpose not involving harm to others: the persons combining being supposed to be of full age, and not forced or deceived. (*CW* xviii, 225–6 [i, 12])

What is the rightful limit of the sovereignty of the individual over himself? In chapter iv Mill addresses this in more detail. He says that "every one who receives the protection of society owes a return for the benefit," requiring conduct "first, in not injuring the interests of one another; or rather certain interests, which, either by express legal provision or by tacit understanding, ought to be considered as rights; and secondly, in each person's bearing his share (to be fixed on some equitable principle) of the labours and sacrifices incurred for defending the society or its members from injury and molestation" (*CW* XVIII, 276 [IV, 3]).

Let us look first at this area of positive obligations. In chapter I, he lists some of these positive acts for the benefit of others that an individual may rightfully be compelled to perform:

such as, to give evidence in a court of justice; to bear his fair share in the common defence or in any other joint work necessary to the interest of the society of which he enjoys the protection; and to perform certain acts of individual beneficence, such as saving a fellow-creature's life or interposing to protect the defenceless against ill-usage … A person may cause evil to others not only by his actions but by his inaction, and in either case he is justly accountable to them for the injury. (*CW* XVIII, 225 [I, 11])

It is important to keep in mind that Mill believes that harm can be done by failure to act as well as by positive actions. But he has limits upon what an individual may be required to do.

In chapter V Mill says that if one

injures his property, he does harm to those who directly or indirectly derived support from it, and usually diminishes, by a greater or less amount, the general resources of the community. If he deteriorates his bodily or mental faculties, he not only brings evil upon all who depended on him for his portion of their happiness, but disqualifies himself for rendering the services which he owes to his fellow-creatures generally. (*CW* XVIII, 280 [IV, 8])

To address this Mill makes a distinction between conduct that violates "a distinct and assignable obligation to any other person or persons" and that which does not. For example, if a man through intemperance or extravagance becomes unable to pay his debts, or, "having undertaken the moral responsibility of a family, becomes from the same cause incapable of supporting or educating them, he is deservedly reprobated, and might be justly punished; but it is for the breach of duty to his family or creditors, not for the extravagance" (*CW* XVIII, 281 [IV, 9]). With regard to merely making himself less able to contribute to the needs of society, Mill says, "the inconvenience is one which society can afford to bear, for the sake of the greater good of human freedom" (*CW* XVIII, 282 [IV, 10]). Thus, although the individual's behavior does affect prejudicially the welfare of society, Mill is giving a utilitarian argument (assuming that freedom has a positive value) for disregarding it when it does not violate a specific obligation.

Returning to the first requirement, "not injuring the interests of one another," Mill in chapter I states his "one very simple principle" using the term "harm": "That the only purpose for which power can be rightfully exercised over any member of a civilized community, against his will, is to prevent harm to others" (*CW* XVIII, 223 [1, 9]). The shift to "interests" which ought to be considered as "rights" is a restriction of the concept of harm, and might be considered Mill's more carefully worded doctrine. This formulation answers the objection that there is no self-regarding action that does not have effects upon others and may cause pain or harm. With the formulation in terms of "interests," Mill can make the distinction between what affects only the individual himself, "or if it also affects others, only with their free, voluntary, and undeceived consent and participation" (*CW* XVIII, 225 [1, 12]). If an individual harms himself, he also harms those who care about him and whose happiness includes his welfare. For example, if an adult child engages in activities disapproved of by his parents, they suffer pain. But Mill can say that although they are harmed, and their interests in his welfare are injured, they do not have a right that is being violated. Their concern for their son is voluntary and undeceived and ought not to be protected by society as a right against his free choice. More generally, people feel some displeasure when others engage in activities that they regard as immoral or degrading. But Mill attempts to distinguish between this displeasure, due to disapproval, and the harm or injury to interests that is not due merely to likings and dislikings, even moral disapproval.

However, Mill's distinction between interests that ought to be considered rights and harm that "affects others, only with their free, voluntary, and undeceived participation" leaves a wide area between them. Where rights are violated, society ought to intervene to protect them. Where it is only a matter of causing displeasure to those who disapprove of the behavior, society has no right to compel conformity. But there is a region where the interests of others are affected without violating anyone's rights. Here society has a right to interfere, but whether to do so is a matter of utilitarian calculation.

The acts of an individual may be hurtful to others, or wanting in due consideration for their welfare, without going to the length of violating any of their constituted rights. The offender may then be justly punished by opinion, though not by law. As soon as any part of a person's conduct affects prejudicially the interests of others, society has jurisdiction over it, and the question whether the general welfare will or will not be promoted by interfering with it, becomes open to discussion. (*CW* XVIII, 276 [IV, 3])

An example is trade. Trade "is a social act. Whoever undertakes to sell any description of goods to the public, does what affects the interest of other persons, and of society in general; and thus his conduct, in principle, comes within the jurisdiction of society" (*CW* XVIII, 276 [V, 4]). Another example is competition: "Whoever succeeds in an overcrowded profession, or in a competitive examination; whoever is preferred to another in any contest for an object which both desire, reaps benefit from the loss of others, from their wasted exertion and their disappointment" (*CW* xviii, 292 [v, 3]). But Mill thinks that there is a utilitarian argument for permitting this: "it is, by common admission, better for the general interest of mankind, that persons should pursue their objects undeterred by this sort of consequences" (*CW* xviii, 292 [v, 3]).

My conclusion from these passages is that Mill's notion of harm that justifies society's interference with individual conduct is not precise. At one end of the spectrum, he wants to deny that mere displeasure due to the attitudes of others is to be counted as prejudicial to a relevant sort of interests, and the harm that an individual does by simply making himself incapable of maximal contributions to society is too rigorous a standard. At the other end of the spectrum, the violation of rights, whether actually recognized or such that society ought to recognize them, is sufficiently harmful to count. In between there are degrees of harm that require utilitarian trade-offs. If others are protected from such harms, will that be in the general interest of society? Or will it be better for society to allow individuals freedom to act as they wish in these areas? Utilitarian calculations are required.

In addition to ambiguities in the notion of harm, there is a fine line that Mill attempts to draw in making a distinction between compulsion and other forms of social reaction to undesired behavior. When someone shows qualities that conduce to his own good, he is the proper object of admiration. When he is grossly deficient in those qualities, a sentiment the opposite of admiration will follow. "There is a degree of folly, and a degree of what may be called (though the phrase is not unobjectionable) lowness or depravation of taste, which, though it cannot justify doing harm to the person who manifests it, renders him necessarily and properly a subject of distaste, or, in extreme cases, even of contempt." We have a right to avoid his society. We have a right to caution others against him. We may give others a preference over him in optional good offices. "In these various modes a person may suffer very severe penalties at the hands of others, for faults which directly concern only himself; but he suffers these penalties only in so far as they are the natural, and, as it were, the spontaneous consequences of the faults themselves, not because they are purposely inflicted on him for the sake of punishment" (*CW* xviii, 278 [iv, 5]). Mill recognizes that these are "penalties," but they are not inflicted on him for the express purpose of punishment. If a person spoils his life by mismanagement, we shall not, for that reason, desire to spoil it still further. As I say, there is a fine line between these penalties and the social control of custom and opinion that Mill is seeking to combat in *On Liberty*. Mill describes everyone, "in our times," as under the eye of a hostile and dreaded censorship (*CW* xviii, 279 [iii, 6]). But this censorship does not have to consist of penalties deliberately inflicted upon nonconformists. It can consist of attitudes that Mill describes as appropriate toward those regarded as foolish or extravagant. People do not always purposefully punish non-conformists by attempting to make their lives painful. They show distaste, disapproval, and in extreme cases contempt; they avoid the person's society and warn others to do likewise. These are the forms of social control exercised by the "tyranny of the majority."

Is it possible to distinguish between the social control exercised by tradition or dislike and the "natural," "spontaneous" reaction to a person of folly and extravagance? In some cases, there may be a difference of intent: the reaction to a nonconformist may be purposefully to penalize. Aside from that, the only difference that I can see is that Mill's person who is wise and of refined taste is living an examined life and passing judgment from experience, whereas the attitude toward nonconformists is a conventional judgment not based on anything except convention.

On the basis of this brief discussion, I shall try to summarize my interpretation of Mill's conception of liberty. If an individual violates the rights of others, his behavior deserves punishment or compulsion. This includes duties of omission as well as commission; so an individual may be forced to carry out specific social duties that others have a right to count on. If an individual's behavior is detrimental to the legitimate interests of others but not in violation of a right, society has jurisdiction but should interfere only if interference is justified by utilitarian considerations. If an individual's behavior does not harm others, or it harms others only with their "free, voluntary, and undeceived consent and participation," and this includes the mere likings and dislikings of others, or if the behavior harms others only by lessening the individual's ability to contribute to the general welfare, society ought not to interfere. In addition, Mill advocates a positive freedom of thought and expression and of liberty of action in choice and exploration of modes of living that are the individual's own. He advocates an "atmosphere" of freedom, with individual choice given positive value.

MILL'S INDIRECT UTILITARIANISM

There are passages in *Utilitarianism* where Mill appears to be an "act-utilitarian." His formula in chapter ii, "actions are right in proportion as they tend to promote happiness, wrong as they tend to produce the reverse of happiness" (*CW* x, 210 [II, 2]) appears to be a reference to individual actions. But it can just as easily refer to *kinds* of actions. Later in that chapter, in answer to the objection that there is not time to calculate the consequences of every action, he says mankind "must by this time have acquired positive beliefs as to the effects of some actions on their happiness; and the beliefs which have thus come down are the rules of morality for the multitude, and for the philosopher until he has succeeded in finding better" (*CW* x, 224 [II, 24]). "Actions" here would seem to be a reference to *kinds* of actions, and morality is to be a set of rules. These rules are "secondary principles" based on the first principle, that of utility. At the end of chapter II of *Utilitarianism*, where he recognizes that rules of morality may come into conflict, but that utilitarianism has an advantage in having an ultimate source of moral obligation that may be invoked to decide between incompatible demands, Mill says, "We must remember that only in these cases of conflict between secondary principles is it requisite that first principles should be appealed to" (*CW* x, 226 [II, 25]). The strongest evidence against an act-utilitarian interpretation of Mill's view of *morality* is in chapter v of *Utilitarianism*. There he says:

We do not call anything wrong, unless we mean to imply that a person ought to be punished in some way or other for doing it; if not by law, by the opinion of his fellow creatures; if not by opinion, by the reproaches of his own conscience. This seems to be the real turning point of the distinction between morality and simple expediency. (*CW* x, 246 [v, 14])

Morality appears to be a set of rules backed by sanctions of one of the three sorts listed. These passages do not rule out the use of act-utilitarian reasoning in exceptional cases. As Mill says, "There is no ethical creed which does not temper the rigidity of its laws, by giving a certain latitude, under the moral responsibility of the agent, for accommodation to peculiarities of circumstances" (*CW* x, 225 [II, 25]). But except in extreme circumstances, morality is a set of rules, not the application of the principle of utility case by case.

Is the principle of *On Liberty* any different? In his *System of Logic*, Mill distinguishes three departments of the "Art of Life," all governed by the principle of utility: "Morality, Prudence or Policy, and Aesthetics; the Right, the Expedient, and the Beautiful or Noble, in human conduct and works."[2] When an individual's actions affect prejudicially the interests of others, they fall within the department of morality as well as policy. "If any

---

[2] *A System of Logic, Ratiocinative and Inductive* (1843; 8th edn. 1871), vols. VII–VIII of *The Collected Works of John Stuart Mill*, ed. J. M. Robson (Toronto: University of Toronto Press; London: Routledge & Kegan Paul, 1973), vol. VIII, 949 (Bk. VI, XXI, 6).

one does an act hurtful to others, there is a *prima facie* case for punishing him, by law, or, where legal penalties are not safely applicable, by general disapprobation" (*CW* xviii, 224 [i, i]). In some cases, legal and social penalties produce other evils, greater than those they are designed to prevent. In such cases, "the conscience of the agent himself should step into the vacant judgment seat, and protect those interests of others which have no external protection; judging himself all the more rigidly, because the case does not admit of his being made accountable to the judgment of his fellow creatures" (*CW* xviii, 225 [i, ii]). These are the sanctions of morality. But in cases where no right is being violated, although "damage, or probability of damage, to the interests of others, can alone justify the interference of society," it does not always justify such interference (*CW* xviii, 292 [v, 3]). It may be better for the general interest of mankind that persons should pursue their objects undeterred. "All restraint, *quâ* restraint, is an evil" (*CW* xviii, 293 [v, 4]). The restraints in question may affect only that part of conduct which society is competent to restrain, namely, that which harmfully affects others, but the restraints do not really produce the results which it is desired to produce by them. Thus in his chapter on "Applications" in *On Liberty* Mill is concerned to address difficult questions of what alternative policies have better or worse consequences. The point in this context is that general rules are needed. "In the conduct of human beings towards one another, it is necessary that general rules should for the most part be observed, in order that people may know what they have to expect; but in each person's own concerns, his individual spontaneity is entitled to free exercise" (*CW* xviii, 227 [iv, 4]). Thus, I think that we may conclude, in the department of Policy as well as of Morality, Mill believes that general rules are necessary. In the department of Prudence, concerning only an individual's wise choice, there may be case-by-case decisions. Thus, even if compelling an individual against his better judgment to conform to the wise counsels of others might be beneficial in the individual case, Mill believes that a general policy of leaving individuals to act on their own judgment is the best general policy, and his version of utilitarianism does not require maximizing utility case by case. This is seen in the case where a man, through injuring himself or his property, diminishes the general resources of the community but violates no specific duty and hurts no assignable individual except himself. Mill says that "the inconvenience is one which society can afford to bear, for the sake of the greater good of human freedom" (*CW* xviii, 282 [iv, ii]). In an individual case, it would produce greater welfare if the individual were prohibited from injuring himself. But the general rule allowing such freedom is the general rule having best consequences.

MILL'S QUALITATIVE HEDONISM

In *Utilitarianism* Mill makes his famous or infamous distinction between pleasures and pains on the basis of quality as well as quantity. He is answering the objection that to suppose that life has no end higher than pleasure is a doctrine worthy only of swine. Mill's reply is that a beast's pleasures do not satisfy a human being's conception of happiness. Human beings have faculties more elevated than the animal appetites and do not regard anything as happiness which does not include their gratification. The "pleasures of the intellect, of the feelings and imagination, and of the moral sentiments" have a higher value as pleasures than those of mere sensation. "It is quite compatible with the principle of utility to recognize the fact, that some *kinds* of pleasure are more desirable and more valuable than others" (*CW* x, 211 [II, 4]).

Mill's argument for this position is complicated, and I do not plan to defend its details. First, there is the question whether there *is* a difference in quality among pleasures. Mill is an introspective psychologist, and he believes that careful attention to our experiences shows that pleasures differ in the kind of *pleasure* that is experienced, not just in the non-pleasure components of qualitatively different experiences. The pleasure of solving an intellectual problem is a different kind of *pleasure* from the pleasure of eating when hungry. Second, he claims that the evidence of preference of those properly qualified gives those pleasures using the higher human faculties a higher status than those which do not.

He says that

> those who are equally acquainted with, and equally capable of appreciating and enjoying both, do give a most marked preference to the manner of existence which employs their higher faculties. Few human creatures would consent to be changed into any of the lower animals, for a promise of the fullest allowance of a beast's pleasures; no intelligent human would consent to be a fool, no instructed person would be an ignoramus, no person of feeling and conscience would be selfish and base, even though they should be persuaded that the fool, the dunce, or the rascal is better satisfied with his lot than they are with theirs. (*CW* x, 211 [II, 6])

Notice that Mill is not saying that on every occasion on which there is a choice between a higher and a lower pleasure, a qualified person chooses the higher pleasure. He is comparing a "manner of existence" in which there are no higher pleasures with one in which there are. (What if one compared a manner of existence in which there were no lower pleasures with one in which there are lower pleasures? Would one choose to be a pure mind, with intellectual, aesthetic, and moral sentiments but no physical pleasures?) One might also question whether the concept of happiness used here is the same as Mill's analysis of happiness where he says that happiness is "an existence made up of few and transitory pains, many and various pleasures, with a decided predominance of the active over the passive, and having as the foundation of the whole, not to expect more from life than it is capable of bestowing" (*CW* x, 215 [II, 12]). In that passage he is clearly attempting to analyze happiness into episodes of pleasure and of pain, but in the earlier passage he says that a being of higher faculties can never really wish to sink into what he feels to be a lower grade of existence. He seems to be treating happiness as including an appraisal of one's life that is not reducible to episodic events. All humans have a sense of dignity, he says, "which is so essential a part of their happiness … that nothing which conflicts with it could be, otherwise than momentarily, an object of desire to them" (*CW* x, 212 [II, 6]). However, it is possible to give a hedonistic interpretation of these statements. There can be "secondary" pleasures and pains when one reflects upon the character of one's life. If one has self-respect, such an appraisal gives one episodes of pleasure. If one has self-disrespect, that gives one pain. In any case, Mill believes that there are higher and lower pleasures, and a flourishing life includes the higher pleasures.

In chapter IV of *Utilitarianism*, his effort to argue for the principle of utility on the ground that there is really nothing desired as an end except happiness, Mill claims that whatever is desired otherwise is desired as a means to some end beyond itself and thus ultimately to happiness, or it "is desired as itself a part of happiness" (*CW* x, 237 [IV, 8]). This claim is based on his associationist psychology. An example is the love of money. There is nothing originally desirable about possession of money. Its worth is solely its ability to buy desirable things. But the possession of money can, through association with the pleasures of its use, become an end in and for itself, stronger than the desire to use it. "It may, then, be said truly, that money is desired not for the sake of an end, but as part of the end. From being a means of happiness, it has come to be itself a principal ingredient of the individual's conception of happiness" (*CW* x, 236 [IV, 6]). This is true of the desire for power and for fame and for virtue:

there was no original desire of [virtue], or motive to it, save its conduciveness to pleasure, and especially to protection from pain. But through the association thus formed, it may be felt a good in itself, and desired as such with as great intensity as any other good; and with this difference between it and the love of money, of power, or of fame, that all of these may, and often do, render the individual noxious to the other members of the society to which he belongs, where there is nothing which makes him so much a blessing to them as the cultivation of the disinterested love of virtue. And consequently, the utilitarian standard, while it tolerates and approves those other acquired desires, up to the point beyond which they would be more injurious to the general happiness than promotive of it, enjoins and requires the cultivation of the love of virtue up to the greatest strength possible, as being above all things important to the general happiness. (*CW* x, 236 [iv, 7])

There are many passage in *On Liberty* in which Mill can be interpreted as having a theory of intrinsic value that is richer than hedonism. These include liberty itself, "individuality," originality, and the intrinsic value of a human being. For example, he regrets that "individual spontaneity is hardly recognised by the common modes of thinking, as having any intrinsic worth, or deserving any regard on its own account" (*CW* xviii, 261 [iii, 2]). He speaks of "a different type of human excellence from the Calvinistic … There is a Greek ideal of self-development" (*CW* xviii, 265–6 [iii, 8]). "It is not by wearing down into uniformity all that is individual in themselves, but by cultivating it … that human beings become a noble and beautiful object of contemplation; and as the works partake the character of those who do them, by the same process human life also becomes rich, diversified, and animating … In proportion to the development of his individuality, each person becomes more valuable to himself" (*CW* xviii, 266 [iii, 9]). "It will not be denied by anybody," he says, "that originality is a valuable element in human affairs" (*CW* xviii, 267 [iii, 1]). In arguing against too much power for the state, Mill says, "The worth of a State, in the long run, is the worth of the individuals composing it" (*CW* xviii, 310 [v, 23]). Mill preaches against mediocrity (*CW* xviii, 268–9 [iii, 13]), and, in talking about human advancement and improvement (e.g. *CW* xviii, 272–3 [iii, 17]), he evidently has a standard by which one is to measure improvement. This standard could be a perfectionist ideal independent of pleasure and pain. It would simplify Mill's case for liberty if he could assume that there is intrinsic worth to free, creative individuals, using their active faculties, exercising their judgment, having true beliefs about the subjects with which they have to deal, with diverse tastes and activities, and engaging in voluntary association with other individuals with impartial concern for the welfare of all. Many readers of *On Liberty* believe that this is the basis for Mill's case for liberty and that his claim to appeal to utility "in the largest sense, grounded on the permanent interests of man as a progressive being," must be interpreted not in a hedonistic way but as utility in promoting non-hedonistic ideals. However, in nearly all of the passages cited above as evidence to interpret Mill as holding perfectionist ideals, Mill could have also said that these promote human happiness. In the first paragraph of chapter iii, "Of Individuality, as One of the Elements of Well-Being," Mill says, "Where, not the person's own character, but the traditions or customs of other people are the rule of conduct, there is wanting one of the principal ingredients of human *happiness*" (*CW* XVIII, 261 [III, 1], emphasis added).

With Mill's conception of qualitative superior pleasures that are obtained only by the exercise of the distinctive human faculties, the development of these faculties is the source of qualitative superior pleasures. With Mill's analysis of happiness such that music and virtue, as well as power, fame, and possession of money, come to be "parts" of an individual's happiness, the absence of developed human capacities results in the absence of fundamental parts of happiness. The development of human capacities and their exercise in individual choices are essential to the greatest happiness.

Mill could be giving the reader alternative possible foundations for liberty: the case for liberty can be grounded on the intrinsic value of the development of human capacities, or the case for liberty can be grounded on the greatest happiness. In Mill's view, these are interrelated: the development of human capacities is necessary for the greatest happiness, but, in case the reader does not accept happiness as an adequate foundation, but accepts, or can be persuaded of, the intrinsic value of human development independently of happiness, either one can serve as a foundation.

MAN AS A PROGRESSIVE BEING

Mill believed in the possibility of progress or development in both individuals and society. He does not take the satisfaction of existing desires as the criterion for the greatest happiness. Qualitatively higher pleasures can be judged higher only by those who are competently acquainted with the higher pleasures, fully capable of enjoying them, and having habits of self-consciousness and self-observation as well as opportunities for experiencing them (*CW* X, 214 [II, 10]). He believes that most human beings are capable of these characteristics, and this is one of the grounds on which he advocates compulsory education for children. Among the requirements for the enjoyment of these higher pleasures is the development of one's "mental culture," and he sees no reason why this "should not be the inheritance of everyone born in a civilized country" (*CW* X, 216 [II, 14]). One of the requirements for the development of this mental culture is that one be able to make one's own decisions. He believed that with liberty individuals can develop their human capabilities and "character." "Where, not a person's own character, but the traditions and customs of other people are the rule of conduct, there is wanting one of the principal ingredients of human happiness, and quite the chief ingredient of individual and social progress" (*CW* XVIII, 261 [III, 1]). Traditions and custom are evidence of what experience has taught people in the past, but "their experience may be too narrow; or they may not have interpreted it rightly" (*CW* XVII, 262 [III, 3]). The customs are suitable for customary circumstances and customary characters, but an individual may be in uncustomary circumstances or be an uncustomary character. And although the custom may be good as a custom, "to conform to custom, merely *as* custom, does not educate or develop in him any of the qualities which are the distinctive endowment of a human being. The human faculties of perception, judgment, discriminative feeling, mental activity, and even moral preference, are exercised only in making a choice" (*CW* XVIII, 262 [IV, 3]). This is what Mill calls "individuality," and he says that it is "the same thing with development, and that it is only the cultivation of individuality which produces, or can produce, well-developed human beings" (*CW* XVIII, 267 [III, 10]). There are also such differences among individuals "in their sources of pleasure, their susceptibilities of pain, and the operation on them of different physical and moral agencies, that unless there is a corresponding diversity in their modes of life, they neither obtain their fair share of happiness, nor grow up to the mental, moral, and aesthetic stature of which their nature is capable" (*CW* XVIII, 270 [III, 14]).

Mill also argues that liberty promotes social progress. Mill was a reformer. In his youth he supported the "Philosophical Radicals," who advocated repeal of the Corn Laws, extension of suffrage, and other, at the time, radical political measures. In his maturity he was famous for his advocacy of the emancipation of women: for their equality in marriage relations, for their admission to professions currently limited to men, for their right to vote. He also held positions that he was afraid to advocate publicly, for example, artificial birth control and atheism. In his youth he was arrested for distributing birth-control information, and in private correspondence he denounced Christian morality as primitive and misguided. In a letter written in 1850 he said:

How can morality be anything but the chaos it now is, when the ideas of right and wrong, just and unjust, must be wrenched into accordance either with the notions of a tribe of barbarians in a corner of Syria three thousand years ago, or with what is called the order of Providence; in other words, the course of nature, of which so great a part is tyranny and inequity – all the things which are punished as the most atrocious crimes when done by human creatures, being the daily doings of nature through the whole range of organic life.[3]

---

[3] *The Later Letters of John Stuart Mill (1849–1873)*, vols. XIV–XVII of *The Collected Works of John Stuart Mill*, ed. Francis E. Mineka and Dwight N. Lindley (Toronto: University of Toronto Press; London: Routledge & Kegan Paul, 1972), vol. XIV, 52 (letter to Walter Coulson, November 1850).

One of Mill's chief objections to ethics based on a moral sense, on divine will, or on Nature, was that such morality is not subject to criticism and improvement.

If it be true that man has a sense given to him to determine what is right or wrong, it follows that his moral judgments and feelings cannot be susceptible of any improvement … According to the theory of utility, on the contrary, the question, what is our duty, is as open to discussion as any other questions … and changes as great are anticipated in our opinions on that subject, as on any other, both from experience, and from alterations in the condition of the human race, requiring altered rules of conduct.[4]

In his work *Auguste Comte and Positivism*, Mill argues for meritorious altruism that goes beyond duty, but he also claims that with moral improvement, what was once meritorious may become a duty: "the domain of moral duty, in an improving society, is always widening. When what once was uncommon virtue becomes common virtue, it comes to be numbered among obligations."[5]

One of the benefits of freedom of thought and discussion would be that radical-minded individuals could make their case for birth control and atheism without fear of social penalties. Mill himself was fearful of disclosing his religious views, postponing the publication of his writings on religion until after his death. For years, in Mill's lifetime, Darwin postponed the publication of the *Origin of Species*. The whole of chapter II of *On Liberty* is devoted to the achievement of Truth as a vibrant feature of intellectual life, with the assumption that knowing the Truth and the grounds for it in scientific, religious, and practical life will make people happier. Mill no doubt has in mind that freedom of discussion would undermine supernaturalist religious beliefs. It would also remove a barrier to the introduction of better modes of social life.

Mill was sympathetic with small-scale socialist experiments, thinking that socialism would be superior to existing forms of capitalism, although not, perhaps, to capitalism at its best, with population control and universal education. If there were freedom for "experiments in living," the socialist proposals could be tested by success or failure. Married couples could more easily practice "perfect equality" in their relationships. Mill believed that

---

[4] "Sedgwick's Discourse" (1835), in *The Collected Works of John Stuart Mill*, ed. John M. Robson, vol. x: *Essays on Ethics, Religion and Society* (Toronto: University of Toronto Press; London: Routledge & Kegan Paul, 1969), 73–4.
[5] *Auguste Comte and Positivism* (1865), in *The Collected Works of John Stuart Mill*, gen. ed. John M. Robson, vol. x: *Essays on Ethics, Religion and Society* (Toronto: University of Toronto Press; London: Routledge & Kegan Paul, 1969), 338.

what is necessary for this is that individuals have the liberty to be different from the crowd. "The initiation of all wise or noble things, comes and must come from individuals" (*CW* XVIII, 269 [III, 13]). The average human can then follow that initiative when the exceptional individual (or individuals) points out the way.

In all of these reform proposals, the ground for his policies was belief that they would increase human happiness and decrease misery. In answer to the objection that happiness is unattainable, Mill replies that a life of happiness is even now the lot of many. "The present wretched education, and wretched social arrangement, are the only real hindrance to its being attainable by almost all" (*CW* X, 215 [II, 12]).

When people who are tolerably fortunate in their outward lot do not find in life sufficient enjoyment to make it valuable to them, the cause generally is, caring for nobody but themselves ... Next to selfishness, the principal cause which makes life unsatisfactory is want of mental cultivation. A cultivated mind – I do not mean that of a philosopher, but any mind to which the fountains of knowledge have been opened, and which has been taught, in any tolerable degree, to exercise its faculties – finds sources of inexhaustible interest in all that surrounds it; in the objects of nature, the achievements of art, the imaginations of poetry, the incidents of history, the ways of mankind past and present, and their prospects in the future. (*CW* X, 215 [II, 13])

There is nothing in the nature of things, Mill asserts, to prevent this unless a person, "through bad laws, or subjection to the will of others, is denied the liberty to use the sources of happiness within his reach ... most of the great positive evils of the world are in themselves removable, and will [be removed], if human affairs continue to improve ... Poverty, in any sense implying suffering, may be completely extinguished by the wisdom of society ... disease, may be indefinitely reduced in dimensions ... All the grand sources, in short, of human suffering are in great degree, many of them almost entirely, conquerable by human care and effort" (*CW* X, 216–17 [II, 14]).

THE CASE FOR LIBERTY

Mill's case for liberty is based on "utility in the largest sense, grounded on the permanent interests of man as a progressive being" (*CW* XVIII, 224 [I, 10]). Some of these permanent interests are obvious. There may be oppression by rulers or by a majority, and "precautions are as much needed against this as against any other abuse of power ... 'the tyranny of the majority' is now generally included among the evils against which society requires to be on its guard" (*CW* XVIII, 219 [I, 4]). There must be restraint upon the actions of other people, but what these restraints should be is the principal question.

Unfortunately, the principle that many want to apply is that everybody should be required to act as he would like them to act. The likings and dislikings of society, or of some powerful portion of it, have practically determined rules laid down under penalties of law or opinion. In the first place, it is against these that Mill is seeking an alternative principle. He thinks that each individual is the best judge of what is good for that individual so far as it concerns only himself. The strongest of all the arguments against the interference of the public in purely personal conduct "is that, when it does interfere, the odds are that it interferes wrongly, and in the wrong place" (*CW* xviii, 283 [iv, 12]). Society is seeking only conformity to its likes and dislikes, without consideration of the peculiar character of the individual.

Mill's case for liberty is not based merely on the odds that society interferes wrongly. If that were the case, there could be sub-classes of instances of interference in which the odds might be different. Mill is seeking a general rule that, if observed, would protect others from interfering on the basis of their paternalistic judgment. He is seeking a principle that would deny others the right to interfere. He supports this rule by arguing for the value of individual choice as an essential ingredient of human happiness and of an individual's fulfilling his individual human capacities. He also supports it by claiming that social progress is furthered by the improvement of the individuals who make up society and that individual improvement comes only through development of individuals through their own choices.

Much can be said in support of Mill's position. The total subservience of one person to others, as in slavery, is contrary to happiness and individual development. The liberation of women may have created problems with the difficulties of choice between traditional roles and new opportunities, but in the long run it can be expected to be good for individual women and for society. Family planning has extended the control over women's lives in a positive way. The lack of freedom of religion or of freedom from religion has perpetuated superstitions that have worked against human welfare and development, and genuine freedom to criticize supernatural beliefs would be liberating. The inability of homosexuals to live their sexual preferences openly without discriminatory penalties frustrates the happiness of those individuals. On the positive side, compulsory education of children, and freedom of adults to practice artificial birth control, have given people greater control over their lives with resulting greater happiness and fulfillment.

Mill limits his principle of liberty to apply only to adults and to people in civilized societies. He may have underestimated the uncivilized subcultures in modern "civilized" societies, where religious teachings prevent adherents from being "capable of being improved by free and equal discussion" (*CW* xviii, 224 [i, 10]). He certainly has underestimated the compulsion that controls those who are addicted to mind-altering chemicals. The alcoholic of Mill's day was in far better control of his addiction that the drug addict of today. But even recognizing this, decriminalization of drug use may be the most sensible policy.

In the near century and a half since Mill wrote, his principle has been applied in many areas of life. His case for it in the end rests upon the test of its consequences in practice. So far, the consequences seem to have been positive.

CHAPTER 2

Mill's liberal principles and freedom of expression

David O. Brink

Chapter II of *On Liberty* contains John Stuart Mill's now classic defense of freedom of expression. This defense of expressive liberties has proved extremely influential and finds important echoes in First Amendment jurisprudence within United States constitutional law. Though important in its own right, Mill's defense of freedom of expression also plays an important, though sometimes overlooked, role in his more general defense of individual liberties. Mill turns to freedom of expression immediately after his introductory chapter in the belief that there is general agreement on the importance of freedom of expression and that, once the grounds for expressive liberties are understood, this agreement can be exploited to support a more general defense of individual liberties.

It will be convenient for the argument if, instead of at once entering upon the general thesis [the defense of various individual liberties], we confine ourselves in the first instance to a single branch of it on which the principle here stated is, if not fully, yet to a certain point, recognized by the current opinions. This one branch is the Liberty of Thought, from which it is impossible to separate the cognate liberty of speaking and writing. Although these liberties ... form part of the political morality of all countries which profess religious toleration and free institutions, the grounds, both philosophical and practical, on which they rest are perhaps not so familiar to the general mind ... Those grounds, when rightly understood, are of much wider application than to only one division of the subject, and a thorough consideration of this part of the question will be found the best introduction to the remainder. (*CW* XVIII, 227 [I, 16])

This means that a proper understanding of the significance of Mill's defense of freedom of expression requires not only reconstructing his arguments on behalf of expressive liberties and exploring their bearing on issues of freedom of expression, but also seeing how these arguments generalize to other kinds of liberties. In this regard, it will be especially instructive to consider how his claims about freedom of expression inform his liberal principles, especially what his discussion of the best grounds for expressive liberties can tell us about the best grounds for opposing paternalism. But it is also worth exploring whether philosophical pressure runs in the other direction as well – whether Mill's discussions of liberalism, in general, and paternalism, in particular, have implications for the proper articulation of principles governing expressive liberties. This perspective requires that we view Mill's defense of freedom of expression in the context of his liberalism.

MILLIAN PRINCIPLES

Mill begins *On Liberty* by distinguishing old and new threats to liberty. The old threat to liberty is found in traditional societies in which there is rule by one (a monarchy) or a few (an aristocracy). Though one could be worried about restrictions on liberty by benevolent monarchs or aristocrats, the traditional worry is that when rulers are politically unaccountable to the governed they will rule in their own interests, rather than the interests of the governed. In particular, they will restrict the liberties of their subjects in ways that benefit the rulers, rather than the ruled. It was these traditional threats to liberty that the democratic reforms of the Philosophical Radicals were meant to address.[1] But Mill thinks that these traditional threats to liberty are not the only ones to worry about. He makes clear that democracies contain their own threats to liberty – this is the tyranny, not of the one or the few, but of the majority (*CW* XVIII, 217–20 [1, 1–5]). Mill sets out to articulate the principles that should regulate how governments and societies, whether democratic or not, can restrict individual liberties (*CW* XVIII, 220–1 [1, 6]).

In an early and famous passage Mill offers one formulation of his basic principles concerning liberties.

The object of this essay is to assert one very simple principle, as entitled to govern absolutely the dealings of society with the individual in the way of compulsion and control, whether the means used be physical force in the form of legal penalties or the moral coercion of public opinion. That principle is that the sole end for which mankind are warranted, individually or collectively, in interfering with the liberty of action of any of their number is self-protection. That the only purpose for which power can be rightfully exercised over any member of a civilized community,

---

[1] See, for example, Jeremy Bentham, *Constitutional Code* and *Plan for Parliamentary Reform*, in *The Works of Jeremy Bentham*, vols. IX and III, ed. J. Bowring (New York: Russell & Russell, 1962); and James Mill, *Essay on Government* (1824), in Jack Lively and John Rees, eds., *Utilitarian Logic and Politics* (Oxford: Clarendon Press, 1978), 53–95.

against his will, is to prevent harm to others. His own good, either physical or moral, is not a sufficient warrant. He cannot rightfully be compelled to do or forbear because it will be better for him to do so, because it will make him happier, because, in the opinions of others, to do so would be wise or even right. These are good reasons for remonstrating with him, or reasoning with him, or persuading him, or entreating him, but not for compelling him or visiting him with any evil in case he do otherwise. To justify that, the conduct from which it is desired to deter him must be calculated to produce evil to someone else. The only part of the conduct of anyone for which he is amenable to society is that which concerns others. In the part which merely concerns himself, his independence, is, of right, absolute. Over himself, over his own body and mind, the individual is sovereign. (*CW* xviii, 223–4 [i, 9])

Notice that Mill is concerned with articulating principles to apply to restrictions on liberty in various contexts. He is perhaps most interested in cases where the state uses civil or criminal law to forbid conduct and applies sanctions for noncompliance. But he is also interested here and elsewhere – for instance, in *The Subjection of Women* – in other sorts of cases, including those in which social groups or individuals use the threat of force or disapprobation to limit liberty and ensure conformity. Having noted these complexities, let us focus, as Mill himself does, on the central case of legal prohibition by the state.

In this passage, Mill distinguishes paternalistic and moralistic restrictions of liberty from restrictions of liberty based upon the harm principle.
- *A*'s restriction of *B*'s liberty is *paternalistic* if it is done for *B*'s own benefit.
- *A*'s restriction of *B*'s liberty is *moralistic* if it is done to ensure that *B* acts morally or not immorally.
- *A*'s restriction of *B*'s liberty is an application of the *harm principle* if *A* restricts *B*'s liberty in order to prevent harm to someone other than *B*.

Here, Mill seems to say that a restriction on someone's liberty is legitimate if and only if it satisfies the harm principle (cf. *CW* xviii, 223–4 [iv, 1–4, 6; v, 2]). Later, he distinguishes between genuine harm and *mere offense*. In order to satisfy the harm principle, an action must actually violate or threaten imminent violation of those important interests of others in which they have a right (*CW* xviii, 225–6 [i, 12], 260–1 [iii, 1], 276 [iv, 3], 281–2 [iv, 10], 283–4 [iv, 12], 293–5 [v, 5]). So he seems to be saying that the harm principle is always a good reason for restricting liberty, but that mere appeals to morality, paternalism, or offense are never good reasons for restricting liberty.

As this recounting of Mill's principles suggests, his defense of individual liberties appears to be part of what might be called a *categorical approach*. To decide whether an individual's liberty ought to be protected, we must ascertain to which category the potential restriction of liberty belongs. The main categories for potential restrictions are these:

- offense (mere offense)
- moralism (mere moralism)
- paternalism (mere paternalism)
- harm principle

The potential restriction is permissible if and only if it is an application of the harm principle; if not, the restriction is impermissible and the liberty must be protected.[2]

It is generally thought that by applying this categorical approach to liberty and its permissible restrictions Mill is led to offer a fairly extensive defense of individual liberties against interference by the state and society. In particular, it is sometimes thought that Mill recognizes a large sphere of conduct that it is impermissible for the state to regulate. We might characterize this sphere of protected liberties as Mill's conception of *liberal rights*. On this reading, Mill is deriving his conception of liberal rights from a prior commitment to the categorical approach and, in particular, to the harm principle.[3]

MILL AGAINST PATERNALISM

Consider Mill's opposition to paternalism. Presumably, Mill's concern with paternalism is general and includes paternalism practiced by individuals or groups, as well as by states. But, as we have already noticed, his focus is on paternalism practiced by the state. Why the blanket prohibition on paternalism? He offers two explicit reasons.

First, state power is liable to abuse. Politicians are self-interested and corruptible and will use a paternalistic license to limit the freedom of citizens in ways that promote their own interests and not those of the citizens whose liberty they restrict (*CW* XVIII, 306–10 [V, 20–3]).

---

[2] Sometimes Mill suggests that the harm principle is equivalent to letting society restrict other-regarding conduct (*CW* XVIII, 224–5 [I, 11], 276 [IV, 2]). On this view, conduct can be divided into self-regarding and other-regarding conduct. Regulation of the former is paternalistic, and regulation of the latter is an application of the harm principle. So on this view it is never permissible to regulate purely self-regarding conduct and always permissible to regulate other-regarding conflict. But this is over-simple. Some other-regarding conduct causes mere offense, not genuine harm (*CW* XVIII, 276 [IV, 3], 283–4 [IV, 12]). So Mill cannot equate harmful behavior and other-regarding behavior and cannot think that all other-regarding behavior may be regulated.

[3] For a contrasting reading, which treats Mill's commitment to liberal rights as constraining the proper interpretation of the harm principle, see Daniel Jacobsen, "Mill on Liberty, Speech, and the Free Society," *Philosophy & Public Affairs*, 29 (2000), 276–309.

Second, even well-intentioned rulers will misidentify the good of citizens. Because an agent is a more reliable judge of his own good, even well-intentioned rulers will promote the good of the citizens less well than would the citizens themselves (*CW* XVIII, 276–7 [IV, 4], 283–4 [IV, 12]).

These are reasonably strong consequentialist arguments against giving the state a broad discretionary power to engage in paternalistic legislation whenever it sees fit. However, they do not support a categorical ban on paternalism. In particular, these arguments provide no *principled* objection to paternalism – no objection to *successful* paternalistic restrictions on *B*'s liberty that do in fact benefit *B*. Perhaps some who object to paternalism are concerned only with unsuccessful paternalism. They would have no objection to successful paternalism. But, for many, doubts about paternalism run deeper. They would be inclined to think that much, if not all, paternalism would be impermissible even if it was successful. For it is common to think that individuals have a right to make choices in their own personal affairs and that this includes a right to make choices that are imprudent.

Mill's view of paternalism is ultimately more complicated than these explicit arguments suggest. In particular, he has the resources for another, stronger argument against paternalism. These resources are clearest in his defense of free speech. As noted earlier, Mill thinks that there is general agreement on the importance of free speech and that, once the grounds for free speech are understood, this agreement can be exploited to support a more general defense of individual liberties (*CW* XVIII, 227 [I, 16], 260–1 [III, 1]). So his defense of expressive liberties is important not only in its own right but also insofar as it lays the foundation of his liberal principles.

MILL AGAINST CENSORSHIP

Mill's discussion of censorship in chapter II focuses on censorship whose aim is to suppress false or immoral opinion (*CW* XVIII, 228–9 [II, 1–2]). Here too, Mill is apparently concerned with censorship whether practiced by individuals, groups, or states. However, here, as elsewhere, he focuses on restrictions on liberty imposed by the state. He mentions four reasons for maintaining free speech and opposing censorship:

1. A censored opinion might be true (*CW* XVIII, 228–43 [II, 1–20], 258 [II, 41]).
2. Even if literally false, a censored opinion might contain part of the truth (*CW* XVIII, 252 [II, 34], 257 [II, 39], 258 [II, 42]).

3. Even if wholly false, a censored opinion would prevent true opinions from becoming dogma (*CW* xviii, 228–9 [ii, 1–2], 231–2 [ii, 6–7], 243–5 [ii, 22–3], 258 [ii, 43]).
4. As a dogma, an unchallenged opinion will lose its meaning (*CW* xviii, 247 [ii, 26], 258 [ii, 43]).

It is natural to group these four considerations into two main kinds: the first two invoke a truth-tracking defense of expressive liberties, while the second two appeal to a distinctive kind of value that free discussion is supposed to have.

(i) The truth-tracking rationale

The first two claims represent freedom of expression as instrumentally valuable; it is valuable, not in itself, but as the most reliable means of producing something else that Mill assumes is valuable (either extrinsically or intrinsically), namely, true belief. Though Mill seems to assume that true belief is valuable, it is not hard to see how true beliefs would possess at least instrumental value, if only because our actions, plans, and reasoning are likely to be more successful when based on true beliefs. Of course, the most reliable means of promoting true belief would be to believe everything. But that would bring a great deal of false belief along too. A more plausible goal to promote would be something like the ratio of true belief to false belief. Freedom of expression might then be defended as a more reliable policy for promoting the ratio of true belief to false belief than a policy of censorship. This rationale for freedom of expression is echoed by Justice Oliver Wendell Holmes, in his famous dissent in *Abrams* v. *United States*,[4] when he claims that the best test of truth is free trade in the marketplace of ideas.

Notice that this instrumental defense of freedom of expression does not require the mistaken assumption, which Mill sometimes makes, that the censor must assume his own infallibility (*CW* xviii, 229 [ii, 3]). The censor need not assume that he is infallible. He can recognize that he might be mistaken, but insist that he must act on the best available evidence about what is true. Mill's better reply is that proper recognition of one's own fallibility should generally lead one to keep discussion open and not foreclose discussion of possibilities that seem improbable.

This instrumental rationale may justify freedom of expression in preference to a policy of censorship whenever the censor finds the beliefs in

---

[4] 250 U.S. 616 (1919) (upholding the conviction of a wartime pamphleteer on behalf of the Russian Revolution under the Espionage Act of 1917).

question implausible or offensive. But it does not justify freedom of expression in preference to more conservative forms of censorship. If the question is what policies are likely to increase the ratio of true to false belief, we would seem to be well justified in censoring opinions for whose falsity there is especially clear, compelling, and consistent or stable evidence. We would be on good ground in censoring flat-earthers (both literal and figurative).

Another way to see the weakness of the truth-tracking justification of freedom of expression is to notice a parallel with Mill's explicit arguments against paternalism. Mill's instrumental opposition to paternalism, we saw, could not explain principled opposition to successful paternalism (cases in which *A*'s restriction of *B*'s liberty does in fact benefit *B*). In a similar way, Mill's instrumental defense of freedom of expression cannot explain what is wrong with censorship that is successful in truth-tracking terms. Suppose we lived in a society of the sort Plato imagines in the *Republic* in which cognitive capacities are distributed unequally between rulers and citizens and in which maximally knowledgable and reliable censors – call them "philosopher-kings" – censor all and only false beliefs. The truth-tracking argument would provide no argument against censorship in such circumstances. This shows that the truth-tracking argument condemns only *unsuccessful* or *incompetent* censorship. For some, this may be the biggest worry about censorship. But many would have residual worries about *successful* or *competent* censorship. They would object to censorship, even by philosopher-kings. Answering this worry requires a more robust defense of expressive liberties.

(ii) The deliberative rationale

The resources for a more robust defense of freedom of expression can be found in Mill's claim that it is needed to keep true beliefs from becoming dogmatic, because this reason for valuing freedom is intended to rebut the case for censorship even on the assumption that all and only false beliefs would be censored (*CW* xviii, 229 [ii, 2], 243 [ii, 21]). Mill's argument here is that freedoms of thought and discussion are necessary for fulfilling our natures as progressive beings (*CW* xviii, 242–3 [ii, 20]). We can and should read Mill as appealing to his perfectionist assumptions about happiness to defend expressive liberties.

In his introduction to *On Liberty*, Mill claims that his defense of liberty relies on claims about the happiness of people as progressive beings:

It is proper to state that I forgo any advantage which could be derived to my argument from the idea of abstract right as a thing independent of utility. I regard utility as the ultimate appeal on all ethical questions; but it must be utility in the largest sense, grounded on the permanent interests of man as a progressive being. (*CW* xviii, 224 [i, 11])

Mill thinks that it is our deliberative capacities, especially our capacities for practical deliberation, that mark us as progressive creatures and that, as a result, the principal ingredients of our happiness or well-being must be activities that exercise these deliberative capacities. At its most general, practical deliberation involves reflective decision-making. In *On Liberty*, Mill thinks of practical deliberation in terms of capacities to form, assess, choose, and implement projects and goals.

He who lets the world, or his own portion of it, choose his plan of life for him has no need of any other faculty than the ape-like one of imitation. He who chooses his plan for himself employs all his faculties. He must use observation to see, reasoning and judgment to foresee, activity to gather materials for decision, discrimination to decide, and when he has decided, firmness and self-control to hold his deliberate decision. And these qualities he requires and exercises exactly in proportion as the part of his conduct which he determines according to his own judgment and feelings is a large one. It is possible that he might be guided in some good path, and kept out of harm's way, without any of these things. But what will be his comparative worth as a human being? (*CW* xviii, 262–3 [iii, 4])

Mill makes similar claims about the importance of self-examination and reflective decision-making in his discussion in *Utilitarianism* of the higher pleasures doctrine, where he recognizes a categorical preference on the part of competent judges for activities that exercise their higher capacities – claiming that "it is better to be a human being dissatisfied than a pig satisfied; better to be Socrates dissatisfied than a fool satisfied."[5]

Even if we agree that these deliberative capacities are unique to humans or that humans possess them to a higher degree than other creatures, we might wonder in what way their possession marks us as progressive beings or their exercise is important to human happiness. Mill thinks an account of human happiness ought to reflect the kinds of beings we are or what is valuable about human nature. Though he is not as clear about this as one might like, his discussion of responsibility in *A System of Logic* ("Of Liberty and Necessity") suggests that he thinks that humans are responsible agents and that this is what marks us as progressive beings. There he claims that capacities for practical deliberation are necessary for responsibility. In

---

[5] John Stuart Mill, *Utilitarianism* (1861), in *The Collected Works of John Stuart Mill*, vol. x: *Essays on Ethics, Religion and Society*, ed. John M. Robson (Toronto: University of Toronto Press; London: Routledge & Kegan Paul, 1969), 212 (ii, 6).

particular, he claims that moral responsibility involves a kind of self-mastery or self-governance in which one can distinguish between the strength of one's desires and their suitability or authority and in which one's actions reflect one's deliberations about what is suitable or right to do.[6] Non-responsible agents, such as brutes or small children, appear to act on their strongest desires or, if they deliberate, to deliberate only about the instrumental means to the satisfaction of their strongest desires. By contrast, responsible agents must be able to deliberate about the appropriateness of their desires and regulate their actions according to these deliberations. If this is right, then Mill can claim that possession and use of our deliberative capacities mark us as progressive beings, because they are what mark us as moral agents who are responsible. If our happiness should reflect the sort of being we are, then Mill is in a position to argue that higher activities that exercise these deliberative capacities form the principal or most important ingredient in human happiness.

Mill's claim that the value of freedom of expression lies in keeping true beliefs from becoming dogmatic reflects his view that freedoms of thought and discussion are necessary for fulfilling our natures as progressive beings (*CW* XVIII, 242–3 [II, 20]). For instance, we can see Mill appealing to a familiar distinction between *true belief*, on the one hand, and *knowledge*, understood as something like *justified true belief*, on the other hand.[7] Progressive beings seek knowledge or justified true belief, and not simply true belief. Whereas the mere possession of true beliefs need not exercise one's deliberative capacities, because they might be the product of indoctrination, their justification would. One exercises deliberative capacities in the justification of one's beliefs and actions that is required for theoretical and practical knowledge. This is because justification involves comparison of, and deliberation among, alternatives (*CW* XVIII, 231 [II, 6], 231–2 [II, 7], 232 [II, 8], 243–5 [II, 22–3], 258 [II, 43]). Freedoms of thought and discussion are essential to the justification of one's beliefs and actions, because individuals are not cognitively self-sufficient (*CW* XVIII, 256–7 [II, 38–9], 260 [III, 1]). Sharing thought and discussion with others, especially about important matters, improves one's deliberations. It enlarges the menu of options, by identifying new options worth consideration, and helps one better assess the merits of these options, by forcing on one's attention new

---

[6] *A System of Logic Ratiocinative and Inductive* (1843; 8th edn. 1871), vols. VII–VIII of *The Collected Works of John Stuart Mill*, ed. John M. Robson, introduction by R. F. McRae (Toronto: University of Toronto Press; London: Routledge & Kegan Paul, 1973), vol. VIII, 839–42 (Bk. VI, III, 3).

[7] See T. M. Scanlon, "A Theory of Freedom of Expression," *Philosophy & Public Affairs*, 1 (1972), 204–26; and C. L. Ten, *Mill On Liberty* (Oxford: Clarendon Press, 1980), 126–8.

considerations and arguments about the comparative merits of the options. In these ways, open and vigorous discussion with diverse interlocutors improves the quality of one's deliberations. If so, censorship, even of false belief, can rob both those whose speech is suppressed and their audience of resources that they need to justify their beliefs and actions (*CW* xviii, 228–9 [ii, 1]).

We should be careful not to overstate the significance of this argument against censorship. Deliberative values may not always speak in favor of expanding one's option set.[8] Cognitively limited agents cannot consider all logically possible options, and careful consideration of many options – especially irrelevant options and options known to have failed – is likely to retard, rather than advance, their deliberations. More options are not always better than fewer. Nonetheless, it is important to note that this perfectionist appeal to deliberative values can explain why it is often wrong to censor even false beliefs. In this way, Mill's defense of expressive liberties that relies on his perfectionist appeal to deliberative values is a more robust defense than the one provided by his truth-tracking arguments alone.

FROM EXPRESSIVE LIBERTIES TO LIBERAL PRINCIPLES

Though important in its own right, Mill's defense of freedom of thought and discussion provides the resources for an argument for various basic liberties. The deliberative rationale for freedoms of thought and discussion is a special case of a more general defense of basic liberties of thought and action that Mill offers in the balance of *On Liberty*. A good human life is one that exercises one's higher capacities (*CW* xviii, 224 [i, 11], 242–3 [ii, 20], 260–82 [iii, 1–10]). A person's higher capacities include her deliberative capacities: in particular, capacities to form, revise, assess, select, and implement her own plan of life. This kind of self-government requires both positive and negative conditions. Among the positive conditions it requires is an education that develops deliberative competence by providing understanding of different historical periods and social possibilities, developing cultural and aesthetic sensibilities, developing skills essential for critical reasoning and assessment, and cultivating habits of intellectual curiosity, modesty, and open-mindedness (*CW* xviii, 301–5 [v, 12–15]). Among the negative conditions that self-government requires are various liberties of thought and action. If the choice and pursuit of projects and plans are to be

---

[8] Cf. Gerald Dworkin, "Is More Choice Better than Less?," in Gerald Dworkin, *The Theory and Practice of Autonomy* (Cambridge and New York: Cambridge University Press, 1988), 62–81.

deliberate, they must be informed as to the alternatives and their grounds, and this requires intellectual freedoms of speech, association, and press that expand the menu of deliberative options and allow for the vivid representation of the comparative merits of options on that menu. If there is to be choice and implementation of choices, there must be liberties of action such as freedom of association, freedom of worship, and freedom to choose one's occupation.

Indeed, liberties of thought and action are importantly related. Mill values diversity and experimentation in lifestyles not only insofar as they are expressions of self-government but also insofar as they enhance self-government. For experimentation and diversity of lifestyle expand the deliberative menu and bring out more clearly the nature and merits of options on the menu (*CW* xviii, 244, 245 [ii, 23, 38], 260–1 [iii, 1]). So experiments in living not only express the autonomy of the agent at the time of action, but they provide materials for the agent and others in future deliberations. But diversity and experimentation presuppose liberties of action, and in this way liberties of action, as well as thought and discussion, are essential to the full exercise of deliberative capacities.

This interpretation provides Mill with a robust rationale for various liberties of thought and action; they are important as necessary conditions for exercising our deliberative capacities and so for producing the chief ingredients of human happiness. In particular, it provides a more robust defense of Mill's general anti-paternalism. For if a person's happiness depends on her exercise of the capacities that make her a responsible agent, then a principal ingredient of her own good must include opportunities for responsible choice and reflective decision-making. But then it becomes clear how autonomy is an important part of a person's good and how paternalism undercuts her good in important and predictable ways. Mill may still not have an argument against successful paternalism, but his perfectionist defense of basic liberties does give him an argument that successful paternalism is much harder to achieve than one might have thought, because it is very hard to benefit an autonomous agent in paternalistic ways.

LIMITS ON LIBERTY

Despite this robust rationale for liberties of thought and action, it is also important to see that Mill is not treating liberty as an intrinsic good or endorsing an unqualified right to liberty.

First, insofar as Mill defends individual liberties by appeal to deliberative values, he can distinguish the importance of different liberties in terms of their role in practical deliberation. A central part of practical deliberation is forming ideals and regulating one's actions and plans in accordance with these ideals. But some liberties seem more central than others to the selection of personal ideals. For instance, it seems plausible that liberties of speech, association, worship, and choice of profession are more important than liberties to drive in either direction on streets designated as one-way, liberties not to wear seatbelts, or liberties to dispose of one's gross income as one pleases, because restrictions on the former seem to interfere more than restrictions on the latter with deliberations about what sort of person to be. If so, Millian principles arguably defend rights to certain *basic liberties*, rather than a right to liberty *per se*. If so, Mill's liberalism should not be confused with traditional libertarianism, which does recognize a right to liberty *per se*.

Second, even the exercise of basic liberties is limited by the harm principle, which justifies restricting liberty to engage in actions that cause harm or threaten imminent harm to others. There are interesting questions about the correct interpretation of the harm principle, such as how we draw the line between harm and offense.[9] But his commitment to some version of the harm principle as a ground for restricting liberty is hard to dispute.

Third, it is important to be clear about how Mill values basic liberties. To account for the robust character of his perfectionist argument, it is tempting to suppose that Mill thinks these basic liberties are themselves important intrinsic goods.[10] But limitations in the scope of Mill's argument show that this cannot be his view.

It is, perhaps, hardly necessary to say that this doctrine is meant to apply only to human beings in the maturity of their faculties … Liberty, as a principle, has no application to any state of things anterior to the time when mankind have become capable of being improved by free and equal discussion. (*CW* xviii, 224 [i, 10])

So, for instance, the scope of Mill's prohibition on paternalism does not include paternalistic restrictions on the choices of the very young. Presumably, Mill is also willing to permit some forms of censorship for the young that he would reject for mature adults. Such restrictions on the

---

[9] Some of these questions about the proper interpretation of the harm principle are taken up in David Lyons, "Liberty and Harm to Others," reprinted in Lyons, *Rights, Welfare, and Mill's Moral Theory* (New York: Oxford University Press, 1994), 89–108; Ten, *Mill On Liberty*, ch. 4; and David Brink, "Mill's Moral and Political Philosophy," in Edward N. Zalta, ed., *Stanford Encyclopedia of Philosophy* (2007).

[10] Cf. Fred Berger, *Happiness, Justice, and Freedom* (Los Angeles: University of California Press, 1984), 41, 50, 199, 231–2; and James Bogen and Daniel Farrell, "Freedom and Happiness in Mill's Defence of Liberty," *Philosophical Quarterly*, 28 (1978), 325–8.

scope of Mill's principles make no sense if basic liberties are dominant intrinsic goods, for then it should always be valuable to accord people liberties – a claim that Mill here denies. These restrictions make perfect sense if the liberties in question, though not intrinsically valuable, are necessary conditions to realizing dominant goods, for then there will be, or need be, no value to liberty where, as in these circumstances, other necessary conditions for the realization of these higher values – in particular, sufficient rational development or normative competence – are absent.

LIMITS ON FREEDOM OF EXPRESSION

Does Mill recognize any limitations on his defense of free speech? If one read only chapter II of *On Liberty* one might be excused for concluding that Mill is a free-speech absolutist who believes that censorship is never permissible (at least for mature competent adults). Were we to combine this free speech absolutism with the assumption that liberty can be restricted if and only if it causes harm, we would have to conclude that Mill believes that speech can never be harmful – "sticks and stone can break my bones, but words can never hurt me." However, Mill does recognize that speech can be harmful, and he applies the harm principle to speech, as well as other action, when he claims that the regulation of incendiary speech is permissible.

Even opinions lose their immunity when the circumstances in which they are expressed are such as to constitute their expression a positive instigation to some mischievous act. An opinion that corn-dealers are starvers of the poor, or that private property is robbery, ought to be unmolested when simply circulated through the press, but may justifiably incur punishment when delivered orally to an excited mob assembled before the house of a corn-dealer, or when handed about among the same mob in the form of a placard. (*CW* XVIII, 260 [III, 1])

One question that the corn-dealer passage raises is how much censorship would be justified by applying the harm principle. Mill would presumably accept at least some aspects of First Amendment jurisprudence. He would agree with some version of the "clear and present danger test" recognized by Justice Holmes in his majority opinion in *Schenck* v. *United States*.[11]

The most stringent protection of free speech would not protect a man in falsely shouting fire in a crowded theater, and causing a panic … The question in every

---

[11] 249 U.S. 47 (1919) (upholding conspiracy convictions, under the Espionage Act of 1917, for the distribution of literature aiming to obstruct the military draft).

case is whether the words used are used in such circumstances and are of such a nature as to create a clear and present danger.

This raises the more general question of how good the match is between Mill's defense of freedom of expression and some central aspects of First Amendment jurisprudence. This is especially relevant to ascertaining which limitations Mill can and should recognize on freedom of expression, because First Amendment jurisprudence is not absolutist.

DELIBERATIVE VALUES AND FIRST AMENDMENT CATEGORIES

It is a general proposition governing the adjudication of cases involving individual rights within constitutional law in the United States that when a court determines that an individual's interest or liberty is a fundamental constitutional value it accords that value special protection by subjecting legislation that interferes with that value to *strict scrutiny* or some comparable standard. To pass strict scrutiny, legislation must pursue a compelling state interest in the least restrictive manner possible. Strict scrutiny and its relatives contrast with a weaker standard of review, known as *rational basis review* that is applied to legislation affecting interests and liberties that are not fundamental. To pass rational basis review, legislation need only pursue a legitimate interest in a reasonable manner. With some notable exceptions in which courts recognize intermediate levels of scrutiny, the analysis of the importance of interests or liberties and associated standards of scrutiny is generally *bivalent*: interests or liberties are either fundamental or they are not; fundamental ones trigger strict scrutiny or some comparable standard, whereas non-fundamental ones trigger rational basis review or some comparable standard.[12] For the most part, liberties of expression are treated as fundamental liberties, because of the central role open discussion plays in both public and private deliberations. Insofar as liberties of expression are fundamental, the court protects them by subjecting legislation that interferes with them to strict scrutiny or some comparably exacting standard, such as the clear and present danger test.

However, not all liberties of expression are treated the same. For instance, First Amendment analysis distinguishes between *content-neutral* restrictions

---

[12] The treatments of commercial speech, under First Amendment jurisprudence, and gender classifications, under Equal Protection jurisprudence, are among the exceptions to this rule, insofar as the court subjects restrictions on commercial speech and regulations distributing social benefits and burdens by gender to an intermediate standard of review.

on speech that restrict the time, manner, and place of speech but not its content, and *content-specific* restrictions that restrict some forms of speech on account of the topic discussed or the viewpoint expressed in the speech. Whereas content-specific restrictions are subject to heightened scrutiny, content-neutral restrictions are subject to weaker forms of scrutiny. Deliberative values would seem to explain the Supreme Court's special concern with content-specific restrictions. Often, time, manner, and place restrictions leave open many avenues of expression and so do not significantly restrict the production, distribution, or consumption of ideas. By contrast, content-specific, especially viewpoint-specific, restrictions make it harder for certain messages to be heard and evaluated. If the representation of diverse perspectives, even mistaken ideas, can improve public and private deliberations, then there is general reason to think that content-specific restrictions constrain deliberative values in unacceptable ways.

However, not all content-specific regulations are thought to restrict fundamental liberties. First Amendment jurisprudence also distinguishes between *low-value* and *high-value* speech. The liberty to engage in low-value speech is not a fundamental liberty; content-specific regulation of low-value speech, as a result, need not satisfy strict scrutiny. By contrast, other forms of speech are high-value, and the liberty to engage in them is a fundamental liberty; as a result, content-specific regulation of high-value speech must satisfy strict scrutiny or some comparable standard. The court formulated the distinction between low-value and high-value speech in *Chaplinsky* v. *New Hampshire*:

There are certain well-defined and narrowly limited classes of speech, the prevention and punishment of which have never been thought to raise any Constitutional problem. These include the lewd and the obscene, the profane, the libelous, and the insulting or "fighting" words – those which by their very utterance inflict injury or tend to incite an immediate breach of the peace. It has been well observed that such utterances are no essential part of any exposition of ideas, and are of such slight social value as a step to truth that any benefit that may be derived from them is clearly outweighed by the social interest in order and morality.[13]

Here the court associates central First Amendment liberties with what is an essential part of the exposition of ideas and what is of value as a step toward truth. Like Mill, the court justifies freedom of expression as a way of promoting true belief. However, if the court values freedom of expression only as a means of promoting true belief, then it becomes difficult to extend

---

[13] 315 U.S. 568 (1942) (upholding a state prohibition on the use of offensive language in face-to-face exchanges in public spaces), at 571–2.

protection to false beliefs, as the court has. But we need not interpret the court as valuing freedom of expression only as a means of acquiring true beliefs. The court appeals to what is an essential part of the exposition of ideas and what is of value as a step toward truth. We can see this rationale as invoking, as Mill also does, deliberative values about the value of free inquiry to the promotion of knowledge, and not just true belief. If we interpret the court's rationale this way, we can provide a more wide-ranging conception of high-value speech that includes the advocacy of some false beliefs.

What would Mill think about low-value speech and the permissibility of regulating it? He might well think that some examples of low-value speech violate the harm principle. For instance, it is not hard to see how libelous speech – roughly, false and defamatory speech in which the speaker knew that her statement was false and defamatory or acted in reckless disregard of these matters – might be harmful. And some kinds of fighting words might also be harmful. Certainly, fighting words that incite pugilistic responses can be harmful, as Mill recognizes in the corn-dealer case (*CW* XVIII, 260 [III, 1]). In other situations, fighting words may cause genuine psychic harm that is serious in its consequences and goes beyond mere offense. It is less clear what Mill would think about the permissibility of anti-discriminatory regulations of speech of the sort embodied in employment discrimination law, hate speech regulations, and policies regulating certain kinds of pornography. Mill's commitments here would depend, in part, on whether the regulations in question targeted mere offense or genuine harm. Insofar as such regulations target genuine harm, and not mere offense, some of them may be defensible according to Millian principles.

Insofar as these forms of speech are harmful, they would be regulable under the harm principle. But the harm principle applies to high-value speech; it says that speech can be regulated no matter how valuable it is if it is harmful. If the harm principle is Mill's only reason for regulating speech, then he would appear to be committed to regulating harmful speech *in spite* of its high value. But then Mill could not really agree with *Chaplinsky's* distinction between high-value and low-value speech and its claim that low-value speech possesses no significant expressive interest.

FROM LIBERAL PRINCIPLES TO EXPRESSIVE LIBERTIES

But this overlooks a way in which Mill might appeal to deliberative values to determine the comparative value of speech interests. To appreciate this possibility, consider how one might understand his free-speech principle in light of his considered views about paternalism. Previously, we examined how his discussion of free speech could inform his liberalism and, in particular, his anti-paternalism. Now I would like to explore a way in which his liberalism and, in particular, anti-paternalism can inform his position on free speech.

Despite Mill's many blanket prohibitions on paternalism, he does not (consistently) reject paternalism *per se*. For instance, he qualifies his blanket prohibition on paternalism to allow that no one should be free to sell himself into slavery.

The ground for thus limiting his power of voluntarily disposing of his own lot is apparent, and is very clearly seen in this extreme case … by selling himself for a slave, he abdicates his liberty; he forgoes any future use of it beyond that single act. He, therefore, defeats in his own case, the very purpose which is the justification of allowing him to dispose of himself. (*CW* xviii, 299 [v, 11])

Because it is the importance of exercising one's deliberative capacities that explains the importance of certain liberties, the usual reason for recognizing liberties provides an argument against extending liberties to do things that will permanently undermine one's future exercise of those same capacities. In this case, an exception to the usual prohibition on paternalism is motivated by appeal to the very same deliberative values that explain the usual prohibition. So this seems to be a principled exception to the usual prohibition on paternalism. We might call these *autonomy-enhancing* or *deliberation-enhancing* forms of paternalism.[14]

There might be similar deliberation-enhancing forms of censorship. There might be speech that does not engage or tends to undermine the very deliberative values that explain why content-specific forms of censorship are normally impermissible. On this view, whereas speech that engages or promotes deliberative values is high-value, speech that fails to engage or frustrates deliberative values would be low-value. I should note that Mill does not explicitly endorse the distinction between high-value and low-value speech or recognize deliberation-enhancing forms of censorship, but doing so would be one way to make his liberal principles more consistent and allow him to accept some central aspects of First Amendment jurisprudence. To see how such limitations on freedom of expression might work, reconsider two categories of low-value speech: libel and fighting words.

---

[14] Notice that Mill claims that the reasons for allowing paternalism in "this extreme case" are "evidently of far wider application" (*CW* xviii, 299–30 [v, 11]). That raises the question of what other forms of paternalism might be justified as principled exceptions to the usual prohibition on paternalism. Mill does not directly address this question.

Though libel can cause harm and so could be regulated even if it were high-value speech, in spite of the fact that it is high-value, it is also arguable that libel does not properly engage deliberative values and so should be treated as low-value speech, which requires no especially compelling justification to regulate. Libel is false and defamatory speech in which the speaker knew that her statement was false and defamatory or acted in reckless disregard of these matters. It is true, as Mill claims, that the careful consideration of claims, advanced in good conscience, that are in fact false can advance deliberation by forcing us to consider the grounds of their falsity. But libelous speech is not advanced in good conscience. It is arguably a case in which more speech is not better insofar as the introduction of false and harmful claims with no concern for their truth and consequences arguably hinders, rather than promotes, reasoned assessment of issues. But then for that reason libel could be viewed as low-value speech and its censorship could be treated as a principled exception to the usual prohibition on censorship.

Deliberative values might also explain why fighting words are low-value speech. *Chaplinsky* characterizes fighting words as those that "by their very utterance inflict injury or tend to incite an immediate breach of the peace." As a matter of subsequent constitutional doctrine, the court has interpreted the category of fighting words narrowly, focusing on their tendency to incite violence. Fighting words, so understood, are words that in their context tend to evoke visceral and violent – rather than articulate – responses. However, it would be a mistake to focus on pugilistic responses, and this is why *Chaplinsky* rightly construes fighting words more broadly, so as to include words whose utterance would cause injury in a reasonable person. A natural response to the use of insulting epithets in many such contexts is visceral but non-violent; the victim of fighting words might be intimidated and silenced as well as provoked. Whether silence or fisticuffs, the natural response is not articulate. But then fighting words simply express, without articulating, the speaker's perspective, and they invite various inarticulate responses. If so, we can see why the court might reasonably claim that they do not contribute to deliberative values, but often hinder them. If so, there is a case to be made for thinking that fighting words are low-value speech and that the censorship of fighting words would be a principled exception to the usual prohibition on censorship.[15]

[15] In this connection, one might note that Mill does consider restrictions on "intemperate" speech that exceeds "the bounds of fair discussion" (*CW* xviii, 258–9 [ii, 44]). He observes that there is more to be

Another potential form of deliberation-enhancing censorship concerns campaign finance reform. Campaign finance reform is obviously a large and complex debate that cannot be satisfactorily addressed here. Nonetheless, we can put parts of this debate in a new perspective by viewing some such reforms as deliberation-enhancing censorship. Campaign finance reform can take many forms, from limitations on private expenditures by candidates, political parties, and individual donors, to the public financing of elections. There are different rationales for different kinds of reforms. Some reforms, such as expenditure limits on private donors, have as their main aim the regulation of influence-peddling. While such reforms and rationales are important in their own right, their connections with deliberative values are unclear or, at best, indirect. Of more direct relevance to our present concerns are those campaign finance reforms that limit spending by candidates and donors or that ban private expenditures and provide for equal public funding for candidates as a way of addressing concerns about the impact of unequal resources on the character of political campaigns and political debate. At least since the landmark case of *Buckley* v. *Valeo*,[16] US courts have been generally skeptical about the permissibility of the limitations on political expression inherent in such reforms. Skeptics of such reforms have generally viewed this as a conflict between equality and First Amendment rights, concluding that the interest "in equalizing the relative financial resources of candidates competing for elective office is clearly not sufficient to justify the provision's infringement of fundamental First Amendment rights."[17] But our Millian defense of limitations on speech that enhance deliberative values suggests a different perspective. In circumstances of significant inequalities in resources, *laissez-faire* political campaigning, in which campaigns are privately funded and in which candidates

said on behalf of such restrictions when they are applied to the expression of prevailing views than when they are applied to the expression of minority views: "In general opinions contrary to those commonly received can only obtain a fair hearing by studied moderation of language and the most cautious avoidance of unnecessary offence, from which they hardly ever deviate even in a slightest degree without losing ground, while unmeasured vituperation employed on the side of the prevailing opinion really does deter people from professing contrary opinions and from listening to those who profess them. For the interest, therefore, of truth and justice it is far more important to restrain this employment of vituperative language than the other" (*CW* XVIII, 259 [II, 44]). But he ultimately rejects all such restrictions, claiming that it is "obvious that law and authority have no business ... restraining either" (*CW* XVIII, 259 [II, 44]). I discuss Mill's concern and caution about regulating intemperate speech and argue that Millian principles may actually support narrowly crafted hate speech regulations in David Brink, "Millian Principles, Freedom of Expression, and Hate Speech," *Legal Theory* 7 (2001), 119–57.
[16] 424 U.S. 1 (1976) (invalidating legislation imposing limits on campaign expenditures by candidates and private donors and creating a system of public funding for presidential campaigns).
[17] Ibid., at 54.

and donors operate under no serious restrictions on the amounts they spend, gives a significant advantage in political debate and electioneering to candidates and causes backed by the most resources. But then a *laissez-faire* regime makes the representation of candidates, issues, and policies hostage to economic interests in a way that is likely to prevent political dialogue from representing diverse views and tracking the merits of viewpoints as required by the sort of free and open inquiry essential to the exercise of deliberative values. Insofar as this is true, *laissez-faire* harms the deliberative interests of Haves, as well as Have-Nots. If we appeal to the deliberative values that justify freedom of expression to help distinguish between fundamental and non-fundamental expressive liberties, then there is an interesting case to be made for the idea that campaign finance reforms designed to redress the effects of economic inequalities on political dialogue do not infringe central First Amendment liberties and that such reforms would be a principled exception to the usual prohibition on the censorship of political expression.[18]

Yet another way in which Mill's conception of freedom of expression might be articulated in light of his liberal principles concerns the obligation of public institutions to represent diverse points of view. Mill insists that in order to exercise our deliberative capacities properly it is essential not only to represent diverse perspectives on important moral, political, and spiritual matters but also to represent their merits faithfully and vigorously. This discipline of fair representation of alternatives is "so essential … to a real understanding of moral and human subjects that, if opponents of all important truths do not exist, it is indispensable to imagine them and supply them, with the strongest arguments which the most skilful devil's advocate can conjure up (*CW* xviii, 245 [ii, 23]).

What is true of the need to represent false opinion applies *a fortiori* to true opinion and opinion whose truth value is not yet known. Mill's defense of proportional, rather than winner-take-all, representation in *Considerations on Representative Government*[19] and state support for the

---

[18] In "Thoughts on Parliamentary Reform" (1859), Mill expresses serious reservations about the effects of economic inequalities among candidates in elections that allow for unrestricted private expenditure by candidates and mentions publicly financed elections as a possible antidote (*CW* xix, 320). However, he does not object to the effects of inequalities among private donors, and he does not make explicit this deliberation-enhancing rationale for restrictions on private campaign finance.

[19] John Stuart Mill, *Considerations on Representative Government* (1861), in *The Collected Works of John Stuart Mill*, vol. xix: *Essays on Politics and Society*, Part II, ed. John M. Robson, introduction by Alexander Brady (Toronto: University of Toronto Press; London: Routledge & Kegan Paul, 1977), 371–577 (vii).

arts in the *Principles of Political Economy*[20] are examples of institutional mechanisms designed to increase the diversity and salience of political, intellectual, and artistic activities and voices so as to enhance the character of public and private deliberations. One application of this concern with the fair representation of alternatives in the domain of expression would be support for a fairness in broadcasting doctrine, of the sort at stake in *Red Lion Broadcasting Co. v. FCC*,[21] that would, at least in some contexts, condition access to broadcast time by some candidates and viewpoints on the provision of access to broadcast time by opposing candidates or points of view. Insofar as making public speech by some conditional on the provision of public speech by others can be understood as a restriction of expressive liberties, it too can be represented as a form of deliberation-enhancing censorship.

Mill's position on the limits of freedom of expression requires reconstruction. He is clearly not a free-speech absolutist, as his application of the harm principle to the corn-dealer case illustrates. The more interesting question is whether he can accept some other limitations on freedom of expression of the sort embodied in some central First Amendment principles and doctrines. Millian principles provide a good rationale for First Amendment doctrines about the importance of high-value speech. While Mill does not himself explicitly distinguish between high-value and low-value speech, one way to reconcile his free-speech principles with his other liberal principles would be to treat speech that fails to engage or retards deliberative values as low-value speech whose suppression could be justified as a form of deliberation-enhancing censorship, akin to the autonomy-enhancing paternalism that he explicitly recognizes.

CONCLUSION

Mill's defense of expressive liberties has been deservedly influential, and it is important in its own right to understand these arguments. But Mill intended his free-speech principles to play a larger role in articulating and grounding more general liberal principles governing thought and action. Once we appreciate the way in which his defense of expressive liberties

[20] John Stuart Mill, *Principles of Political Economy with Some of Their Applications to Social Philosophy*, Part II (1848), vol. III of *The Collected Works of John Stuart Mill*, ed. John M. Robson, introduction by V. W. Bladen (Toronto: University of Toronto Press; London: Routledge & Kegan Paul, 1965), 968–10 (Bk. V, XI, 15).
[21] 395 U.S. 367 (1969) (upholding the FCC's fairness doctrine and, in particular, the personal attack rule against First Amendment challenge).

appeals to the distinctive value of our nature as progressive beings – specifically, our capacities as agents – we can see how he thinks that free-speech principles, properly understood, support a broader array of individual liberties. In particular, we can see how the importance of deliberative values provides Mill with a reasonably robust defense of his general anti-paternalistic doctrine. But just as Mill's free-speech principles can shed light on his liberal principles, so too his liberal principles can shed light on his free-speech principles. Reconciling his expressive and liberal commitments suggests some ways of extending and qualifying his explicit commitments about freedom of expression. Though Mill initially says that he will defend one "very simple" liberal principle – the harm principle – as governing the limits of the authority that the state or anyone else may have over another, this turns out to be an over-simple statement of his liberal principles. Several potential qualifications are in order.[22] One qualification is that the harm principle need not be invoked to justify restricting liberty, for Mill endorses deliberation-enhancing forms of paternalism, as in his discussion of the permissibility of restrictions on selling oneself into slavery. This feature of his considered liberal principles has a direct bearing on freedom of expression. Mill can and does recognize permissible forms of censorship whose aim is to prevent harm, as in the corn-dealer example. But if we try to square Mill's expressive principles with his other liberal principles, this suggests that he can and should recognize the permissibility of other forms of censorship whose aim is not to prevent harm but to advance the very deliberative values that explain why censorship is normally impermissible. When Mill's free-speech principles are understood in this light, they provide an interesting and generally supportive perspective on some central First Amendment categories and doctrines. Viewing Mill's principles governing freedom of expression in the context of his more general liberal principles provides distinctive and instructive information about the proper interpretation of both sets of commitments.

---

[22] See Brink, "Mill's Moral and Political Philosophy," for fuller discussion of ways in which Mill's commitment to the harm principle must be qualified.

CHAPTER 3

Racism, blasphemy, and free speech

Jonathan Riley

INTRODUCTION

J. S. Mill evidently accepts that society and government may legitimately use coercive measures to prevent individuals from behaving in ways that pose a risk of direct and immediate harm to other people without their genuine consent and participation. The most important thing a society can do to promote the general welfare, he makes clear in the fifth chapter of *Utilitarianism*, is to establish laws and customs that distribute weighty equal rights not to suffer unprovoked violence, undue discrimination, and other grievous harms. These rules of justice might sanction unusually harsh punishment for wrongdoers – whether members of the popular majority or a minority – who make a show of harming others merely because the others are perceived as belonging to alien races, religions, or ethnic backgrounds.

But Mill also gives the impression that he draws a sharp distinction between actions and speech. In the second chapter of *On Liberty*, he argues that mature individuals – people capable of rational persuasion, which excludes children and delirious, insane, or otherwise incompetent adults – ought to be absolutely free to form and discuss any opinions they wish: "there ought to exist the fullest liberty of professing and discussing, as a matter of ethical conviction, any doctrine, however immoral it may be considered" (*CW* XVIII, 228n. [II, 1n.]). He "altogether condemn[s]" even the practice of referring to "the immorality or impiety of an opinion" as such (*CW* XVIII, 234 [II, 11]). Complete liberty of thought and discussion is the sole way in which fallible human beings can acquire warranted beliefs: "Complete liberty of contradicting and disproving our opinion, is the very condition which justifies us in assuming its truth for purposes of action; and on no other terms can a being with human faculties have any rational assurance of being right" (*CW* XVIII, 231 [II, 6]). No doubt warranted beliefs that have survived all criticisms offered to date are not known with certainty to be true. But perfect certainty is not possible for fallible beings, who must proceed by learning from their mistakes. A completely open dynamic discussion process of indefinite duration is the only way to attain the imperfect "amount of certainty attainable by a fallible being" (*CW* XVIII, 232 [II, 8]). By implication, individuals should be at liberty to express racist or blasphemous opinions that others may reasonably be expected to find offensive and demeaning. Offense and disgust are disagreeable feelings, he suggests, but such feelings do not amount to perceptible injury or harm.

Some have drawn the conclusion, quite understandably, that Mill is a free-speech absolutist, in other words, a liberal extremist who maintains that the individual ought to have opportunities to express opinions of any content.[1] This need not mean that the individual must have unlimited opportunities. Content-neutral time, place, and manner restrictions are compatible with such absolutism, for instance, provided the individual remains free to express opinions of any content at some times, in some places, and in some manners. Similarly, in cases of "symbolic conduct" such as "burning the flag" or "burning a draft card," where the conduct arguably has expressive and non-expressive components, it may be possible to justify restrictions aimed at the non-expressive component as content-neutral despite the incidental restriction of freedom of expression, provided the individual is free to express in other ways the same opinions which he intended to express by burning the flag or burning his draft card. Still, it may not always be possible to draw a bright line between content-based restrictions and content-neutral ones: at least some time, place, and manner restrictions and some restrictions aimed at non-expressive conduct may limit the content of permissible messages, as McLuhan's well-known phrase "the medium is the message" suggests.[2]

---

[1] Daniel Jacobson, "Mill on Liberty, Speech, and the Free Society," *Philosophy & Public Affairs*, 29 (2000), 276–309; and K. C. O'Rourke, *John Stuart Mill and Freedom of Expression: The Genesis of a Theory* (London: Routledge, 2001), interpret Mill as subscribing to a quasi-Kantian idea of autonomy and defending free-speech absolutism on that basis. But such a reading makes Mill vulnerable to devastating objections of the sort that S. J. Brison, "The Autonomy Defence of Free Speech," *Ethics*, 108 (1998), 312–39, mounts against any autonomy-based defence of free-speech absolutism (see n. 4, below). For further discussion of the interpretations of Jacobson and O'Rourke, see Jonathan Riley, "Mill's Doctrine of Freedom of Expression," *Utilitas*, 17 (2005), 152–9; *Mill's Radical Liberalism* (London: Routledge, forthcoming).

[2] Marshall McLuhan, *Understanding Media: The Extensions of Man*, ed. L. H. Lapham (Cambridge, MA: MIT Press, 1994).

Assuming for the sake of argument that a bright line can be drawn, various justifications can be offered for the absolute rejection of content-based restrictions. Perhaps expression is special in some sense. This might mean that it does not cause any direct and immediate harm to others without their consent. Speech might annoy or upset them but it never causes them any type of perceptible damage unless they are persuaded to participate in the production of the damage. Because it puts no external impediments in their way, others can freely avoid any expression that displeases them. If they are persuaded to adopt foolish opinions, then, as mature individuals, they, not the speaker, are accountable for any damage to themselves or others that flows from their own choices. At least people may learn from their mistakes, even if the expression has no other social benefits. So there is no reason to use coercion to suppress any expression because expression never involves direct and immediate harms to others without their consent. Mill himself uses just this form of argument to defend absolute liberty of what he calls "purely self-regarding" conduct and he does seem inclined to treat discussion as if it were purely self-regarding activity. Indeed, he goes so far as to say that "the liberty of expressing and publishing opinions … is practically inseparable from … the liberty of thought itself" (*CW* xviii, 225–6 [1, 12]). There is no doubt that the liberty of thought is a purely self-regarding liberty in Mill's sense.

Nevertheless, a moment's reflection shows that it is impossible to maintain that expression never harms others without their consent: direct threats of physical injury or financial ruin, incitement of third parties to commit violence, fraudulent commercial advertising, malicious libel, and invasion of privacy are types of speech whose content implies a risk of direct and immediate harm to others without their consent. Indeed, a speaker always poses a risk of harm to his competitors because his speech may prove more persuasive than theirs does to the audience, thereby depriving them of consumers in the market for ideas. A careful reading confirms that Mill does not deny these obvious points. He admits that expression is not purely self-regarding conduct. Instead, "it belongs to that part of the conduct of an individual which concerns other people" (*CW* xviii, 225–6 [1, 12]). Expression is the sort of conduct which Mill calls "social" or other commentators call "other-regarding." Properly understood, such conduct "concerns other people" because it directly and immediately affects them without their consent and participation.

But perhaps expression remains special in a different way. Perhaps it ought to be given special protection even though non-expressive social conduct that resulted in similar harms to others could properly be regulated or even prohibited by society. This intuition is merely a species of super-stition, however, if it is asserted without any supporting reasons for the differential treatment of expressive conduct and non-expressive conduct. Speech could reasonably be seen as special in the sense required, however, if it produces extraordinary benefits not associated with non-expressive con-duct, and these special benefits are sufficient to justify the conclusion that speech of any content always produces, at least in some contexts, more benefits than harms to the members of society.

Yet what could the extraordinary benefits of expression of any content be? Some might reply that expression, unlike non-expressive conduct, always conveys valuable information broadly construed to include sentiments and feelings as well as ideas and propositions. The free flow of information of any content is needed for the discovery of truth in the sense of warranted beliefs, it might be argued, or for the effective operation of a democratic political system, or for individuals to learn more about their feelings and develop greater autonomy in the sense of exerting rational control over their own lives, or for some combination of these various important social benefits. Yet these beneficial effects seem instead to be contingent on the content of the speech. Some content-based restrictions, including restraints against credible threats, incitement, malicious lies, and even promotional (let alone fraudulent) commercial advertising, may actually enhance truth-discovery, democratic deliberation, and personal self-development and autonomy. If so, an absolute rejection of content-based restrictions is not justified for promoting these beneficial consequences.[3]

Against this, it might be objected that any content-based restrictions put society on a slippery slope toward unjustified censorship because legislators and juries cannot be trusted to make the sharp distinctions required to identify credible threats, incitement, and other forms of expression whose content is too damaging to others to permit. There may be something to this worry. Yet nobody thinks it is reasonable to employ the slippery-slope objection to defeat all so-called content-neutral restrictions. As suggested earlier, time, place, and manner restrictions and restrictions targeted at non-expressive elements of symbolic conduct arguably limit content as well, and may well be viewed as politically acceptable ways of smuggling in content-based restrictions. In any case, without further argument, it is unpersuasive

---

[3] For a persuasive argument that free-speech absolutism is not justifiable in terms of autonomy, see S. J. Brison, "The Autonomy Defence of Free Speech," *Ethics*, 108 (1998), 312–39. She argues in particular that autonomy may be undermined by the free expression of some forms of "hate speech." Analogous arguments can be made, it seems, that democratic deliberation and the discovery of warranted beliefs may also be undermined by free expression of some types of speech.

to suggest that people can possess sufficient powers of discrimination to identify criminal non-expressive conduct yet be incapable of identifying criminal expression that severely injures others without their consent.

I shall argue that Mill does not endorse free-speech absolutism. Rather, he endorses a general policy of *laissez-faire*, according to which expression should generally be left alone except in situations in which free expression directly and immediately inflicts grievous harm on others without their consent. Indeed, content-based criminal sanctions may promote the general welfare in the exceptional situations calling for suppression and punishment of speech. Mill's defense of complete liberty of thought and discussion can be reconciled with this general policy of *laissez-faire* for expression. Such a reconciliation depends on defining "discussion" so that the types of expression which involve grievous harm to others without their consent do not count as "discussion." At the same time, coercive measures are justified against types of expression which do not count as "discussion." Before concluding, I shall illustrate this point with specific reference to credible threats of violence against others, incitement of third parties to "imminent lawless action" against them where there is probable cause to believe that the "imminent lawless action" will be produced, and for-profit promotional advertising of such threats and incitements. Mill's liberalism provides support for coercive measures that would serve to marginalize, if not stamp out altogether, the expression and publication of opinions that force others to endure a risk of severe direct and immediate harm merely because of their ethnicity, religion, race, gender, or sexual orientation. These identifying characteristics are inno-cent in the sense that they have no value as predictors of harmful activity toward others on the part of any individual who possesses them.[4]

A *LAISSEZ-FAIRE* DOCTRINE FOR EXPRESSION

To understand how Mill's doctrine of freedom of expression works, it is necessary to situate it within his more general liberal theory of individual liberty and social control.[5] As indicated earlier, he is explicit that "expressing

---

[4] The motivation for expression can, of course, be crucial for the assessment of its permissibility. Credible threats of injury are permissible if issued by judges, juries, or prosecutors in accord with their official discretion during a trial or some other phase of due process against individuals who are indicted or convicted for harmful social conduct, for example. Fraudulent commercial advertising that increases the likelihood that individuals wanted for criminal conduct will be duly captured and punished by the authorities might also be permissible.

[5] I can give here only a bare outline of Mill's liberalism as I interpret it. For further details of my interpretation of its main elements, including the central principle of absolute self-regarding liberty, the doctrine of free speech, and the theory of constitutional representative democracy, see Jonathan

and publishing opinions' is not conduct of the 'purely self-regarding' kind which, according to his central liberty principle, a mature individual has a basic right to engage in as he pleases, free from all forms of coercive interference by others. Self-regarding conduct, he says, does not "affect" others at all "directly, and in the first instance," or, if it does, "only with their free, voluntary, and undeceived consent and participation" (*CW* XVIII, 225 [1, 12]). In particular, it does not directly and immediately cause them any harm unless they genuinely consent and participate in the production of the harm. The idea of "harm" which is most consistent with the text of *On Liberty* is a broad empirical one, to wit, any form of perceptible damage, including physical injury, financial loss, damage to reputation, loss of employment or social position, disappointment of contractual expectations, and so forth, but excluding "mere dislike" or emotional distress without any accompanying evidence of perceptible injury.[6] Any act of expression, however, unlike self-regarding conduct, does directly and immediately harm others in this broad sense without their genuine consent, or at least poses a risk of doing so. A speaker may convince an audience to reject or even refuse to consider the opinions of his competitors, for example, or he might mislead his listeners, or he might injure third parties by slandering their reputations or inciting violence against them, all without the consent of the competitors, listeners, or third parties.

Expressive conduct is "social" or other-regarding in nature insofar as it directly and immediately affects others without their consent. It follows that freedom of expression is not a self-regarding freedom covered by the central liberty principle. Thus, Mill is not committed to any view that speakers must have rights to speak as they please, choosing whatever time, place, manner, and content of speech seem best in terms of their own judgment and inclinations.

Riley, "Introduction" to J. S. Mill, *Principles of Political Economy and Chapters on Socialism* (Oxford: Oxford University Press, 1998), vii–xlvii; "Mill's Doctrine of Freedom of Expression"; "Mill: *On Liberty*," in J. Shand, ed., *Central Works of Philosophy* (Chesham: Acumen, 2005), vol. III, 127–57; "Utilitarian Liberalism: Between Gray and Mill," *Critical Review of International Social and Political Philosophy*, 9 (2006), 117–35; "Mill's Neo-Athenian Model of Liberal Democracy," in N. Urbinati and A. Zakaras, eds., *J. S. Mill's Political Thought: A Bicentennial Reassessment* (New York: Cambridge University Press, 2007); *Mill's Radical Liberalism.*

[6] Such a broad reading of Mill's idea of harm is often rejected by commentators in favor of a narrow reading that restricts harm to mean setbacks to certain interests that ought to be construed as rights, even though the narrow reading is explicitly rejected by Mill himself in *On Liberty*. Mill also admits that self-regarding conduct may indirectly, and in the second or higher instance, harm others without their consent. An individual might do something (such as gamble away his money) that directly injures himself and at the same time injures others (such as his wife and children) through himself. If his self-injurious act is inseparable from his violation of a moral duty to others, his act is taken out of the self-regarding sphere and put into the social sphere, where it is subject to morality if not law. For further discussion, see Riley, "Mill: *On Liberty*," 136–8; "Utilitarian Liberalism."

Rather, society properly has authority to consider regulating any act of expression to protect others from suffering harm without their consent. Society may legitimately consider whether to establish and enforce rules that restrict not only the time, place, and manner but also the content of expression.

Speech falls within the ambit of what may be termed the principle of social authority, according to which "the individual is accountable, and may be subjected either to social or to legal punishment, if society is of opinion that the one or the other is requisite for its protection" (*CW* xviii, 292 [v, 2]). The proper application of this social authority maxim, which is not the central concern of *On Liberty*, must be gathered from Mill's other writings.

Rules of justice

Any civil society may legitimately use force to prevent and punish conduct, including expression, that, without consent, directly and immediately harms others *so seriously* in the estimation of most citizens or their legislative representatives that they agree that individuals should have equal rights not to suffer such grievous injuries. As Mill explains in *Utilitarianism*, society's most important moral rules are its rules of justice, which promote the general welfare by regulating social conduct that causes perceptible injuries of an especially *severe* kind to other people without their consent. To protect any individual from suffering such grievous types of harm, the rules of justice distribute individual rights and correlative duties backed up by the threat of suitable legal penalties and social stigma, except when good reasons exist from "the special expediencies of the case" to rely solely on individual conscience for enforcement. Mill implies that general utility provides a moral criterion for deciding when a harm is so severe that every individual ought to have a right – a claim on society – not to suffer it. Thus, individuals ought to have legal rights not to be killed merely because of their ethnicity, for example, and rights not to be arbitrarily deprived of their good reputations because enemies are spreading malicious lies, among many other rights, given that general rules distributing such rights and correlative obligations are reasonably expected to promote the general good.

Mill's argument in *On Liberty* is consistent with his account of social justice in *Utilitarianism*, contrary to the charges of many commentators. In his view, any coercive interference with the individual's self-regarding liberty is a type of harm so serious that the individual ought to have a right not to suffer it. Utilitarian rules of justice distribute equal rights to absolute self-regarding liberty for all mature individuals in any civil society. To promote the general welfare, every individual must have a legal claim not to be impeded by others when choosing among his self-regarding acts and omissions as he pleases, and others must have correlative duties not to impede him. For Mill, the benefits of self-development or individuality, achieved through spontaneous self-regarding choice and experimentation, always outweigh the mere dislike and emotional distress thereby occasioned for other people together with any "natural penalties" that flow to the agent from others' dislike and distress. Others are not obstructed in the making of their own choices by feeling mere dislike, as they would be obstructed by experiencing some form of perceptible damage without their consent. Anyone who feels mere dislike remains free to avoid the agent of the self-regarding conduct without "parading" the avoidance to others, and thus can continue to pursue his own good freely in his own way without suppressing the individuality of that agent. The natural penalties that flow to the agent are, however, harms to him which his own intentional self-regarding conduct has caused him to suffer. The agent remains perfectly free to alter his self-regarding conduct if he chooses, in order to remove the cause of others' aversion and perhaps avoid the natural penalties that flow from it. If he persists in the conduct, he may be taken to consent to the natural penalties as annoyances that, while damaging to his interests, do not justify for him his sacrifice of his self-regarding liberty.

Again, though, speech is not self-regarding conduct, and utilitarian rules of justice are not required to distribute equal rights to absolute freedom of speech. The benefits of individuality achieved through free speech and experiments of social conduct do *not* always outweigh the various forms of perceptible damage which speech or other social conduct may directly and immediately cause to other people without their consent. Rather, rules of justice can legitimately be established and enforced to regulate the time, place, manner, and content of speech, if most agree that such regulations are essential to protect others from being forced to suffer severe harms that nobody should be forced to suffer in a society that seeks the general welfare.[7]

---

[7] Evidently, Mill is working with a non-standard version of utilitarianism that assigns great weight to rules of justice in its calculations of the general welfare. There may be some similarity in this respect between his utilitarian liberalism and some modern versions of liberalism such as John Rawls's contractualist liberalism (Rawls, *Political Liberalism* [New York: Columbia University Press, 1993]), which assigns absolute priority over other social considerations to rules of justice distributing equal rights and liberties. But there are important differences too. Rawlsian liberalism shies away from anything like a right to absolute liberty of self-regarding conduct, for example, and also downgrades certain social and economic rights as being inherently less valuable than other political and civil rights. At the same time, there is continuing controversy over the precise structure of Mill's utilitarianism. I am inclined to read it as a sophisticated rule utilitarianism or disposition utilitarianism, in which consequentialist reasoning is restricted to the selection of an optimal social code, or optimal type of personal character comprising a suitable mixture of self-regarding and social dispositions. But this might also coincide with a sophisticated act utilitarianism.

Laissez-faire *policies*

A second point to stress about applying the social authority maxim is that society's legitimate authority to consider regulating social conduct does not imply that society must always establish and enforce rules to govern every type of social act or omission that poses a risk of harm to others without their consent. If an individual's social conduct is reasonably expected to yield more social benefits than harms in at least some circumstances, for instance, then it is generally expedient for society to adopt a policy of *laissez-faire* rather than of regulation with respect to that type of social conduct in those situations. A social policy of "letting people alone" is, with some exceptions, better for the general welfare than a policy of coercive interference is in the cases of both trade and expression, Mill suggests, even though these types of social conduct do pose risks of direct and immediate damage to others without their consent. When some sellers gain market share over their rivals, or when some speakers are preferred to others by an audience, "society admits no right ... in the disappointed competitors, to immunity from this kind of suffering" (*CW* xviii, 293 [v, 3]). Indeed, a policy of *laissez-faire* may be best even if the relevant social conduct is reasonably expected to generate more social harm than benefit. This may happen when the various costs of establishing and running a regulatory regime exceed the net harms to be prevented by regulating the conduct.

For Mill, then, any civil society may properly decide to permit individuals and organizations to choose as they please with respect to some types of social conduct, including some types of speech, in at least some contexts, even though the moral right to *absolute* liberty is confined to purely self-regarding conduct. This moral and legal permission to choose among a limited set of social actions is contingent on relevant social benefit–cost estimates which may vary across different societies or the same society at different times and places. Moreover, even if individuals and groups are entrusted with legal rights to perform these social actions in at least some contexts, those legal claims are properly qualified in such a way that the right-holder remains obligated to obey society's code of justice. Sellers who are permitted freely to compete with others in the market remain obligated to obey laws that forbid fraudulent dealing, for example, just as speakers remain obligated to obey laws that forbid malicious libel or incitement to violence. Nobody has a moral right to absolute liberty with respect to social conduct that, by definition, directly and immediately affects others without their consent.

Given his endorsement of broad (though not unqualified) policies of *laissez-faire* for social conduct such as trade and expression, it is a fatal error to interpret Mill as confining individual liberty to self-regarding conduct. Contrary to an influential reading of his purpose, he is not attempting in *On Liberty* to mark out in detail the boundary between individual liberty and social regulation. The self-regarding sphere is, he implies, a *minimum* sphere of absolute liberty which ought to be recognized and protected by every civil society as a matter of *justice and right*. He is very clear that some liberty may also be appropriate in some parts of the sphere of social conduct. The optimal boundary between individual liberty and social regulation does *not* run, therefore, between the self-regarding and social spheres.

Legitimate regulation versus prohibition

The central self-regarding liberty maxim sets an absolute limit on the scope of social morality and thereby limits the extent to which any civil society can legitimately employ coercion to regulate social conduct, including speech, under the social authority maxim. Society may, for example, properly establish and enforce laws of justice which require business firms to publish accurate information about the products they sell. Such rules are designed to protect consumers from being forced to endure severe harm as a direct result of fraudulent market conduct. Society may also legitimately prevent firms from polluting the environment, compel them to provide safe working conditions for their employees, and force them to collect personal information from the buyers of their products as a condition of sale to facilitate police investigations of any ensuing crimes in which the products are abused to harm other people seriously. But society can never rightfully implement rules that *prohibit* altogether the sale of products that can be used in ways that involve no direct and immediate harms for others without their consent. Social regulation of the sellers cannot properly be extended to a social ban on their sales activities because such a ban would interfere with the consumer's self-regarding liberty. The individual consumer has a moral right to buy as he pleases any products that have purely self-regarding uses.

Similarly, the self-regarding liberty principle forbids any civil society to prohibit altogether any type of speech that can be heard or viewed in at least some circumstances without forcing the consumer or third parties to endure a risk of direct and immediate perceptible damage. Society's regulation of speakers cannot legitimately be extended so far that the consumer's right to self-regarding liberty is violated. The consumer must be free to hear or view as he wishes speech of any content in at least some contexts, provided the content does not directly harm third parties by maliciously damaging their reputations, for example, or credibly threatening them with violence without their consent. At the same time, the consumer must be presumed not to consent to hear or view expression that poses a risk of direct and immediate severe harm to himself. This presumption may be open to rebuttal but only if the listener or viewer explicitly gives his unforced and undeceived consent, preferably in writing, after fair warning.

This role played by the self-regarding liberty principle, to forbid the outright prohibition of any speech whose content can be consumed in at least some circumstances without forcing anyone to suffer direct and immediate harm, is perhaps what is most distinctive about Mill's liberal doctrine of free speech. According to the principle, the mature individual has a basic right to receive from others any messages and ideas he consents to receive in the course of forming whatever opinions seem warranted to him in terms of his own judgment and inclinations, provided no form of perceptible damage is directly caused by his consumption to third parties without their consent. Note that there is no denial that a speaker directly and immediately harms his competitors. But the speech, once produced, can be consumed without direct and immediate harm to others. The act of consumption, unlike that of production, does not pose a risk of direct and immediate harm to any of the speakers.[8]

What is crucial for Mill is the complete freedom of any member of the *audience* to receive and use any communications he pleases without forcing anyone else to experience directly any form of perceptible damage. *Speakers* do not have any moral right to express or disseminate any messages they please. Rather, the extent of their freedom to speak is legitimately adjusted and controlled by society, subject to the condition that the consumer's moral right to absolute liberty of self-regarding conduct must be respected. The individual listener or viewer ought to be free to receive any messages he likes so that he can think and form his opinions as he pleases, so long as the content of the message and its time, place, and manner of expression involve no direct and immediate harm for others without their consent.

Speakers, authors, film producers, and so forth enjoy extensive privileges under this doctrine to express and distribute their ideas because those activities are "practically inseparable" from the absolute self-regarding liberty of listeners and viewers. As Mill puts it, "being almost of as much importance as the liberty of thought itself, and resting in great part on the same reasons, [the liberty of expressing and publishing opinions] is practically inseparable from it" (*CW* XVIII, 226 [1, 12]). But speakers do not have moral rights to express and disseminate whatever content they like, whenever and wherever

---

[8] For relevant discussion, see Jonathan Riley, *Mill on Liberty* (London: Routledge, 1998), 116–19.

they please, free from all legal and social regulation. Rather, various forms of regulation may be generally expedient, including time, place, and manner restrictions as well as content-based sanctions that apply independently of time, place, and manner. A sanction against content can properly be considered, however, only if the type of speech in question cannot possibly be heard or seen in any circumstances without forcing the consumer or third parties to experience directly and immediately at least the risk of perceptible injury.

Permissible censorship

The central self-regarding liberty principle gives no protection to products, including types of speech, that have no self-regarding uses. In this regard, there do seem to be some types of speech, including credible threats of injury, malicious attacks on reputation, invasions of privacy, and incitement to violence, which imply a risk of direct and immediate harm for others without their consent, whatever the time, place, or manner of expression. If this is right, then it is legitimate for society to consider measures to censor speech of this content altogether. Moreover, given that the direct harm to others is severe enough to justify employing force to protect anyone from suffering it without his consent, rules of justice should distribute equal rights not to be forcibly exposed to these types of speech, with suitable punishment for anyone who fails to satisfy his duties correlative to the rights. This does not imply that utilitarian laws of justice must include prior restraints against these types of speech. The threat of duly harsh legal punishment after the fact can be used instead to deter such expression.

Waiver of legitimate censorship authority

A final point is that society may properly decide, at least in some circumstances, not to use legal sanctions to deter admittedly very harmful social conduct, including speech that most agree should be censored to protect others from being forced to endure severe direct and immediate harm. Rather than employ the criminal or civil law, which can be relatively costly to enforce, society might establish customs against some harmful types of expression and enforce the customs by means of social stigma. Speakers who repeatedly engage in malicious gossip might properly be punished by certain organized displays of public humiliation and even expulsion from "polite society," for example, and speakers who repeatedly spread malicious lies in their teachings or broadcasts about particular ethnic, racial, or religious groups might be punished by organized protests and boycotts of their classes and broadcasts.

In some cases, society must rely solely on the internal sanctions of a guilty conscience to deter speakers from very harmful speech. It is impossible to employ legal sanctions or stigma against credible threats issued without witnesses, for instance, unless the speech is recorded surreptitiously. Similarly, malicious lies about others kept between close friends, plots of violence kept secret by the plotters, and the like must escape external sanctions.

COMPLETE LIBERTY OF THOUGHT AND DISCUSSION

Mill can defend complete liberty of thought and discussion consistently with the general *laissez-faire* doctrine for expression laid out in the preceding section. The trick is to define "discussion" so that it excludes all types of expression which cannot be heard or viewed without forcing the consumer or third parties to endure a risk of direct and immediate harm ("Permissible censorship," above). This excludes such speech as credible threats, incitement to violence, malicious libel, and fraudulent commercial advertising. But "discussion" still includes expression that may be very upsetting and offensive to others even though it causes them no direct and immediate perceptible damage without their consent. It includes personal insults, for instance, as well as ethnic or racial slurs, blasphemy, and diatribes against the government or particular policies and officials.[9]

It is also possible to define "discussion" more broadly without contradicting the *laissez-faire* doctrine. It can be defined to exclude only those types of expression which force others to endure a risk of direct and immediate harm so *serious* that everyone ought to have a right not to suffer the grievous harm in society's estimation. Discussion then includes not only emotionally distressing types of speech but also expression that directly and

---

[9] It might be objected that blasphemy should not count as "discussion," because of the risk that an offended god will directly and immediately retaliate against those who fail to interfere forcibly with the speaker when they could have done so. But there is no evidence that a divine being has ever directly harmed a blasphemer, let alone harmed others for failing to silence him. This might be taken as a sign that god is not offended by the freedom to express blasphemous opinions. Against this, it might be retorted that an offended god will deny blasphemers and those who fail to silence them entry into a heavenly paradise. Even so, god, not the speaker, is then ultimately accountable for the relevant harms, especially if god is assumed to have created the speaker. In any case, in "Theism" (1874), in *The Collected Works of John Stuart Mill*, vol. x: *Essays on Ethics, Religion and Society*, ed. John M. Robson (Toronto: University of Toronto Press; London: Routledge & Kegan Paul, 1969), 429–89, Mill argues that insufficient evidence exists to warrant a rational belief in the existence of god or an afterlife. Indeed, observation of the natural world rules out any possibility of an omnipotent and benevolent god, he insists, although it is not irrational to imagine that a benevolent deity with great but limited power needs man's help in a struggle to overcome malignant forces or intractable matter. Mill also finds it pleasing to hope that such a Manichean or Platonic god might even have enough power to reward with an afterlife those who help in the fight to bring about the general good.

immediately forces others to put up with harms which in society's estimation are not sufficiently serious to be prevented or punished as a matter of justice. Thus, the popular majority and its legislative representatives might decide to enact laws that permit raucous street demonstrations or turbulent marches and parades as elements of the public discussion in a democratic society, despite the risk of harm to others without their consent. The damage to innocent persons and their properties expected to result directly from such forms of expression may be fairly trivial and therefore tolerated in light of the expected social benefits.

Whether "discussion" is defined more narrowly or more broadly, it is not strictly speaking purely self-regarding conduct. Speakers still pose a risk of direct and immediate harm to their competitors in the discussion. Nevertheless, "discussion" is "almost" self-regarding activity, especially under the narrower of the two definitions where the speech is not forcing listeners, viewers, or third parties to endure any risk of direct and immediate harm. It seems a small step in this context to hold that speakers have a duty as citizens to accept that they are not entitled to any immunity from the suffering which they may experience as disappointed competitors. Although their opinions may lose out to others, they should ignore any damage which this implies for their own interests because the damage is inseparable from the important social benefits of an open public debate.

In any case, complete liberty of discussion does not imply that discussants should never express disgust with the opinions which the other discussants are entitled to express. There is no requirement that participants must be indifferent to what is said, let alone agreeable or polite to each other. It is rarely possible, for example, to detect whether a speaker is deliberately distorting his opponent's position or simply making honest mistakes in a debate relating to some issue in science, politics, morality, or religion. Even if his misrepresentations are serious and frequent, so much uncertainty remains as to his moral culpability that legal sanctions and organized public stigma should not be used to discourage his misleading expression. But listeners and viewers may freely choose to express disagreement with the speaker, avoid his company thereafter, refuse to participate in other discussions with him, warn their acquaintances of his tendency to mislead, and so forth, without stigmatizing him in public as a liar and a cheat. Such "natural penalties" will not force the speaker to change his ways. He may well continue to have opportunities to participate in discussions with others. But those who suspect him of deliberately lying and manipulating the debate are not forced to associate with him.

The "real morality of public discussion" is freely to praise everyone who honestly states his opponent's views, and freely to condemn and avoid everyone who displays evident "want of candour, or malignity, bigotry, or intolerance of feeling," Mill insists, without inferring these virtues or vices from the side of the argument which the person takes (*CW* xviii, 259 [ii, 44]). Public discussion, however misleading, intolerant, and offensive, can be distinguished from credible threats of serious injury, incitement to violence, malicious libel, fraudulent advertising for commercial gain, gross invasion of privacy, and so forth.

LEGITIMATE COERCION AGAINST EXPRESSION THAT IS NOT DISCUSSION

Consider any type of speech that does not count as "discussion." More specifically, consider threatening expression that forces others to endure a risk of imminent severe harm, either from the speaker himself or from those whom he incites. The motivation for the expression is some innocent aspect of the other's identity, for instance, his perceived ethnicity, race, or religion.

Credible threats and incitements of serious harm against others merely for possessing these innocent characteristics are legitimately prohibited and punished by law. To assess the severity of the intended harm, it is reasonable to consider factors such as the speaker's current and past behavior towards members of the relevant groups; his connections with organizations that have a history of prejudice and violence against innocents and that may currently be stockpiling weapons or giving other signs of mobilizing for imminent criminal activity; and his possible incentives and opportunities to profit from deliberately distorting the public discussion so as to produce a general climate of fear in which innocents are forced to endure a higher risk of severe injury at the hands of others.

Any speaker with a personal history of violence against Jews, Muslims, or other religious groups, for instance, is legitimately placed under a special legal restriction that subjects him to unusually harsh punishment if he ever again threatens to inflict even minor harm on people for their religious beliefs. He may also be legitimately forbidden to associate with others with similar histories and subjected to punishment if he nevertheless does associate with them.[10]

---

[10] Mill suggests that any individual who has been convicted of violence toward others when under the influence of alcohol could be subjected to extraordinary penalties under "a special legal restriction" if found drunk again: "The making himself drunk, in a person whom drunkenness excites to do harm to others, is a crime against others" (*CW* xviii, 295 [v, 6]). Thus, a personal history of violence can justify special legal penalties to discourage the person from drinking too much, even though drinking alcohol remains self-regarding conduct for people who do not become violent when drunk and they must be

A speaker who joins a neo-Nazi organization or brandishes Nazi paraphernalia is duly punished for demonstrating against Jews and can reasonably be jailed and fined if he marches, parades, shouts out antisemitic slurs, and so forth anywhere in public – not only on public property but also on private property even with the permission of the owner. The Nazis have a terrible history of persecuting Jews. Anybody who associates himself in public with such an odious organization and its symbols should be presumed on that basis alone to be expressing a credible threat of severe injury against Jews or anyone suspected of being Jewish, and the presumption should be viewed as very difficult to rebut. Society properly employs force to make clear that nobody should be forced by his tormentors to endure such a threat.[11]

Similarly, a speaker who joins the Ku Klux Klan or burns a cross while marching or shouting out racial epithets anywhere in public should be presumed on that basis to be expressing a credible threat of severe injury against blacks (or, more generally, against others whom the speaker classifies as "black") living in the vicinity.[12]

---

perfectly free to get drunk if they please. *A fortiori*, a personal history of violence toward innocents can justify special legal penalties against speakers who threaten to cause perceptible injuries to innocents again. Speech is not self-regarding conduct deserving of absolute protection in any case, and credible threats or incitement of violence can never be heard or viewed without forcing either the consumer or third parties to endure a risk of severe perceptible injury.

[11] P. Strum, *When the Nazis Came to Skokie: Freedom for Speech We Hate* (Lawrence: University Press of Kansas, 1999), provides a succinct discussion of the controversy surrounding demands made by members of the National Socialist Party of America during 1977–8 to be permitted to march through the village of Skokie, a suburb of Chicago, where many Holocaust survivors resided. A march never took place in Skokie, although the US Supreme Court and lower courts effectively cleared the way for one to happen over the protests of Skokie officials, and even gave the American neo-Nazis permission to wear uniforms and display the swastika. The courts seem never to have considered the objection that the marchers, as well as others of similar views who might be encouraged or incited by their demonstration, presented a credible threat of violence against at least some Jewish residents, quite apart from any emotional distress caused by the march. In light of the history of the Nazis, it is reasonable to presume that a march by their American sympathizers always poses a risk of severe physical injury and financial loss to Jews living nearby, whatever assurances to the contrary might be given by the marchers.

[12] The US Supreme Court has recognized that cross-burning can in some circumstances constitute a credible threat of violence against blacks and other targets of the speaker's hatred, since the burning cross is a Klan symbol of intimidation and the Klan has a history of mayhem against blacks, Jews, immigrants, and others. If a credible threat can be shown to exist in the circumstances of the case, cross-burning receives no protection under the First Amendment. See *Virginia* v. *Black* et al., 538 U.S. 343 (2003). But the court also insists that cross-burning even by Klan members can sometimes be political speech deserving of protection, as in ceremonies where the Klan's way of life is celebrated as new members are admitted into the organization. Yet this seems to ignore the fact that the Klan is a terrorist organization with a history of violence that by itself justifies the presumption that cross-burning by Klansmen is always a credible threat of severe injury against innocents. That presumption should be very difficult to rebut. Perhaps if the Klan formally renounced its violent history and promised never to engage again in harmful social conduct against innocents, cross-burning by Klansmen could eventually become protected speech. But then the leopard would have changed his spots, and the new Klan itself would have no interest in cross-burning.

Perhaps it is expedient to reject prior restraints in these cases. In other words, perhaps the state should generally not bother to try to prevent neo-Nazi or Klan demonstrations. Even so, this is compatible with legal punishment after the fact for any such demonstrations that attract the attention of the authorities. Society might also properly decide to forgo legal penalties and rely instead solely on organized displays of stigma, especially if the demonstrations are pathetic events with relatively few marchers and a predominantly hostile audience.[13] In any case, there is certainly no call for the state to subsidize such threatening speech by supplying free police protection for the demonstrators, bearing the costs of insurance against damage to person and property, and so forth.

Yet it is not obvious that prior restraints would be inexpedient against a large well-financed demonstration by neo-Nazis or the Klan. Why should society, unless it has no choice in the matter, ever permit such a demonstration? Perhaps as a safety-valve, to relieve social tensions and forestall civil war? If society is already infected by a large, well-financed group of neo-Nazis, however, it may be better to fight sooner than later, before it is time to flee the country. The contrary strategy is a gamble, that a well-financed minority determined to harm innocents will never be able to take over the government of a society that permits these demonstrations. As the example of Nazi Germany itself shows, that gamble can be lost.

In addition to credible threats and incitements of severe injury against innocents, promotional advertising of such hateful speech is also legitimately suppressed and punished to prevent the creation of a climate of fear and intimidation in which members of particular ethnic, racial, or religious groups are exposed to an increasing risk of severe harm without their consent. This ban against promotional advertising applies not only to government itself and to non-profits subsidized by the taxpayer, but also to commercial for-profit enterprises. It applies to promotional advertising across the mass media, including print, radio, television, the internet, and so forth. There is a particular danger that profit-seekers will make it their business to create, exploit, and manipulate prejudice against innocents through promotional advertising on some or all of these media.[14]

[13] During the Skokie controversy, the neo-Nazis were permitted to demonstrate in St. Louis and Chicago. But these pathetic demonstrations involved a small number of neo-Nazis and were sparsely attended. The main risk of perceptible damage seems to have been to the neo-Nazis themselves from hostile spectators. Stigma may well have been a sufficient social response in those circumstances.

[14] Mill (*CW* XVIII, 296–7 [v, 6]) indicates that promotional advertising of gambling and prostitution may be legitimately suppressed, even though these are self-regarding activities under certain conditions. For further discussion, see Riley, *Mill on Liberty*, 125–9. The 'moral anomaly' of punishing casino-owners and pimps for advertising their businesses when their customers must be allowed to go

Again, it may be expedient to rely on posterior punishments rather than prior restraints to enforce the ban against promotional advertising. Thus, an author and publisher are legitimately fined and even imprisoned for marketing printed materials that credibly threaten violence against innocents, for example, and a radio or television broadcaster can properly be punished for promoting a film that threatens or incites violence against innocents. Depending on the circumstances, society might also properly decide to forgo legal penalties and rely instead solely on stigma to enforce the ban. Hostile audiences might legitimately organize public protests and boycotts against the publisher or broadcaster, for example, as well as against the author or film-producers and their products.

Under a Millian approach, society properly permits, even encourages, promotional advertising of materials that are critical of genuinely threatening speech whereas promotional marketing of such threatening speech is properly prohibited and punished. A Millian liberal society is thus not neutral in any straightforward sense with respect to different types of speech, including the different things profit-seekers might say to promote different conceptions of a good life.

Despite legal and social sanctions, some speakers may still choose to indulge in credible threats and incitements of serious harm as well as promotional advertising of such unjust speech. But relatively few will do so if the punishments are sufficiently harsh. It may be said that the sanctions will merely drive this type of speech underground. But this is highly expedient, since it is then more likely to be confined to small and isolated groups of acquaintances. It will rarely make an appearance in a public forum, and even then will meet with due punishment after the fact.

CONCLUSION

Mill's liberal doctrine of free expression can be summarized as follows. A general policy of *laissez-faire* should apply to speech because freedom results in net social benefits for most types of speech in at least some circumstances,

free does not arise in the case of promoters of threats and incitements because consuming such speech is not self-regarding conduct. For a brief period, the US Supreme Court adopted a doctrine that the state has legitimate authority to restrict promotional advertising of vices like gambling, because the state has authority to prohibit gambling itself. See *Posadas de Puerto Rico Assoc.* v. *Tourism Co.*, 478 U.S. 328 (1986). This is incompatible with a Millian policy, since gambling is a self-regarding activity under certain conditions and thus should be a constitutionally protected activity. But the court's doctrine could be endorsed by Millians in the case of promotional advertising of threats and incitements because such expression cannot be heard or viewed without forcing innocents to endure a risk of severe harm. Such speech should not be constitutionally protected at all.

even though it is undeniable that speech always poses a risk of some harm to others without their consent. But the *laissez-faire* policy clearly admits of exceptions. To prevent serious forms of perceptible damage that nobody should be forced to suffer, laws of justice should include time, place, and manner restrictions that distribute equal rights not to be confronted or bothered by speakers outside the restricted contexts. True, the central principle of self-regarding liberty limits the scope of legitimate social regulation, to wit, society is forbidden to prohibit speech of any content that can be heard or seen in at least some circumstances without forcing the consumer or third parties directly and immediately to endure a risk of perceptible injury. But this limit set by the self-regarding liberty principle does not imply free-speech absolutism. Some types of speech can be legitimately censored altogether, it seems, because their content necessarily forces someone other than the speaker to experience at least a risk of serious harm: the speech cannot be consumed under any circumstances without forcing the consumer or third parties to endure the risk of severe perceptible damage. Society may properly decide to use posterior punishments rather than prior restraints to suppress these unjust types of speech. It might also choose at times not to make use of any legal punishment but rather rely on customs enforced by stigma. In some special situations, it may even have to rely solely on the speaker's conscience to prevent him from engaging in unjust types of speech exemplified by credible threats or incitements of violence.

A civilized society properly adopts coercive measures to suppress unjust speech, that is, any type of speech that implies a risk of such severe harm to others that most citizens – individuals capable of rational persuasion – agree that nobody in the society should be forced to put up with the risk. In addition to credible threats and incitements and promotional advertising of them for private gain, unjust speech may include malicious libel, fraudulent commercial advertising, and speech that grossly invades another's privacy without his consent. These types of speech do not facilitate democratic deliberation, discovery of truth, personal self-development or autonomy, or any other important interest shared in common. More speech of these types is not generally expedient. Rather, individuals should be given equal rights not to be forcibly exposed to such harmful types of speech. Indeed, the basic right of absolute self-regarding liberty itself arguably protects the individual from grossly invasive speech that coercively interferes with his control over his intimate affairs.[15]

---

[15]   Riley, "Mill's Doctrine of Freedom of Expression."

Consistently with the suppression of unjust speech, speakers should remain perfectly free to express disgusting, insulting, and misguided opinions about others, including members of ethnic, racial, or religious groups. No doubt racist or blasphemous speech may offend and upset many who happen to hear or view it. But the audience is free to avoid the speaker, and nothing he says forcibly prevents others from responding with speech of their own – whereas serious threats, incitements, or other unjust speech would forcibly prevent them by presenting them with a risk of severe direct and immediate harm without their consent. People can freely attempt to persuade and cajole the offensive speaker to mend his ways, and even hurl invective and insults back at him if he proves recalcitrant. More speech is desirable to counteract distressing and even hateful speech that does not rise to the level of credible threats, incitements, or other unjust types of speech. This is not to deny that bright lines may be difficult to draw at times between unjust expression and expression that forces others to put up with a risk of more or less benign forms of perceptible damage, and between the latter types of speech and merely upsetting invective that can be heard or viewed without forcing the consumer or third parties to endure a risk of any harm at all. But no policy can be expected to eliminate entirely the need for practical judgment in grey areas. Moreover, it should generally not be difficult to draw a bright line between unjust speech and merely offensive invective. Legal coercion is properly reserved for the relatively easy cases in which speech obviously poses a risk of severe harm to others without their consent.[16]

Finally, for Millian liberals, there must be complete freedom to discuss the pros and cons of credible threats or incitements of violence, malicious libel, or any other type of unjust speech in the context of a public debate. No doubt degrading and offensive opinions may be expressed as part of the discussion. But this is a long way from free-speech absolutism. Freedom to debate the reasons for and against unjust speech is not the same thing as

---

[16] In cases where it is difficult to decide whether the speech is merely offensive to others or instead forces the consumer or third parties to endure a risk of fairly minor perceptible injury, it may not be unreasonable to lean in the direction of freedom even if a plausible argument can be made for organized displays of stigma against the speaker. A plausible argument for stigma can perhaps be made, for example, when journalists and editors publish scurrilous opinions and cartoons about a great religious figure such as Jesus Christ or Muhammad. Perhaps such speech should be punished by stigma because it poses some risk of perceptible damage to the figure's reputation, although whether a person can suffer harm in this sense after his death remains an open question. The mere dislike and emotional distress of the figure's followers, however, should not count in favor of any form of coercive interference. Moreover, religious clerics cannot properly be permitted to respond with credible threats and incitements of violence against the speakers. Offers of paradise or riches to anyone who will kill the journalists or editors, for example, should clearly meet with harsh legal punishment.

freedom actually to engage in unjust speech. The liberty to discuss it at some times and places, and in some manners, is entirely compatible with legal and social punishment for actually engaging in it in any context. Coercive measures against speakers who credibly threaten or incite severe harm against members of ethnic, racial, or religious groups, or who make it their business to whip up a climate of hatred by promotional advertising of such threats and incitements, will tend to discourage such unjust speech and remove it from public debate. Its removal implies not only a restriction on the manner in which any public debate about unjust speech may permissibly be conducted. A restriction of content is also implied, insofar as speakers in the debate are not permitted to make their points by issuing credible threats or incitements of violence or by promoting such hateful speech for private gain.

CHAPTER 4

State neutrality and controversial values in On Liberty

Gerald F. Gaus

I MILL: A "COMPREHENSIVE" DEFENSE OF LIBERAL NEUTRALITY?

In an important essay Charles Larmore tells us that

Kant and Mill sought to justify the principle of political neutrality by appealing to ideals of autonomy and individuality. By remaining neutral with regard to controversial views of the good life, constitutional principles will express, according to them, what ought to be of supreme value throughout the whole of our life.[1]

On Larmore's influential reading, Mill defended what we might call *first-level neutrality*: Millian principles determining justified legal (and, we might add, social) intervention are neutral between competing conceptions of the good life. However, Larmore insists that Millian neutral political principles do not possess *second-level neutrality*: they do not have a neutral justification. "The problem with Mill's value-based defense of liberalism," Larmore holds, is that because the value of individuality is "far from uncontroversial,"[2] Mill's case liberalism is open to reasonable objection. In contrast Larmore and, of course, John Rawls, seek to develop a "political liberalism" that defends liberal neutrality without appeal to a "general 'philosophy of man' or a 'comprehensive moral ideal.'"[3] The justification of liberal principles "must be acceptable by reasonable people having different views of the good life, not just those who share, for example, Mill's ideal of the person."[4] Liberals, argues Larmore, need "a *neutral justification of neutrality*."[5]

I would like to thank Michael Gill and Charles Larmore for their helpful comments on an earlier draft of this chapter.
[1] Charles Larmore, "Political Liberalism," in his *The Morals of Modernity* (Cambridge: Cambridge University Press, 1996), 127–8.
[2] Ibid., 128.
[3] Ibid., 132. See also John Rawls, *Political Liberalism* (New York: Columbia University Press, 1993), xliv–xlv, 78.
[4] Larmore, *Patterns of Moral Complexity* (Cambridge: Cambridge University Press, 1987), 51.
[5] Ibid., 53, emphasis added.

This chapter challenges this widely accepted view of Mill as presenting a "comprehensive" defense of liberalism, to be sharply contrasted with the "political liberalism" of Larmore and Rawls.[6] I do not, of course, wish to deny that there are fundamental differences between, on the one hand, Larmore's and Rawls's political liberalism and, on the other, the case for liberal neutrality that Mill presents in *On Liberty*. I do, however, dispute the currently accepted view that Mill's case for liberal neutrality necessarily depends on a controversial perfectionist ideal of individuality or a utilitarian calculus, whereas political liberalism is grounded on a core morality that is a common ground to all reasonable citizens.[7] I shall argue that Mill provides a broad defense of liberal neutrality that appeals to a wide range of citizens' interests and, in that regard, Mill shares Larmore's and Rawls's concern with a non-sectarian defense of liberal neutrality. This interpretation is endorsed by a careful reading of *On Liberty*, which presents a wide array of arguments for liberty, appealing to an equally wide array of citizens' beliefs and values. No interpretation that depicts Mill's liberalism as resting on a single value does justice to the complexity of *On Liberty*.

Section II briefly analyzes the notions of first- and second-level political neutrality. Section III takes up the question whether Mill's liberalism – centered on the harm principle – constitutes a first-level neutral liberalism: I argue that it is strongly neutralist. Section IV then turns to Larmore's core claim that Mill's justification of neutral principles is not itself neutral (in the sense of second-level neutrality). I shall argue that Mill's justification of the value of liberty and the harm principle is surprisingly broad: because he appeals to diverse values, his case is broadly "neutral."

II FIRST- AND SECOND-LEVEL LIBERAL NEUTRALITY

(i) A conception of neutrality

For the last few decades political theorists have vigorously debated whether liberalism is committed to some doctrine of "state neutrality," and whether neutrality provides a plausible constraint on legitimate laws and policies. As I have commented on these debates elsewhere, I shall not rehearse these matters

---

[6] Although this view is almost a commonplace today, it has not gone unchallenged. See, for example, John Patrick Rudisill, "The Neutrality of the State and its Justification in Rawls and Mill," *Auslegung*, 23 (2000), 153–68.
[7] Larmore, "Political Liberalism," 133.

here.[8] However, I do think that a feature of this long-running debate is that there has been too much controversy about an ill-defined notion; it would behoove us to try to get a little clearer about our topic. Let us, say, focus on two citizens, *A* and *B*, who have a value-based disagreement, *D*. Consider law *L*, a coercive imposition. Let us say that *L* is neutral[9] between citizens *A* and *B* on *D* regarding treatment *T* if and only if *L* does not treat *A* and *B* differently (engage in differential *T*) on the basis of *D*. So:[10]

Political neutrality: *L* is neutral between *A* and *B* on dispute *D* in relation to *T* if and only if it does not *T* them differently on the basis of *D*.

A few points of clarification.

(1) As I have characterized it, political neutrality is a generic principle that can be filled in with different conceptions of neutrality, depending on how the variables are specified. Of particular importance is determining what is the relevant treatment: what are the morally important ways of treating people differently that a neutrality principle identifies? Must a neutral law treat people the same in all ways? We can better understand the ideal of neutrality in political philosophy if we pause to reflect on a different, traditional, application of the notion of neutrality – combatants under international law. A government is neutral between the combatants (*A* and *B*) concerning the differences in their war aims or combatant status (*D*) when the government's decision, say, about shipments of arms or war-related matters (*T*) does not treat *A* and *B* differentially on the basis of their war aims, alliances, etc. The range of *T* is a matter of dispute between different notions of state neutrality in war (just as it is in debates about liberal neutrality). In 1914 President Wilson insisted that "The United States must be neutral in fact, as well as in name ... We must be impartial in thought, as well as action, must put a curb upon our sentiments, as well as upon every transaction that might be construed as a preference of one party to the struggle before another."[11] But that is extreme (and certainly was not adhered to). A very different view was taken by the Swedish government in 1941: "Neutrality does not demand that nations not participating in an

---

[8] I note the diversity of conceptions of neutrality in Gerald F. Gaus, "Liberal Neutrality: A Radical and Compelling Principle," in George Klosko and Steven Wall, eds., *Perfectionism and Neutrality* (Lanham, MD: Rowman & Littlefield, 2003), 137–65.

[9] Jeremy Waldron also applies neutrality constraints to laws (rather than, say, actions). "Legislation and Moral Neutrality," in his *Liberal Rights* (Cambridge: Cambridge University Press, 1993), 149–67.

[10] I have defended this characterization of liberal neutrality in Gerald F. Gaus, "The Moral Necessity of Liberal Neutrality," in Thomas Christiano and John Christman, eds., *Contemporary Debates in Political Philosophy* (Oxford: Blackwell, forthcoming).

[11] Woodrow Wilson, *Message to Congress, 63rd Cong.*, 2nd Session, Senate Doc. No. 566 (Washington, 1914), 3–4.

armed conflict should be indifferent to the issues of the belligerents. The sympathies of neutrals may well lie entirely with one side, and a neutral does not violate his duties as long as he does not commit any unneutral acts that might aid the side he favors."[12] On this view T is restricted to some actions, and certainly does not include thoughts and sentiments. The Swedish doctrine explicitly allows that the neutral government need not always refrain from different treatment of A and B on the basis of their war aims (D): the neutral government's public schools might still favor A's aims, and treat A and B differently in its curriculum, but this would not impair the state's neutrality regarding T – e.g., arms shipments or war materials. Note also that even when we have identified T, the idea of neutrality does not require a neutral always to treat (T) A and B the same. Suppose the neutral government sells arms to both A and B, but A has paid and B has not (international law allows neutrals to sell arms). Then the neutral state may treat A differently than B even regarding T, because the difference in treatment is not grounded on D (their war aims), but on whether payment has been made.

Depending on how "treatment" (T) is explicated, political neutrality might be understood as, for example, neutrality of (some or all) effects, neutrality of justification, or neutrality of aims.[13] Depending on how D is filled out, conceptions can be neutral between people's conceptions of the good, comprehensive conceptions, values, religious beliefs, and so on. The philosophical work of a conception of neutrality will be to make out a good case for focus on a particular form of treatment (T) and a particular dispute (D).

(2) It is an advantage of the above characterization that it makes clear that neutrality is always between people in a certain set (A and B). At the limit, neutrality might be the set of all persons, but it will almost always concern a smaller set, such as the set of reasonable citizens, or the set of tolerably rational citizens, and so on. Until we identify the set, we cannot apply a neutrality principle.

(3) Note also that political neutrality is not concerned with neutrality between conceptions of the good or values. Liberalism is neutral between *persons*, and this neutrality requires not treating them differentially on the basis of their differing values, conceptions of the good, and so on. (As the Swedish government made quite clear, a neutral need not be neutral between war aims, but must be neutral between combatants.) Liberalism is not concerned

---

[12] http://lawofwar.org/Neutrality.htm.
[13] On these distinctions see Larmore, *Patterns of Moral Complexity*, 43ff.; Will Kymlicka, "Liberal Individualism and Liberal Neutrality," *Ethics*, 99.3 (1989), 833–905; Simon Caney, "Consequentialist Defenses of Liberal Neutrality," *Philosophical Quarterly*, 41 (1991), 457–77; George Sher, *Beyond Neutrality: Perfectionism and Politics* (Cambridge: Cambridge University Press, 1997), ch. 2.

with neutrality between values or conceptions of the good, as if conceptions of the good themselves had claims to neutral treatment. It is only because citizens hold such conceptions that neutrality between citizens has consequences for the way conceptions of the good can enter into laws and political principles. This might seem pedantic, but, I think, it helps us avoid confusion. Suppose at time t_1 there are two conceptions of the good in society, C_1 and C_2, but at time t_2 everyone has come to embrace C_1. It would seem that, if liberalism is really committed to neutrality between conceptions of the good *per se*, then even at t_2 it must be neutral between C_1 and C_2, but this seems all wrong. As I interpret the liberal understanding of political neutrality, since it requires neutrality between persons, appealing at t_2 to C_1 does not run afoul of neutrality, since there are no differences among citizens on this matter. So it is not in itself non-neutral to appeal to conceptions of the good; it all depends on the differences that obtain among moral persons or citizens.

(4) Another advantage of the above formulation is that it helps us avoid common errors, such as the claim that neutral laws cannot appeal to controversial conceptions of the good. Laws can be neutral with regard to controversial conceptions of the good *and yet still appeal* to them. For example, consider neutrality of justification: on this view a law treats (T) citizens neutrally if its justification for its action does not depend on the differences between citizens (i.e., its justification cannot depend on its "taking sides" on D). Now a justification may be based on either *consensus* or *convergence* of values. A consensus justification maintains that L is justified because everyone has the same grounds to endorse it; a convergence justification maintains that L is justified because Alf has his own grounds to endorse it while Betty endorses it for different reasons. Suppose, though, that *both* parties to the dispute D endorse the law on the basis of their *differing* views. A convergence justification is perfectly neutral: the justification does not rely on our disagreements about values (D), but, instead, on our agreement about the implications of our different values. Thus we must reject the plausible idea that liberal neutrality prohibits appeal to "controversial conceptions of the good." This point will prove important.

(ii) First-level neutrality

At the most basic level, a law (or, more generally, a political principle which determines the acceptability of laws) is neutral with respect to Alf and Betty on matter D if it does not T (treat) them differently on the basis of their positions on D. But what are the relevant forms of treatment, and what are the relevant differences?

It is often supposed that there must be a single answer to this query: "When liberals talk of treating people neutrally they mean neutrality *qua* —" where the blank is filled in with, say, neutrality of effect, or neutrality of aim. There are, though, many different ways to treat people "the same," and there is no reason why a doctrine of political neutrality should not endorse several.

Although some political philosophers still endorse versions of it,[14] we should certainly reject as implausibly strong "neutrality of effect": i.e., to be neutral between *A* and *B* on *D*, *L* must have the same effects on *A* and *B* (or, perhaps, no differential effects are caused by *D*). This supposes a very expansive notion of a "treatment." Return to the idea of neutrality in war: for state S to be neutral between *A* and *B* would require that S's actions and policies have no differential effect on them (or at least none that can be traced back to their combatant status). Suppose the neutral state refuses to sell arms to either of the combatants – this certainly looks neutral. But if country *A* has lots of alternative sources for arms while *B* does not, then this refusal to sell arms would violate neutrality of effect because the arms policy affects *B* more than *A*. Thus neutrality (*qua* "of effect") might require the neutral state to sell arms only to *B*! That cannot be right.

Let me propose three ways – which have been important in the liberal tradition – in which laws can be neutral: if a law is neutral in all three ways I shall call it a neutral law. If it is neutral in some but not all these ways, I shall call it a partly neutral law.

1. A law can be *neutral on its face*. A law to establish Episcopalianism would not be neutral on its face: it would treat Episcopalians and those of other faiths differentially on the basis of their religious differences. In cases such as this the law refers to a disputed position, and gives differential benefits and burdens on the basis of it. Fundamental to liberalism is the idea that some disputes among citizens (such as religious differences) should not ground differences in legal rights and duties.

2. A law can be *neutral in its intent*. This, of course, is much harder to discern, and it has been a matter of controversy whether such intent can be discerned by courts. In contrast – and I concur – others recently have argued that "it makes perfectly good sense to speak of legislative intent."[15] A law is neutral in intent between *A* and *B* regarding *D* if the goal of the legislation was not to favor either side in the *D* dispute; whatever

---

[14] See Michael Pendlebury, "In Defense of Moderate Neutralism," *Journal of Social Philosophy*, 33.3 (2002), 360–76.

[15] Lawrence M. Solan, "Private Language, Public Laws: The Central Role of Legislative Intent in Statutory Interpretation," *Georgetown Law Journal*, 93.2 (2005), 427–85.

differential effects the law may have, it was not the goal of the legislature that the differential effects be based on D.[16] A law that is not neutral on its face can be neutral in intent. Suppose that the legislature has accepted the claims that (1) strong families are needed to protect the general welfare (for example, to reduce crime and poverty) and (2) strong families require a married father and mother in residence with the children. A resulting law may give special advantages to heterosexual couples with children, being clearly non-neutral on its face in relation to differences over the value of homosexual households. Yet insofar as the aim was, say, to prevent crime and poverty, the law was neutral in its intent.

3. A law may also be *neutral or non-neutral in its interpretation.* Suppose a law is neutral on its face and in intent – say a law provides for freedom of religious expression, and the goal was such freedom. But suppose further that the interpretations of the law draw on controversial conceptions of religion (say, monotheism). In that case interpretations of the law treat differentially monotheistic and polytheistic citizens on the basis of this difference. If so, the law fails to be fully neutral.

Of course all of this still leaves open the set of citizens and range of disputes over which the law is neutral in these ways. No law can be neutral without limit. Some citizens are criminals: a law that seeks to reduce crime clearly is not neutral between criminals and the rest of the population. Any notion of neutrality must identify the range of valuational disputes among citizens regarding which the law must be neutral. However, once the range of relevant valuational disputes is identified, it would seem that an acceptable liberal theory, at this first level, must be *neutral among all citizens on that dispute.* If there is some valuational dispute D that has been identified as worthy of respect (in the sense that laws seek to be fully neutral in relation to it), the law should be neutral with respect to all citizens party to the dispute. That, crucially, is what is meant by equal citizenship in a liberal regime and equality before the law.

(iii) Second-level neutrality

Larmore's important contribution is to insist that once we have identified an ideal of first-level neutrality, another, deeper, issue of neutrality arises: is the commitment to first-level neutrality itself neutrally justified? Hence Larmore's criticism of Mill: he thinks it is manifest that Mill offers a deep

---

[16] Neutrality of aim or intent is not, as we shall see, to be equated with neutrality of justification. There can be a neutral justification of non-neutral aim, as I explain in the text. Cf. Sher, *Beyond Neutrality*, 4.

justification of first-level neutrality that is based on a controversial ideal of individuality. Put bluntly, Larmore's core claim is that Mill thinks the best way to promote his ideal of individuality is through neutral political principles (that mandate first-level neutral laws). But such a defense of first-level neutrality (laws that operate neutrally) would ultimately not advocate a deep neutrality between citizens on fundamental disputes, such as whether individuality is really a value to be cherished. In this sense, it is charged, Mill is not truly a neutralist liberal or, if he is, his is only a surface sort of neutralism. It is this latter claim about Mill that I shall dispute in section IV.

III MILL'S FIRST-LEVEL LIBERAL NEUTRALIST PRINCIPLES

(i) Mill's three principles

Before disputing Larmore's interpretation of Millian liberalism, we should note that it is based on an important insight: at the first level Mill's theory is strongly, though we shall see not perfectly, neutralist.[17] Although we have heard it many times, we must not forget Mill's insistence that he defends "one very simple principle, as entitled to govern *absolutely* the dealings of society with the individual in the way of compulsion and control." And, of course, "That principle is, that the sole end for which mankind are warranted, individually or collectively, in interfering with the liberty of action of any of their number, is self-protection ... That the only purpose for which power can be rightfully exercised over any member of a civilized community, against his will, is to prevent harm to others" (*CW* XVIII, 223 [1, 9]). More precisely, Mill's liberalism can be explicated in terms of three principles:

1. the presumption in favor of liberty;
2. the principle that only harm to others can overcome the presumption (and so self-regarding actions are left free);
3. the principle that harm to others is necessary,[18] but not sufficient, to justify a coercive limitation of liberty; there may be good reasons for allowing harm.

---

[17] See also Sher, *Beyond Neutrality*, 34. But compare Pendlebury, "In Defense of Moderate Neutralism."
[18] I am putting aside here important complications, such as whether the harm principle concerns only *causing* harm to another, or concerns omissions as well. There is also a question whether Mill thinks that causing mere offense to others can ground legitimate intervention; if so, harm to others is not, in the end, a necessary condition for intervention. On these important issues, see C. L. Ten, *Mill on Liberty* (Oxford: Clarendon Press, 1980), 61–7, 102–7.

(ii) The presumption in favor of liberty

According to the first principle (as Mill says in the *Principles of Political Economy*) "the onus of making a case always lies on the defenders of legal prohibitions,"[19] or (as he says in *The Subjection of Women*), "in practical matters, the burthen of proof is supposed to be with those who are against liberty."[20] Now to say that the basic presumption in favor of freedom is (at this first level) neutral is to say that (1) it is neutral on its face between various conceptions of the good life, (2) it is neutral in its intent, and (3) it is neutral in its interpretation – its interpretation does not require appeal to a rationally contentious conception of the good life. For now I put aside the question whether Mill offers a neutral *justification* for the presumption in favor of liberty (a question of second-level neutrality); our concern now is whether the presumption in favor of liberty is a first-level principle of neutral legislation.

I take it that the idea that each person should be free to act on his controversial values unless good reasons can be provided for interfering is the basis of liberal tolerance.[21] Certainly this principle is neutral on its face among a range of controversial views about what makes life worth living, and the intent is to allow each to pursue his vision of the good life. To be sure, as with any neutral principle, its neutrality covers only a certain range of disputes (*D*) among citizens. The presumption is not neutral between those who wish to be free and those who wish to control others. No principle is neutral between its defenders and opponents. Mill recognizes that some people object to presuming that others should be free; he spends a good deal of time arguing that a denial of the presumption of freedom makes a tolerant society impossible. Such denials, he argues, rest on a "principle of tyranny" (*CW* XVIII, 290–1 [IV, 20]); they insist that there is no asymmetry between the choice of a person as to how he will live and the choice of others as to how he will live. But, insists Mill, "there is no parity between the feeling of a person for his own opinion, and the feeling of another who is offended at his holding it; no more than between the desire of a thief to take a purse, and the desire of the

[19] John Stuart Mill, *Principles of Political Economy with Some of Their Applications to Social Philosophy*, Part II (1848), vol. III of *The Collected Works of John Stuart Mill*, ed. John M. Robson, introduction by V. W. Bladen (Toronto: University of Toronto Press; London: Routledge & Kegan Paul, 1965), 938 (Bk. V, XI, 2).

[20] John Stuart Mill, *The Subjection of Women* (1869), in *The Collected Works of John Stuart Mill*, vol. XXI: *Essays on Equality, Law, and Education*, ed. John M. Robson, introduction by Stefan Collini (Toronto: University of Toronto Press, London: Routledge & Kegan Paul, 1984), 262 (I, 3); see also *CW* XVIII, 299 (V, 11).

[21] See S. I. Benn, *A Theory of Freedom* (Cambridge: Cambridge University Press, 1988), 87–90. See also my *Justificatory Liberalism* (New York: Oxford University Press, 1996), 162–6.

right owner to keep it" (*CW* xviii, 283 [iv, 12]). This is a bedrock liberal
principle, and liberal laws are certainly not neutral on the issue of whether
there is a presumption in favor of tolerating individual choice. So the
presumption is not neutral on its face or intent on *this* issue, but it *is* neutral
among all disputes concerning which values can ground a person's choices
about how he is to act. The presumption applies to all choices, and no
citizen is treated differently because he has made a certain choice about
how to live his life, what, if any, religion to follow, etc.

Now, it may be charged, the presumption cannot be neutral in its
interpretation. If liberty is an essentially contested concept, then to know
what the presumption in favor of liberty entails, we must employ some
contested conception of liberty resting on some controversial values.[22] Thus
any application of the first principle would necessarily be non-neutral. But,
surely, if this is a problem it plagues all liberal theories; if we accept this
critique, there can be no such thing as a neutralist liberalism. Our concern
in this chapter, though, is whether Mill's liberalism is non-neutral in some
sense that contrasts with Rawls's or Larmore's neutralism. As Mill sees it, he
is appealing to widely shared understandings of freedom and coercion,
which do not rest on any controversial moral values.

There is, I think, one point where Mill's application of principle 1 is
manifestly non-neutral, viz., his claim that "Liberty, as a principle, has no
application to any state of things anterior to the time when mankind have
become capable of being improved by free and equal discussion," and so
applies only to peoples who "have attained the capacity of being guided to
their own improvement by conviction or persuasion" (*CW* xviii, 224 [i, 10]).
To determine the range of application of the presumption in favor of
liberty Mill appeals to his controversial theory of individual and social
development (see section IV [iii] below). This should not be ignored: Mill
does not have a neutral account of the distinction between properly liberal
and non-liberal states. Yet Mill is also quick to point out that his concern is
the workings of the liberty principle within liberal states and here the
application of it is neutral.

(iii) What is a harm?

Principle 2 is the heart of the harm principle – Mill's very simple principle.
Because Mill insists that it is a simple principle that governs absolutely, the
presumption in favor of liberty can never be overturned unless the person

---

[22] I analyze this claim in *Political Theory and Political Concepts* (Boulder, CO: Westview, 2000) chs. 1–5.

whose liberty is being limited has done "definite damage" or posed "definite risk of damage" to others (*CW* xviii, 282 [iv, 10]). Now here critics of Mill have long insisted that the conception of a "harm," or an "injury" to the interests of another (*CW* xviii, 276 [iv, 3]), is hopelessly controversial. Long ago Robert Paul Wolff complained:

Mill takes it as beyond dispute that when Smith hits Jones, or steals his purse, or accuses him in court, or sells him a horse, he is in some way affecting Jones' interests. But Mill also seems to think it is obvious that when Smith practices the Roman faith, or reads philosophy, or eats meat, or engages in homosexual practices, he is not affecting Jones' interests. Now suppose that Jones is a devout Calvinist or a principled vegetarian. The very presence in his community of a Catholic or a meat-eater may cause him fully as much pain as a blow in the face or the theft of his purse. Indeed, to a truly devout Christian a physical blow counts for much less than the blasphemy of a heretic. After all, a physical blow affects my interests by causing me pain or stopping me from doing something I want to do. If the existence of ungodly persons in my community tortures my soul and destroys my sleep, who is to say that my interests are not affected?[23]

Thus Wolff and other critics imply that Mill's most distinctive contribution to liberalism – the harm principle – draws on secular values (a real harm is a bodily harm), and so begs the question against religious conceptions of harms and interests. Thus even at our first level of interpretation and application, Mill looks non-neutralist.

Mill's analysis of such cases is much more sophisticated than this criticism indicates. He is fully aware that offenses to religious sensibilities can be intense, and he does not dismiss them as, say, superstitious or irrational. Rather, Mill reflects on the acceptability of a principle allowing interference with liberty to protect religious sensibilities. Suppose we adopt a principle "Offense to religious sensibilities are harms." If so, Mill argues, the same principle that would protect Protestant sensibilities against Catholic "outrages" would protect Catholics against Protestant "outrages" such as married clergy. But Protestants cannot accept a principle that would allow suppression of their cherished activities: "we must beware of admitting a principle of which we would resent as a gross injustice the application to ourselves" (*CW* xviii, 285 [iv, 15]). Thus, Mill thinks, the only tenable principle for everyone is one that does not count such outrages as harms, but as "self-regarding concerns of individuals [with which] the public has no business to interfere" (*CW* xviii, 285 [iv, 14]). Mill is doing here precisely

[23] Robert Paul Wolff, *The Poverty of Liberalism* (Boston: Beacon Press, 1968), 23–34.

what Larmore recommends: retreating to a common ground in the face of disagreement.[24] A principle that allows intervention on grounds of protecting sensibilities will seem a "gross injustice" when applied to us; hence the only principle that can be accepted by all is mutual tolerance.

Readers often overlook the importance of impartial principles in *On Liberty*. Mill repeatedly criticizes proposals in favor of intervention that are based on mere preferences (*CW* XVIII, 220–2 [1, 6–7]). He begins *On Liberty* with the complaint that "There is, in fact, no recognized principle by which the propriety or impropriety of government interference is customarily tested. People decide according to their personal preferences" (*CW* XVIII, 223 [1, 8]). Throughout *On Liberty* Mill repeatedly reformulates proposals to prohibit a certain action in terms of a general underlying principle, and then finds the principle wanting, often on the grounds that once we see it as a principle, it will become clear that it is unacceptable, even to those who are friendly to some of the interventions it warrants. Lord Stanley, for example, argued that the sale of liquor harmed him because, among other reasons, it impeded his "right to free moral and intellectual development" by surrounding his "path with dangers, and by weakening and demoralizing society." Mill replies that the principle underlying Stanley's complaint is that "all mankind [has] a vested interest in each other's moral, intellectual, and even physical perfection, to be defined by each claimant according to his own standard" (*CW* XVIII, 288 [IV, 19]). But such a principle is impossible to accept, because it makes mutual toleration impossible.[25] For Mill the idea that principles governing intervention must be general and impartial is absolutely crucial in eliminating a host of proposed claims to being harmed by the actions of others. Importantly, Mill is contemptuous of "principles" based on the "logic of persecutors" which "say that we may persecute others because we are right, and that they must not persecute us because they are wrong" (*CW* XVIII, 285 [IV, 15]). Such principles are manifestly non-neutral since they presuppose that one party is correct in the dispute; only principles of interpretation that are not partial in this way are acceptable.

Mill, then, aims for a neutral interpretation of the harm principle. The only acceptable interpretations of "harm" are those that, once formulated in general terms, are not partial to one side in a religious or other valuational dispute about how to live life. The test of this partiality is whether the

[24] Larmore, *Patterns of Moral Complexity*, 53.
[25] In a similar way, Mill argues that the only principle he can discern in proposals to conduct a "civilizade" against the Mormon practice of polygamy is a principle of tyranny (*CW* XVIII, 280–91 [IV, 8–21]).

proponent of a conception of harm really endorses it when it would be employed against him; if not, it is objectionably partial. Thus Mill argues that all religious citizens should see that they could not accept a conception of harm in which their own religious practice could be seen as harmful to others. Consequently, he argues that a general principle of, say, not counting as a harm offense to religious sensibility is indeed neutral because it does not take a side in the dispute between religions. Of course there will be limits to the range of dispute that any interpretation of the harm principle can respect: the harm principle is not neutral between those who like to be harmed and those who do not, or between those who think that it would be better to die than to live among heathens and their more worldly brethren.[26] We shall consider later just how wide Mill seeks to cast his net (section IV), but for now the crucial point is that Mill repeatedly resists simply appealing to his own controversial conception of individuality when determining what constitutes a harm, something we might have expected from a "comprehensive" liberal. Indeed, Mill implies in *Principles* that appealing to a controversial conception of harm as the basis of a law – even if that notion of harm is verified by an appeal to utility – is to be avoided unless it is endorsed by the general citizenry.

Unless the conscience of the individual goes freely with the legal restraint, it partakes, either in a great or in a small degree, of the degradation of slavery. Scarcely any degree of utility, short of absolute necessity, will justify a prohibitory regulation, *unless it can also be made to recommend itself to the general conscience; unless persons of ordinary good intentions either already believe, or can be induced to believe, that the thing prohibited is a thing that they ought not to wish to do.* (*CW* III, 938 [Bk. V, XI, 2], emphasis added)[27]

(iv) When can society bear the harm?

We have seen that Mill's principles do not achieve first-level neutrality in relation to their range of application (i.e., liberal v. non-liberal societies). However, the deep worry about whether Mill's doctrine achieves first-level neutrality arises at the stage in which it has been shown that an action has harmed others and we now must decide whether this harm is significant enough to prohibit the action, or whether society can bear the harm. Remember, according to Mill

---

[26] A conception of harm that appeals to the basic welfare interests of citizens does not take sides in religious or other disputes about how to live; therefore such interpretations of the harm principle are neutral. I argue for this claim in my *Social Philosophy* (Armonk, NY: M. E. Sharpe, 1999), ch. 8.

[27] Mill bases this restriction on an appeal to individuality – but that is a matter of second-level neutrality that we shall consider in section IV.

it must by no means be supposed, because damage, or probability of damage, to the
interests of others, can alone justify the interference of society, that therefore it always
does justify such interference. In many cases, an individual, in pursuing a legitimate
object, necessarily and therefore legitimately causes pain or loss to others, or intercepts a good which they had a reasonable hope of obtaining. (*CW* xviii, 292 [v, 3])

In deciding which harms *to allow*, it seems impossible for Mill to avoid some
sort of cost–benefit calculation, and so he straightforwardly appeals to the
general interest (*CW* xviii, 293 [v, 3]). We might say that, for Mill, while all
laws must be neutral on their face, in their intent, and in their interpretation, the decision whether to refrain from legislating (in cases allowed by
principle 2) is a matter of social utility and requires appeal to the public
welfare. This raises an interesting problem for Millian neutralist liberalism.
We could have a body of laws each of which is neutral, but the system
nevertheless reflects general utilitarian (or even perfectionist) concerns
because such concerns inform the decision not to legislate; only legislation,
not its absence, requires a neutral justification.

Interestingly, this asymmetry seems built into the fabric of Mill's
account, and perhaps liberalism in general. If leaving people free does not
require a justification – if, as Mill says, "the onus of making a case always lies
on the defenders of legal prohibitions" (*CW* iii, 938 [Bk. V, xi, 2]), then no
one need defend a decision to leave people free. And that means that they
might be legitimately left free for a variety of reasons. I do not think Mill
would be worried about this. At least in his day, he thought over-regulation
was rampant; and since regulation limits liberty, I believe that he generally
supports bearing "inconveniences" for the "greater good of human freedom" (*CW* xviii, 282 [iv, 11]) whenever possible. Notice that the appeal to
liberty now plays a different role in the argument: it is not simply a
presumption (as in principle 1), but a great social value ("a greater good")
that can often outweigh even legitimate harms to others. Insofar as liberty is
a great social value that outweighs harms to others, and *that* is why we do
not legislate, we may have a neutral justification for a wide range of cases *not*
to legislate – if, that is, there is a neutral case for seeing liberty as so
important. We are thus led to the heart of Mill's liberalism: is there a
neutral justification for liberty as a great social value?

(v) Is anyone not a neutralist in this sense?

Before going on to look at Mill's case for neutral legislation, it is important
to stress that many liberals have defended distinctly non-neutral principles
of legislation. Consider the British idealists, whose version of liberalism

dominated late nineteenth-century English political theory. Their principles of liberal legislation really were perfectionist and non-neutral. Indeed,
their master political principle was that, with regard to compulsory government policies, the state should "hinder hindrances" to "the best life."[28] And
so, in his doctrine of liberal legislation T. H. Green maintained: "There is
no right to freedom in the purchase and sale of a particular commodity,
if the general result of allowing such freedom is to detract from freedom
in the higher sense, from the general power of men to make the best of
themselves."[29]

IV MILL'S SECOND-LEVEL NEUTRALIST LIBERALISM

(i) What would be a neutral case for first-level neutrality?

Thus far we have been examining the extent to which Mill defends neutral
legislation; what is required, as Larmore says, to provide a neutral justification of neutral principles? Recall:

Political neutrality: L is neutral between A and B on dispute D in relation to T if
and only if it does not T them differently on the basis of D.

Applying this idea, we can say that the justification (J) of a principle of
(first-level) neutral legislation is itself neutral between A and B on dispute D
if J does not treat A and B differently. In this context, for J to treat A and B
differently would be for the justification to presuppose, or favor, A's or B's
position on the disputed matter. Now it is obvious that just "how neutral"
the justification is will turn on how broadly we specify D and the members
of A and B. If D covers only a small range of disputes (say, about the proper
interpretation of Christian doctrine), the justification would be neutral in
relation to Christians, but not *vis-à-vis* non-Christians.[30] Again, if the
parties to the disputes are characterized narrowly – for example, fully
rational citizens who have no false beliefs – the justification would not be
neutral between the views of this group and the positions of less than fully
rational citizens on D.

---

[28] Bernard Bosanquet, "*The Philosophical Theory of the State*," in Bernard Bosanquet, *The Philosophical Theory of the State and Related Essays*, ed. Gerald F. Gaus and William Sweet (Indianapolis: St. Augustine Press, 2001), 190.

[29] T. H. Green, "Lecture on 'Liberal Legislation' and Freedom of Contract," in Paul Harris and John Morrow, eds., *Lectures on the Principles of Political Obligation and Other Writings* (Cambridge: Cambridge University Press, 1986), 210.

[30] A view that Mill explicitly criticizes at *CW* XVIII, 240–1n. [II, 19].

We can see, then, that rather than asking simply whether a justification is neutral, we should think about how broadly neutral it is: the broader the range of disputes, and the broader the class of citizens among whom the justification is neutral, the broader the second-level neutrality. I shall argue that Mill's second-level justification of his three core principles is very broadly neutral, and goes far beyond the set of citizens who embrace his ideal of individuality. Indeed, he seeks to appeal to the general public – that "miscellaneous collection of a few wise and many foolish individuals" (*CW* xviii, 232 [ii, 8]). The point of *On Liberty* is that public opinion cannot be allowed to rule freely over the lives of others. So, as we have seen, Mill clearly does not respect the opinions of ordinary members of the public about how others should live. However, this does not mean that Mill does not wish to show ordinary members of the public – even those who fail to value individuality – that they have good reasons to embrace neutral legislation. Mill offers justifications for neutral legislation that appeal to general members of the public, and which do not require taking sides on a wide range of disputes about the best way to live, including the value of individuality.

It is important to stress that not every justification that Mill offers needs to be neutral with regard to every dispute. As we shall see (sections IV (ii) and (iv) below), Mill does indeed offer consensus justifications, but *On Liberty* is partly devoted to *convergence justifications* (section II (i) 4, above), which show how the public in general have various strong reasons to adopt his principles, based on their differing interests and aims. Different parts of the public will respond to different arguments. A convergence justification can be neutral between Alf and Betty and yet draw on Alf's controversial belief β to justify a neutral principle, if it can provide Betty, who does not share β, with another reason, perhaps based on a controversial belief that she holds but Alf does not, to endorse the principle. The important point is that, by the end of the day, every member of the general public has reason to endorse the principles.

(ii) The master argument for liberty: shared epistemic interests

The "official Mill" of the political liberalism of Rawls and Larmore rests his case for the value of liberty on the ideal of individuality. But that is not the first case for liberty that Mill presents; chapter ii of *On Liberty* is devoted to freedom of speech. Many political philosophers are apt to dismiss this first, lengthy, defense of freedom of speech as not directly relevant to a defense of *freedom of action*. Recall that after concluding his defense of freedom of speech Mill explicitly says: "No one pretends that actions should be as free as opinions. On the contrary, even opinions lose their immunity, when the circumstances in which they are expressed are such as to constitute their expression a positive instigation to some mischievous act" (*CW* xviii, 260 [iii, 1]). He then seems to begin his defense of freedom of action, which draws on the ideal of individuality (see section IV (iii) below), leading to the impression that the ideal of individuality is *the* defense of free action. However, Mill explicitly tells us that

the same reasons which show that opinion should be free, prove also that he should be allowed, without molestation, to carry his opinions into practice at his own cost. That mankind are not infallible; that their truths, for the most part, are only half-truths; that unity of opinion, unless resulting from the fullest and freest comparison of opposite opinions, is not desirable, and diversity not an evil, but a good, until mankind are much more capable than at present of recognizing all sides of the truth, are principles applicable to men's modes of action, not less than to their opinions. As it is useful that while mankind are imperfect there should be different opinions, so is it that there should be different experiments of living; that free scope should be given to varieties of character, short of injury to others; and that the worth of different modes of life should be proved practically, when any one thinks fit to try them. (*CW* xviii, 260–1 [iii, 1])

Thus the grounds of freedom of speech "when rightly understood, are of much wider application than to only one division of the subject" (*CW* xviii, 227 [i, 16]).

What are these grounds? Mill provides two general epistemic cases for freedom of speech. We can see one as based on our interest in truth, and one on our interest in justified belief.

1. The argument for the interest in truth is a social epistemology argument.[31] A society which gives great scope for freedom allows citizens to engage in many experiments of living. Just as true beliefs will tend to be produced in an epistemic climate in which they can be challenged and defended by anyone, so too Mill thinks that correct ways of living will arise in an atmosphere of freedom of action. This argument appeals to anyone who thinks that some ways of living are truer or more correct than others – one need not be a proponent of individuality or eccentricity. If one believes that there are better or truer ways of living – including non-Millian ways of living – then the social epistemological argument of chapter ii of *On Liberty* is relevant. Indeed, Mill is explicit that even if we only have opinions about

---

[31] See Allen Buchanan, "Social Moral Epistemology," *Social Philosophy & Policy*, 19.2 (2002), 126–52. I have greatly benefited from discussions with Piers Norris Turner about social epistemological issues.

what is a more *useful* way of living, the social epistemological argument applies (*CW* xviii, 233 [ii, 10]).

2. To be sure, one may argue that Mill's case does not succeed – that some traditional ways of living that are genuinely useful or good for humans cannot be shown to be better in a society with freedom to experiment. Perhaps they have a hard time competing in a free society.[32] Mill has another, and I think even more important, argument to deploy at this point: if one believes that some ways of life are more useful or better for humans, *this belief is itself justified only in a society that allows freedom to experiment and challenge it.* "Complete liberty of contradicting and disproving our opinion, is the very condition which justifies us in assuming its *truth for purposes of action*; and *on no other terms* can a being with human faculties have any rational assurance of being right" (*CW* xviii, 231 [ii, 6], emphasis added). Any agent with an interest in action on the basis of justified belief has an interest in the condition that makes such belief possible – liberty. Of course one might reply here that this shows that someone who thinks there are better and worse ways of living ought to allow debate about the matter, but not allow others actually to try out alternative ways of living: it shows only the need for freedom of opinion, not of action. But surely this is the point of Mill's reference to "experiments in living" (*CW* xviii, 267 [iii, 1]). To say that one could have justified grounds for believing that one's way of living was better or more useful by allowing debate but not to allow competing practice is like saying one can have justified grounds for one's views about physics by allowing discussion but not permitting those who disagree to conduct experiments. Thus, interestingly, on Mill's view, if a way of life cannot exist under conditions of freedom, none of its adherents could be justified in believing its way of life is good, useful, and so on.

I am not claiming here that Mill's arguments cannot be disputed; our concern is whether they are neutral. And they are neutral among all citizens who think that some ways of living are better, that we have an interest in finding out which they are, and that we can have justified beliefs about what they are.

(iii) Individuality, social progress, and diversity of tastes

Let us now turn to the Mill of Rawls and Larmore, who rests his case for liberty on the value of individuality. There is no doubt that Mill thinks (1) that individuality is a genuine value, (2) that it endorses far-reaching

---

[32] On this issue see John Gray, *Two Faces of Liberalism* (Cambridge: Polity Press, 2000).

liberty of tastes and pursuits, and (3) that it is a controversial value insofar as many are not interested in individuality (*CW* XVIII, 267 [III, 10]).[33] However, this does not show that Mill's case for liberty is non-neutral: only if it is necessary to accept the value of individuality in order to justify a person's endorsing the principles of neutral legislation would Mill's case fail to achieve second-level neutrality. But as I have been stressing, controversial values can be an element of a neutral *convergence* justification. Mill is not precluded from advocating what he thinks are the best and true grounds for liberty in order to achieve second-level neutrality.

It has been argued, though, that Mill's defense of individuality shows that his case is clearly not neutral in relation to the "Calvinistic theory," which holds that "the one great offence of man is Self-will" (*CW* XVIII, 265 [III, 7]).[34] In contrast to Millian individuality, which defends the flowering of human nature, the Calvinist thinks that humanity has its nature bestowed on it in order for it to be "abnegated" (*CW* XVIII, 266 [III, 8]). However, even supposing that Mill believes the Calvinistic theory to be worthless, and that he thinks truth lies only in the value of individuality, this would not show that his case is overall non-neutral – it would imply that advocates of the Calvinistic view cannot embrace neutral principles on the grounds of individuality. Moreover, a more careful reading does not bear out the claim that Mill thinks that the Calvinistic view is without worth. "'Pagan self-assertion' is one of the elements of human worth, *as well as 'Christian self-denial.'* There is a Greek ideal of self-development, which the Platonic and Christian ideal of self-government blends with, but does not supersede" (*CW* XVIII, 266 [III, 8], emphasis added). This sounds much like the Mill of chapter II (*CW* XVIII, 252ff. [II, 34]), where he argues that the truth is many-sided, and only freedom for the partial truths to compete and present their cases can uncover the real complex truth (in this case, about the human good).

The deep flaw of the Larmore-Rawls reading, though, is that it ends midway though chapter III of *On Liberty*. In the first half of the chapter Mill presents his case for individuality, but then he pauses and asks:

Having said that Individuality is the same thing with development, and that it is only the cultivation of individuality which produces, or can produce, well-developed human beings, I might here close the argument: for what more or better can be said of any condition of human affairs, than that it brings human beings themselves nearer to the best thing they can be? or what worse can be said of any

---

[33] I have explored this ideal of individuality at some length in Gerald F. Gaus, *Modern Liberal Theory of Man* (London: Croom-Helm 1983), ch. 1. I argue there that Rawls concurs in endorsing this ideal.
[34] Rudisill, "The Neutrality of the State and its Justification in Rawls and Mill," 161ff.

obstruction to good, than that it prevents this? Doubtless, however, these considerations will not suffice to convince those who most need convincing; *and it is
necessary further to show*, that these developed human beings are of some use to the
undeveloped – to point out to those who do not desire liberty, and would not avail
themselves of it, that they may be in some intelligible manner rewarded for allowing
other people to make use of it without hindrance. (*CW* xviii, 267 [iii, 10], emphasis
added)

The remainder of chapter iii then seeks to do what Mill says is "necessary" –
to show those who do not value individuality for itself that they ought to
value it (in others). Mill endeavors to uncover a broad common ground of
values that should lead general members of the public to allow individuality,
even if they do not have a taste for it themselves. (Remember, the public is
composed of the few wise and the many ignorant and foolish.) Mill again
invokes the epistemic benefits of experiments (*CW* xviii, 267 [iii, 11]), but
then spends a great deal of effort in arguing that general social progress,
which brings a number of conveniences to everyone, depends on the
discoveries and actions of exceptional individuals, and we can expect such
genius only in an "*atmosphere* of freedom" (*CW* xviii [iii, 11], emphasis
original).

  Lastly, Mill explicitly says late in chapter iii that the case for liberty does
not depend on the pursuit of individuality and genius:

But independence of action, and disregard of custom are not solely deserving of
encouragement for the chance they afford that better modes of action, and customs
more worthy of general adoption ... nor is it only persons of decided mental
superiority who have a just claim to carry on their lives in their own way ... Human
beings are not like sheep; and even sheep are not undistinguishably alike ... If it
were only that people have diversities of taste, that is reason enough for not
attempting to shape them all after one model. (*CW* xviii, 269–70 [iii, 14])

Mill, then, concludes with a general argument that, simply given differences
in tastes as well as in our basic constitutions, people cannot get "their fair
share of happiness" if they are not allowed to go about their own lives in
their own way. Does this mean that Mill believes that (1) everyone will come
to value diversity of tastes and (2) the argument for liberty depends on this?
Certainly Mill thinks that (1) will characterize a developed society. But recall
that Mill's claim is that a person will have a tolerably happy life only if she is
free to live her own life in her own way. Thus if each is concerned merely
with her own life and individual happiness, the only principle on which we
can converge is individual liberty. It does not seem necessary (although Mill
certainly thinks it would be desirable and perhaps will occur in the future)
that we all, in addition, positively value diversity itself.

(iv) Arguments for the harm principle

I have been focusing on arguments that liberty is a great value that should not be limited except in the face of serious harms to others (section III (iv) above). But the harm principle too must be justified: why should society interfere only with harm to others and not some self-regarding actions? How broadly neutral are Mill's arguments?

1. Mill tells us that "the strongest of all arguments" against allowing public interference with purely self-regarding "conduct, is that when it does interfere, the odds are that it interferes wrongly, and in the wrong place" (*CW* XVIII, 283 [IV, 12]). "On questions of social morality, of duty to others, the opinion of the public, that is, of an overruling majority, though often wrong, is likely to be still oftener right; because on such questions they are only required to judge of their own interests; of the manner in which some mode of conduct, if allowed to be practised, would affect themselves" (*CW* XVIII, 283 [IV, 12]). But when interfering with a self-regarding action of others, people tend to follow their own preferences (which, it will be recalled, is the worry at the heart of *On Liberty*; see section III (iii) above). Mill takes pains to warn us against assuming an ideal state that makes only justified interventions: real states governed by real publics will tend to make systematic and persistent errors. This is a general government failure argument that does not depend on an appeal to individuality and is consistent with a variety of values.

2. Mill explicitly appeals to an ideal of reciprocity as a basis for the harm principle. At the very outset of chapter IV, which examines the harm principle, Mill tells us that "everyone who receives the protection of society owes a return for the benefit, and that each should be bound to observe a certain line of conduct towards the rest" (*CW* XVIII, 276 [IV, 3]). And this conduct is not to harm the essential interests of others.[35] Mill holds that this is so basic to social life that anyone who refuses to observe this line of conduct is to be treated "like an enemy of society" (*CW* XVIII, 280 [IV, 7]) or, less extremely, he is a "nuisance to other people" (*CW* XVIII, 260 [III, 1]). When arguing against unjustified interferences such as those based on intolerance, Mill again points out the absence of reciprocity: people demand of others what they do not demand of themselves (*CW* XVIII, 257 [II, 38], 285 [IV, 15]). That principles of political right are founded on reciprocity is, of course, fundamental to political liberalism.[36]

---

[35] It also includes what might be called "the public harm principle," which concerns provision of public goods. See Gaus, *Social Philosophy*, ch. 10.

[36] This is clearest in John Rawls, "The Idea of Public Reason Revisited," in his *Collected Papers*, ed. Samuel Freeman (Cambridge, MA: Harvard University Press, 1999), 573–615.

Taken together, these two arguments are a compelling, very broadly neutral, *consensus* justification of the harm principle. In Rawlsian terms, by argument 2, all reasonable people – those who seek to live social life on reciprocal terms – must accept that coercive legislation is justified by the harm principle.[37] And, by argument 1, recognition of the basic facts of government failure provides a case that only harm to others – not self-regarding harms – can justify public intervention in the lives of citizens.

V CONCLUSION

In the first chapter of *On Liberty* Mill proclaims: "I forgo any advantage which could be derived to my argument from the idea of abstract right, as a thing independent of utility. I regard utility as the ultimate appeal on all ethical questions; but it must be utility in the largest sense, grounded on the permanent interests of man as a progressive being" (*CW* XVIII, 224 [I, 11]). But this does not mean that one must be a utilitarian to be reasoned into accepting liberty; only that a utilitarian such as Mill (thought himself to be) need not worry that his utilitarianism failed to endorse the doctrine. But, as Mill suggests, a contract view should also accept the harm principle (*CW* XVIII, 276 [IV, 3]). Millian liberalism (as a view based on a strong principle of liberty and the harm principle) has been the subject of what Rawls would call an "overlapping consensus": utilitarians, contract theorists,[38] and less systematic liberalisms[39] have all embraced its strongly neutralist theory of justified legislation.

On Liberty is filled with arguments. Throughout, Mill appeals to a variety of possible objecting positions, trying to show *them* that they should embrace liberty. Larmore's dictum that political liberals should retreat to common ground in the face of disagreement is in many ways the method of argument in most of *On Liberty*. Because Mill also presents his own favored, controversial, defense of freedom, he has come to be seen as resting his neutralist liberalism on the narrow foundation of a controversial "comprehensive" theory. I have challenged this reading by surveying some of Mill's most important arguments. I hope it is clear that the foundations of his neutralist liberalism are neither narrow nor sectarian.

[37] See Rawls, *Political Liberalism*, 58ff. [38] See Gaus, *Social Philosophy*, ch. 6.
[39] Most famously, of course, Joel Feinberg, *The Moral Limits of the Criminal Law*, 4 vols. (New York: Oxford University Press, 1984–90).

CHAPTER 5

Rawls's critique of On Liberty

Robert Amdur

John Rawls's *A Theory of Justice* was published in 1971. It was immediately recognized as a classic, a work of enormous importance. Robert Nozick, who disagreed with Rawls on many points, described it as "a powerful, deep, subtle, wide-ranging, systematic work in political and moral philosophy which has not seen its like since the writings of John Stuart Mill, if then."[1] Many others echoed this view.

Between 1971 and his death in 2002 Rawls published several more books and many articles, along with a revised edition of *A Theory of Justice*.[2] In Rawls's later works, the main outlines of his theory remained intact, but he clarified some points, changed his position on others, and addressed several questions he had largely ignored in *Theory*, among them international justice, political legitimacy, and the role of religion in a democratic society. Rawls scholars have debated, and will no doubt continue to debate, the significance of these changes and additions, and the extent to which they represent departures from the letter and spirit of *Theory*.

Rawls clearly regarded Mill as a theorist of the first rank. He learned from Mill, and saw himself, in part, as building on Mill's ideas in *On Liberty*. It is also clear, both in *A Theory of Justice* and in his later works, that he saw Mill's arguments as flawed in important ways. In *A Theory of Justice* he identifies what he sees as the main weaknesses in Mill's defense of liberty. In *Political Liberalism* and *Justice as Fairness: A Restatement*, he argues, from a different perspective, that Millian liberalism cannot form the basis of a stable society. In this chapter I want to examine both lines of criticism.

I would like to thank Beth Rubenstein for her comments on an earlier version of this chapter.

[1] Robert Nozick, *Anarchy, State, and Utopia* (New York: Basic Books, 1974), 183.

[2] The most important books are *Political Liberalism* (New York: Columbia University Press, 1993), cited in the text as *PL*; *Justice as Fairness: A Restatement* (Cambridge, MA: Harvard University Press, 2001), cited in the text as *JFR*; and *A Theory of Justice*, rev. edn. (Cambridge, MA: Harvard University Press, 1999), cited in the text as *TJ* (unless otherwise noted, all references to *A Theory of Justice* refer to the revised edition). The main articles can be found in *Collected Papers*, ed. Samuel Freeman (Cambridge, MA: Harvard University Press, 1999).

I

We can think of Rawls as beginning with the question: what terms of cooperation would citizens, viewed as free and equal persons, agree to, to regulate the basic structure of society? To answer this question Rawls introduces the original position, a thought experiment, the equivalent of the state of nature in traditional social contract theory. He asks us to imagine a group of hypothetical men and women instructed to deliberate until they agree on a set of principles to govern the main political and social institutions of their society. The parties in the original position operate behind a "veil of ignorance" which deprives them of all particular information – concerning, for example, race, gender, natural abilities, and life plans – about themselves (Rawls sometimes describes this information as "morally irrelevant"). They are, however, permitted certain minimal information about fundamental human needs and interests, and also about human psychology and the way institutions work. The idea is that, deprived of information that could permit them to select principles tailored to their own interests, the parties will be forced to reach a fair agreement. Hence the name: justice as fairness.

Rawls argues that his hypothetical contractors would choose the following two principles:

(a) Each person has the same indefeasible claim to a fully adequate scheme of equal basic liberties, which scheme is compatible with the same scheme of liberties for all; and
(b) Social and economic inequalities are to satisfy two conditions: first, they are to be attached to offices and positions open to all under conditions of fair equality of opportunity; and second, they are to be to the greatest benefit of the least-advantaged members of society (the difference principle) (*JFR*, 42–3).

The basic liberties protected by the first principle include "freedom of thought and liberty of conscience; political liberties (for example, the right to vote and to participate in politics) and freedom of association, as well as rights and liberties specified by the liberty and integrity (physical and psychological) of the person; and finally, the rights and liberties covered by the rule of law" (*JFR*, 44). They do not include what have sometimes been called economic liberties: freedom of contract, freedom to own productive property, freedom to appropriate what one has produced, freedom to leave one's possessions to persons of one's choice. Rawls clearly believes that the first set of liberties is more important, more central to what it means to be a human being.

The first principle takes what Rawls calls lexical priority over the second: the basic liberties can be restricted only for the sake of liberty.

> [T]his priority rules out exchanges ("trade-offs," as economists say) between the basic rights and liberties covered by the first principle and the social and economic advantages regulated by the difference principle. For example, the equal political liberties cannot be denied to certain groups on the grounds that their having these liberties may enable them to block policies needed for economic growth and efficiency. (*JFR*, 47)

There are obvious similarities between Rawls's first principle and Mill's "one very simple principle." Both Mill and Rawls aim to provide strong protection (perhaps the strongest possible protection) for a largely overlapping set of liberties. Both place an extremely high value on freedom of conscience and free thought and discussion. Both want to rule out some of the most common justifications for interference – paternalistic and moralistic justifications in particular. No doubt there are differences between their principles. But when he discusses Mill in his chapter on "Equal Liberty," Rawls does not emphasize those differences. He clearly sees Mill as someone whose goals – at least when it comes to liberty – are similar to his own, but also as someone whose efforts to provide the strongest possible protection for liberty are vitiated by his utilitarianism.

Using freedom of conscience as an example, Rawls begins by suggesting that his own theory provides strong arguments for equal liberty. "Equal liberty," he writes, "is the only principle that the persons in the original position can acknowledge" (*TJ*, 181). But, he adds: "I do not deny … that persuasive arguments for liberty are forthcoming on other views. As understood by Mill, the principle of utility often supports freedom" (*TJ*, 184). What, then, is the problem with Mill's defense of liberty? After summarizing several of the arguments in chapter III of *On Liberty*, Rawls explains:

> … Mill's contentions, as cogent as they are, will not, it seems, justify an equal liberty for all. We still need analogues of familiar utilitarian assumptions. One must suppose a certain similarity among individuals, say their equal capacity for activities and interests of men as progressive beings, and in addition a principle of the diminishing marginal value of basic rights when assigned to individuals. In the absence of these presumptions the advancement of human ends may be compatible with some persons' being oppressed, or at least granted but a restricted liberty. Whenever a society sets out to maximize the sum of intrinsic value or the net balance of the satisfaction of interests, it is liable to find that the denial of liberty for some is justified in the name of this single end. The liberties of equal citizenship are insecure when founded upon teleological principles. The argument for them relies upon precarious calculations as well as controversial and uncertain premises. (*TJ*, 185)

In this passage Rawls does not actually criticize the arguments in chapter III. Rather, he seems to be making two general points. First, even if Mill has made a strong case for liberty (or for certain specific liberties), it may not be a case for *equal* liberty; the argument for equal liberty requires additional assumptions. Second, and more important, the case for liberty is itself precarious, relying as it does on the result of utilitarian calculations. Even if the calculations appear to support liberty today, tomorrow a new set of calculations could demonstrate that repression produces greater overall utility. (Even the knowledge that this might happen at some point in the future could threaten citizens' self-esteem and leave them less secure.) Under justice as fairness, on the other hand, "the equal liberties have a different basis altogether ... They are not a way of maximizing the sum of intrinsic value or of achieving the greatest net balance of satisfaction." Rather "these rights are assigned to fulfill the principles of cooperation that citizens would acknowledge when each is fairly represented as a moral person" (*TJ*, 185).

Rawls's criticism would appear to apply most forcefully to the argument from truth in chapter II of *On Liberty*. Even here matters are complicated, for Mill is doing a number of different things in chapter II. At one point he suggests that freedom can raise "even persons of the most ordinary intellect to something of the dignity of thinking beings" (*CW* XVIII, 243 [II, 20]). About people who hold true opinions without understanding the grounds of those opinions, he writes: "this is not the way in which truth ought to be held by a rational being" (*CW* XVIII, 244 [II, 22]). These are not utilitarian arguments, and they could not easily be refuted by utilitarian calculations. But the main argument in chapter II – the argument connecting free discussion to the discovery and spread of truth – does seem to be open to Rawls's objections. One can imagine calculations that would demonstrate (1) that free discussion is not the most efficient road to the discovery of truth; or (2) that free discussion works most effectively when the liberties of some people (or some groups) are restricted. In either case, the consequences for Mill's argument would be devastating. As Martha Nussbaum puts it, under the argument from truth free thought and discussion are "made hostage to contingent facts concerning what best promotes truth and progress."[3]

But the most important arguments in chapter III are different. They focus on self-development, on the intrinsic worth of spontaneity, on character, and, above all, on the value of individual choice:

[3] Martha C. Nussbaum, *Hiding from Humanity: Disgust, Shame, and the Law* (Princeton: Princeton University Press, 2004), 326.

The human faculties of perception, judgment, discriminative feeling, mental activity, and even moral preference are exercised only in making a choice. He who does anything because it is the custom makes no choice. He gains no practice either in discerning or in desiring what is best. The mental and moral, like the muscular, powers are improved only by being used …

He who lets the world, or his own portion of it, choose his plan of life for him has no need of any other faculty than the ape-like one of imitation. He who chooses his plan for himself employs all his faculties. (*CW* xvIII, 262 [III, 3–4])

Mill's point is not simply that people who choose for themselves are likely to make "better" choices than others could make for them, but also that choosing itself is important. One becomes a fully developed human being only when one makes choices for oneself. These include especially (but not only) choices about one's "plan of life." Further, Mill believes that these choices are never (or never need be) final; we must have the opportunity to reconsider and revise our prior decisions about what to believe or how to live our lives. In order to choose for themselves people require both freedom from outside interference and access to the widest possible range of ideas, opinions, and modes of living. People who make choices for themselves may not be happier in the ordinary sense of the word, but Mill clearly believes they are superior human beings.

Two points deserve emphasis. First, while Mill sometimes treats liberty as a means to happiness, the most important arguments in chapter III suggest that freedom is intrinsically valuable, a constituent or an essential ingredient of each person's well-being. Important as this is, however, it does not fully answer the Rawlsian challenge. Even if freedom, or individual choice, is an essential element of well-being, there may still be reasons to restrict some people's freedom to enhance the well-being of (or to increase the range of choices available to) others. This seems especially likely if we believe that some people are more capable of choosing, or more likely to choose well, than others. Based on what he says about the importance of men and women of genius, one might be tempted to attribute that view to Mill. This leads to the second point: while there are no doubt elitist elements to Mill's thought, the key arguments in chapter III contain a strong democratic component. When Mill tells us that some of the most important human faculties "are exercised only in making a choice," he seems to be referring not only or even primarily to geniuses, but to human beings in general. Later on in the same chapter, Mill makes this explicit:

Nor is it only persons of decided mental superiority who have a just claim to carry on their lives in their own way. There is no reason that all human existence should be constructed on some one or some small number of patterns. If a person possesses any tolerable amount of common sense and experience, his own mode of laying out his existence is best, not because it is the best in itself, but because it is his own mode. (*CW* xviii, 270 [iii, 14])

If we agree that liberty is an essential element of well-being (not just a means to well-being), and that every person has a "just claim" to carry on her life in her own way, then Rawls's criticisms of Mill would seem to lose much of their force. Again, Rawls seems concerned above all that future calculations might undermine the case for liberty; he believes this possibility exists whenever society is committed to maximizing the sum of value, however defined. But Mill's main arguments for equal liberty do not rely on "precarious calculations" or empirical claims of any sort. Nothing is being maximized. Like any liberal theory, including Rawls's, Mill's theory requires certain minimal assumptions about human equality, but it does not require any controversial assumptions about individual capacities or diminishing marginal utility. As Nussbaum rightly observes, the main argument in chapter iii of *On Liberty* "has a Kantian flavor." Here at least "Mill is veering round to a … theory, more Kantian in spirit, in which each person is inviolable, and an end."[4]

This is the side of Mill's theory that Rawls misses, at least in *A Theory of Justice*; later on, as we shall see, he suggests a different understanding of what Mill was doing in chapter iii. His criticisms of utilitarian arguments for liberty are utterly convincing – if the criticisms sound familiar, that is a tribute to Rawls's influence. But those criticisms do not apply to the most important arguments in the crucial chapter of *On Liberty*.

What about Rawls's alternative? Even if his criticisms of Mill are flawed, even if he is mistaken about the kind of argument Mill was making in chapter iii, he still could be right on the larger question. One could still argue that he has provided firmer grounding for his liberty principle than Mill does for his one simple principle. With the priority rule in place, his theory may still offer stronger protection for the most important basic liberties. After all, as Colin Bird points out, the priority rule precludes trade-offs between liberty and other goods, while "Mill's argument allows us to restrict liberty for considerations other than those of liberty."[5] This alone might lead one to conclude that Rawls's principle is stronger.

Are these claims plausible? Clearly, a lot depends on the meaning of the priority rule and the force of the arguments supporting it. Without attempting to offer a final verdict on this part of Rawls's theory I want to argue, first,

---

[4] Ibid., 331, 334.
[5] Colin Bird, *An Introduction to Political Philosophy* (Cambridge: Cambridge University Press, 2006), 198.

that in one important respect the priority rule is weaker than Rawls's initial formulation suggests; and second, that despite various changes and clarifications, the priority of liberty remains one of the more problematic features of justice as fairness.

(i) Equal liberty and the priority rule

In *A Theory of Justice*, Rawls suggests that Mill's arguments do not justify an equal liberty for all. In his later work, he repeatedly emphasizes his commitment not just to liberty but to equal basic liberties. But what exactly does this commitment entail? In particular, how does it fit with what Rawls says about permissible restrictions on liberty under the priority rule? Rawls insists that once society reaches the point at which liberties can be effectively exercised, liberty can be restricted only for the sake of liberty itself (or in the more recent formulation, only for the sake of basic liberties). Still, under the priority rule, it is possible to justify restrictions on basic liberties, including some that involve a lesser liberty for everyone, and others that permit unequal liberties. A general restriction – one that affects everyone – is justified only when it strengthens the total system of basic liberties shared by all. To justify unequal liberties one needs to demonstrate that the freedom of those with the lesser liberty is "better secured."

Rawls acknowledges that, historically, those who have opposed equal political liberty have often put forward the right kind of justification. When Mill proposed giving extra votes to people with greater intelligence and education, he seems to have assumed that this would leave the other liberties of the uneducated more secure. If we accept that assumption, "plural voting may be perfectly just" (*TJ*, 205). Of course, Rawls adds, some liberties are more central than others. Limits on liberty of conscience and the rights defining the integrity of the person are more difficult to defend than unequal voting rights. But under the right circumstances even these might be justified. Again, the crucial point is that in every case it is "those with the lesser liberty who must be compensated. We are always to appraise the situation from their point of view" (*TJ*, 218).

In fact, Rawls interprets the priority rule so as to permit restrictions that cannot plausibly be described as better securing the freedom of those with the lesser liberty. Two examples make this clear. First, Rawls says that the tolerant can restrict the freedom of an intolerant sect when they "sincerely and with reason believe that their own security and that of the institutions of liberty are in danger" (*TJ*, 193). As Pogge points out, "there is no suggestion here that the unequal restriction of the freedom of the intolerant must be to their own benefit."[6] The second and in some ways more troubling example involves conscription. While Rawls is extremely sensitive to the class-based injustice that characterized the American selective service system, he believes that this "drastic interference with the basic liberties of equal citizenship" can be justified when necessary to defend those liberties against a foreign threat (*JFR*, 47; *TJ*, 333–4). Again he does not attempt to argue that conscription better secures the liberties of those who are forced to serve.

My point here is not that Rawls is wrong about conscription, or about tolerating the intolerant. On these two issues his conclusions seem reasonable enough. But those conclusions are extremely difficult to reconcile with Rawls's official view about when restrictions on liberty can be justified. Here, Rawls seems to be saying that the liberties of some citizens can be restricted when necessary to protect society (or the majority) from serious threats to its security. And as the conscription example demonstrates, the people whose liberties are restricted need not be the source of the threat – clearly, in this instance they do not pose a danger to anyone; they have not violated the rules of justice or done anything to forfeit their rights. In these cases, Rawls's conclusions seem easier to justify under Mill's harm principle than under the priority rule; and I suspect that Rawls may be (implicitly) relying on a version of that principle when he discusses specific examples.

(ii) The priority of liberty

I have suggested that in one important area Rawls's commitment to equal liberty under the priority rule is weaker than advertised. More serious, however, are concerns about the priority of liberty itself. Rawls clearly believes that this is one of the main things that distinguishes him from earlier liberals, including Mill. At one point, he writes: "The force of justice as fairness would appear to arise from two things: the requirement that all inequalities be justified to the least advantaged, and the priority of liberty" (*TJ*, 220). But there remains the question, why should the basic liberties be assigned lexical priority over all other primary social goods?

In *A Theory of Justice* Rawls puts forward several arguments for the priority of liberty. The argument that received the most attention, at least initially, posits an increasing preference for liberty, as opposed to other goods. "As the conditions of civilization improve, the marginal significance for our good of further economic and social advantages diminishes relative

---

[6] Thomas Pogge, *John Rawls: His Life and Theory of Justice* (New York: Oxford University Press, 2007), 98–9.

to the interests of liberty, which become stronger as the conditions for the exercise of the equal freedoms are more fully realized."[7] Recognizing this, the parties in the original position would not permit basic liberties to be sacrificed for economic gains, once the most urgent human wants have been satisfied.

A second argument concerns moral, religious, and philosophical interests and obligations. The parties in the original position do not know anything about their particular conceptions of the good, but they know that they may have moral and religious commitments that they regard as important. One could say that they regard themselves "as having moral or religious obligations which they must keep themselves free to honor." Since they also have no way of knowing whether their religious and moral beliefs are in the majority or the minority in their society, they will not take chances "by permitting the dominant religious or moral doctrine to persecute or to suppress others if it wishes." To gamble in this way "would show that one did not take one's religious or moral convictions seriously, or highly value the liberty to examine one's beliefs" (*TJ*, 180–1).

Rawls's final argument in *A Theory of Justice* concerns self-respect, which he identifies as "perhaps the most important" of the primary goods. Writers in the socialist tradition have argued for economic equality on the ground that unequal rewards undermine the self-respect of those at the bottom. While Rawls seems to believe that this may be true in extreme cases, he rejects it as a general proposition: "The basis for self-respect in a just society is not one's income share but the publicly affirmed distribution of fundamental rights and liberties." Since that distribution is equal under justice as fairness, "everyone has a similar and secure status when they meet to conduct the common affairs of the wider society" (*TJ*, 477).

In his more recent works, Rawls explicitly rejects the first argument, which he now regards as mistaken (*PL*, 371; *TJ*, xiii). The other two remain, though their status is not entirely clear. In these works, however, a different set of arguments – hinted at but not developed in any detail in *A Theory of Justice* – have come to dominate the discussion of the priority of liberty. These arguments begin with the claim that free and equal persons should be understood as having two "moral powers": the capacity for a sense of justice and the capacity for a conception of the good.

[T]he capacity for a sense of justice is the capacity to understand, to apply, and normally to be moved by an effective desire to act from (and not merely in

---

7 John Rawls, *A Theory of Justice* (Cambridge, MA: Harvard University Press, 1971), 542. This passage does not appear in the revised edition of *TJ*.

accordance with) the principles of justice as the fair terms of social cooperation. The capacity for a conception of the good is the capacity to form, to revise, and rationally to pursue such a conception, that is, a conception of what we regard for us as a worthwhile human life. (*PL*, 302)

In *Justice as Fairness: A Restatement* Rawls asserts that "the basic liberties and their priority are to guarantee equally for all citizens the social conditions essential for the adequate development and the full and informed exercise of their two moral powers" (*JFR*, 112). The equal political liberties and freedom of thought guarantee citizens the opportunity to exercise their capacity for a sense of justice; that is, they enable citizens to apply the principles of justice to the basic structure, to judge the justice of basic institutions and social policies. Liberty of conscience and freedom of association ensure them the opportunity to form, revise, and pursue a conception of the good, "individually, or more often, in association with others" (*JFR*, 45). Finally, "the remaining and supporting basic liberties – the liberty and integrity (physical and psychological) of the person and the rights and liberties covered by the rule of law – are necessary if the other basic liberties are to be properly guaranteed" (*JFR*, 113). In short, the two moral powers identify certain interests that we regard, on reflection, as having a special significance. The parties in the original position give priority to the first principle in order to protect those fundamental interests.

I believe these newer arguments represent an improvement over the original argument about an increasing preference for liberty, and perhaps over Rawls's other arguments in *A Theory of Justice* as well. They are also closer to Mill's argument in chapter III of *On Liberty*. In reworking his argument for the priority of liberty, Rawls seems to be relying on something very similar to Mill's ideal of the person. The fundamental interest protected by Rawls's second moral power – the interest in forming, revising, and pursuing a conception of the good – resembles the interest Mill describes when he talks about the importance of choosing and reexamining one's own plan of life.

Whether any of Rawls's arguments succeed is a more difficult question. As others have noted, the priority rule precludes a minuscule sacrifice of basic rights or liberties in return for enormous gains in wealth and income for the least advantaged. Many readers have found this counterintuitive, to say the least. Here it may be possible to say about Rawls roughly what he says about Mill: these are compelling arguments, they identify important considerations, but they do not do the work they are intended to do. Rawls has provided good reasons for protecting certain basic liberties. But he has not made a convincing case for granting liberty (or, in the current formulation, the basic liberties) priority over all other goods. As Robert S. Taylor explains, Rawls seems to believe "that once he has shown the instrumental value of the basic liberties for some essential purpose (e.g., securing self-respect), he has automatically shown the reason for their lexical priority."[8] As Taylor makes clear, this is an error. One can accept everything Rawls says about the value of the various basic liberties, and still believe that we should sometimes permit trade-offs between basic liberties and other goods. To describe the interest served by a particular liberty as "fundamental" does not solve the problem; one needs to demonstrate that this fundamental interest always takes precedence over all other fundamental interests or combinations of fundamental and non-fundamental interests.

At one point Rawls seems to acknowledge that the priority rule may be unduly rigid and that modifications may be in order. Near the beginning of *Political Liberalism*, he suggests that the first principle "may easily be preceded by a lexically prior principle requiring that citizens' basic needs be met, at least insofar as their being met is necessary for citizens to understand and to be able to fruitfully exercise" their basic rights and liberties (*PL*, 7). Rawls does not pursue the point, and it is difficult to know whether to take it as an addition to the theory – to meet the criticisms of Marxists like Rodney Peffer – or as an off-hand speculation as to how we might think about improving it.[9] The words "may easily" are disarming in that they seem to leave the matter open, even though a basic needs principle lexically prior to the liberty principle could represent a major change in the theory.

Suppose we take Rawls's comment as an addition to the theory, as Pogge and others have argued. That would make basic liberties (or some of them) "hostage to contingent facts," facts about the level of material and social well-being, and of training and education, needed before people can understand and fruitfully exercise their basic rights. Elsewhere in *Political Liberalism* Rawls appears to suggest that the necessary level of well-being will vary from society to society (*PL*, 166). The possibility that liberty might be sacrificed to secure basic needs does not seem purely hypothetical – it does not have the science-fiction-like quality of many of the examples used by philosophers in discussions of utilitarianism, say, or the morality of abortion. Certainly, one can imagine situations in which limits on freedom of thought, freedom of political speech, and freedom of assembly might be

---

[8] Robert S. Taylor, "Rawls's Defense of the Priority of Liberty: A Kantian Reconstruction," *Philosophy and Public Affairs*, 31.3 (2003), 247–8.
[9] Rawls cites Rodney Peffer, *Marxism, Morality, and Social Justice* (Princeton: Princeton University Press, 1989).

necessary to meet the basic needs of citizens – which is, of course, exactly what critics like Peffer had in mind.

Some readers will see a basic needs principle lexically prior to the liberty principle as an improvement in Rawls's theory. Others are likely to view it as a wrong-headed concession to people who do not take liberty seriously enough. Either way, it clearly represents a retreat from the position on liberty that Rawls embraced in *A Theory of Justice*. For those who regard it as a step forward the next question is: why stop at basic needs? Why not extend the argument to permit the logic behind a basic needs principle be extended to permit (or require) additional trade-offs, once basic needs are satisfied? Since Rawls never explains his reasons for supporting a basic needs principle, it is difficult to know how he would answer this question.[10] But without an answer of some sort, a successful defense of the priority of liberty may prove impossible. I believe that this element of Rawls's theory will remain highly controversial.

II

In *A Theory of Justice*, Rawls was already concerned about the problem of stability; he believed that an adequate conception of justice had to be capable of generating its own support, that a just society had to be capable of remaining stable over time. In his later works, however, the stability problem takes on a new dimension. To understand why, we need to look briefly at two recent additions to Rawls's theory: the notion of a "comprehensive doctrine" and what Rawls calls "the fact of reasonable pluralism."

For Rawls, a doctrine is comprehensive "when it includes conceptions of what is of value in human life, ideals of personal virtue and character, and the like, that inform much of our nonpolitical conduct (in the limit, our life as a whole)."[11] Or, as he puts it in *Justice as Fairness: A Restatement*, a comprehensive doctrine is "one that applies to all subjects and covers all values" (*JFR*, 14). After the publication of *Theory*, Rawls came to believe that any society with free institutions will be characterized by "a diversity of conflicting and irreconcilable yet reasonable comprehensive doctrines"; in any democratic society there will be "profound and irreconcilable differences in citizens' reasonable comprehensive religious and philosophical conceptions of the world, and in their views of the moral and aesthetic values to be sought in human life" (*JFR*, 3, 34). These differences are not

---

[10] Pogge offers some suggestions in *John Rawls*, 104–5.

[11] John Rawls, "The Domain of the Political and Overlapping Consensus" (1989), in *CP*, 480; see also *PL*, 175.

caused by defects in human reasoning – hence they cannot be eliminated by perfecting our reasoning or correcting our mistakes through free and open discussion; they are a fact of life in the modern world. Pluralism of this sort "is a permanent feature of a free democratic culture" (*JFR*, 36). This means that even under the most favorable circumstances the stability of a free society cannot rest on agreement on a single comprehensive doctrine.

Given the fact of reasonable pluralism, how can a democratic society achieve stability? Rawls's answer is as follows: Even if consensus on a comprehensive doctrine is impossible, it may be possible to achieve and maintain agreement on a more limited "political" conception of justice. People holding different comprehensive views may still be able to support a liberal political conception. Because it limits itself to the design of society's basic structure, because it does not presuppose any particular comprehensive worldview, and finally because it derives from ideas implicit in society's public political culture, justice as fairness can serve as the subject of an overlapping consensus. That is, people holding different reasonable comprehensive views can endorse the two principles, and "the fundamental ideas within which justice as fairness is worked out," including "such ideas as those of society as a fair system of social cooperation and of citizens as reasonable and rational, and free and equal" (*PL*, 149) (it is not clear what else Rawls sees as the "fundamental ideas," though they would almost certainly have to include the main outlines of the original position and probably the fact of pluralism itself). Rawls does not believe that justice as fairness can be endorsed by everyone; there may be people with unreasonable comprehensive views – or others who do not hold any comprehensive views, but whose values are incompatible with a liberal political conception. These people will not be part of Rawls's overlapping consensus; they will have no commitment to the constitution of a liberal society and will follow the laws only when it is in their interest to do so. But Rawls believes that justice as fairness can generate a wide enough consensus for a society based on it to achieve what he calls stability "for the right reasons."

In Rawls's view, this is precisely what cannot be said of Kant and Mill. Rawls is not saying that Mill's arguments are wrong or in any way defective on philosophical grounds; indeed, they might well be true. Here, however, their truth or falsity is not the issue. The problem is that the liberalisms of Kant and Mill "both comprehend far more than the political. Their doctrines of free institutions rest in large part on ideals and values that are not generally, or perhaps not even widely, shared in a democratic society."[12] This has important implications. For, as Rawls explains:

[12] John Rawls, "The Idea of an Overlapping Consensus" (1987), in *CP*, 427.

[A] continued shared adherence to one comprehensive doctrine can be maintained only by the oppressive use of state power, with all its official crimes and the inevitable brutality and cruelties, followed by the corruption of religion, philosophy and science … Let us call this the fact of oppression. In the society of the Middle Ages, more or less united in affirming the Catholic faith, the Inquisition was not an accident; its suppression of heresy was needed to preserve the shared religious belief. The same holds true for any comprehensive philosophical and moral doctrine, even secular ones. A society united on a form of utilitarianism, or even on the moral views of Kant and Mill, would likewise require the oppressive sanctions of state power to remain so. (*JFR*, 34; see also *PL*, 37)

Rawls clearly believes that Mill is putting forward a comprehensive doctrine in *On Liberty* (here again, he refers specifically to chapter III). But his description of that doctrine will come as a surprise to readers of *A Theory of Justice*. As we have seen, in *Theory* Rawls treats Mill as a utilitarian – though obviously a utilitarian of a special sort, given Mill's reference to the permanent interests of man as a progressive being. In his later works he does not describe Mill's comprehensive doctrine as a variant of utilitarianism; he refers instead to Mill's "ideal of individuality."[13] While Rawls does not explain exactly what he means, it seems clear that this is not simply a change in terminology; the new description suggests a different understanding of Mill's theory. Again, Rawls's examples of comprehensive doctrines include "a form of utilitarianism, or even … the moral views of Kant or Mill," clearly implying that these are alternatives.

On the one hand, the newer description seems more accurate, at least when applied to chapter III of *On Liberty*. On the other hand, one might think that the shift on Rawls's part undercuts the claim that Mill's doctrine is truly comprehensive (if it is really comprehensive, one might say, there should not be so much uncertainty about how to describe it). However, I want to leave this issue aside. Assuming that Mill is putting forward a comprehensive doctrine in *On Liberty*, and further that the doctrine is one of individuality, do Rawls's criticisms make sense? Could a Millian society really require the oppressive use of state power in order to maintain itself?

Surely, it seems reasonable to think that a continued shared adherence to some comprehensive doctrines can be maintained only by the oppressive use of state power, with official crimes, brutality and so on. And surely the list may include secular comprehensive doctrines. If the Inquisition was not an accident, neither was the Terror or the Cultural Revolution. But it hardly follows that shared adherence to any comprehensive doctrine can be

---

[13] Ibid. See also *PL*, 78, 98; *JFR*, 156.

maintained only by the oppressive use of state power. There is no reason to assume that all comprehensive doctrines are equal in this regard. Whether the "fact of oppression" applies in a particular case ought to have something to do with the *content* of the comprehensive doctrine in question. The issue is whether a doctrine emphasizing individual development, choice, diversity, and toleration could possibly be maintained by the oppressive use of state power.[14]

Of course, a government can adopt policies that will encourage citizens to develop their faculties, to make choices for themselves, to engage in experiments in living, to adopt a skeptical attitude toward received opinion, to avoid doing anything merely "because it is the custom." There are many ways of doing this that might be palatable to liberals. But the operative word here is "encourage." The point is not just that government officials committed to Millian principles would be reluctant to use coercion to produce superior human beings – though that may be true. But regardless of the temperament or dispositions of those in charge, Mill's goals do not lend themselves to the kinds of coercion, brutality, and cruelties that gave totalitarianism a bad name. Terror may have its uses, but it is not an effective method for producing citizens who make choices for themselves.

Rawls does not provide any examples – real or hypothetical – of the oppressive use of state power to enforce a Kantian or Millian value system. He comes closest to doing so in a brief discussion of the education of children. After noting that "various religious sects oppose the culture of the modern world and wish to lead their common life apart from its unwanted influences," he writes: "the liberalisms of Kant and Mill may lead to requirements designed to foster the values of autonomy and individuality as ideals to govern much if not all of life" (*PL*, 199; *JFR*, 156). Groups such as the Amish would no doubt find such requirements objectionable. But, Rawls adds, "political liberalism has a different aim and requires far less."

One problem with this line of argument is that it runs counter to what Mill actually says about education in *On Liberty*. In chapter v Mill begins by suggesting that the state should require and compel the education, up to a

---

[14] According to Thomas Nagel: "One of the most important points Rawls has made is that the alternative, of deriving the political order from a particular comprehensive value system, is often supported by nostalgia for a communitarian past that never existed, in which all the members of society were united in devotion to their common conception of the good: the Christian world of the middle ages – in fantasy. Rawls points out that the maintenance of orthodoxy of that kind has always required oppression because harmonious agreement over fundamental values does not maintain itself naturally" ("Rawls and Liberalism," in *The Cambridge Companion to Rawls*, ed. Samuel Freeman (Cambridge: Cambridge University Press, 2003), 83). Perhaps, but does it make sense to describe Millian liberalism as an orthodoxy "of that kind"?

certain standard, of every child. But, he immediately adds, permitting the state to direct that education is a "totally different thing."

That the whole or any large part of the education of people should be in State hands, I go as far as anyone in deprecating. All that has been said of the importance of individuality of character, and diversity in opinions and modes of conduct, involves as of the same unspeakable importance, diversity of education. (*CW* xviii, 302–3 [v, 13])

Quite pointedly, Mill does not insist that children be taught the value of individual choice, the provisional nature of all claims to truth, the need for skepticism, or the importance of experimentation; in fact, he does not even insist that they be taught the importance of toleration. Rather he opts for a system of competing private institutions, many of which would presumably be run by churches or other secondary associations. In these schools, children would be taught "comprehensive doctrines"; but the doctrines would be chosen by their parents, not by the state. Members of a religious sect opposed to the culture of modernity could establish their own school; they would not have to worry about their children being taught that individuality is the ideal that should govern much if not all of life. As for Mill, he seems willing to allow children to be taught comprehensive doctrines different from his own; what he really opposes is an arrangement in which all children are taught the same doctrine in state-run schools – even if that is the doctrine advanced in *On Liberty*.

Of course, it is possible that Mill has misunderstood the implications of his own argument. One could argue that "all that has been said" in the previous chapters does not point toward a system of competing private schools, each teaching its own comprehensive doctrine, but rather to state-run schools that teach the value of choice, diversity, individuality, experimentation and so on. If we agree that this is the position Mill should have taken concerning education, then his argument may well be open to Rawls's criticism.

The question is whether the same objection applies to Rawls's own view of education. In the passage cited earlier, after asserting that political liberalism requires "far less" than Millian liberalism, Rawls continues: "It will ask that children's education include such things as knowledge of their constitutional and civic rights." He adds that "their education should also prepare them to be fully cooperating members of society and enable them to be self-supporting; it should also encourage the political virtues so that they want to honor the fair terms of social cooperation in their relations with the rest of society" (*PL*, 199; *JFR*, 156).

Some critics have denied that a Rawlsian educational program could be this modest. They have argued that Rawlsian civic education would necessarily involve far more: an effort to instill the necessary political virtues would require teaching mutual respect and toleration; Rawlsian citizens would need to be trained in (and strongly encouraged to engage in) critical thinking. A few have gone further, suggesting that "the skills and concepts associated with personal autonomy would inevitably have to be included in a political liberal civic education curriculum."[15]

To the extent that these claims are plausible, what follows? It is possible that a Rawlsian educational scheme would closely resemble (our reconstructed version of) Mill's. But even if there were significant differences, there is reason to believe that the two educational systems would be equally demanding. One suspects that Rawlsian civic education would be opposed by – and would have to be forcibly imposed upon – many of the same people who would find Millian education objectionable. These would include religious sects that oppose the culture of the modern world, and perhaps many others as well.

Different versions of the paragraph about the oppressive use of state power appear in several of Rawls's later works. In one version (though not the most recent one) Rawls appears to acknowledge that there is something odd about this argument, at least as it applies to Kant and Mill. After stating that "a society united on the reasonable liberalisms of Kant or Mill, would ... require the sanctions of state power to remain so," he adds in a footnote: "This statement may seem paradoxical. If one objects that, consistent with Kant's or Mill's doctrine, the sanctions of state power cannot be used, I quite agree. But this does not contradict the text, which says that a society in which everyone affirms a reasonable liberal doctrine if by hypothesis it should exist, cannot long endure" (*PL*, 37–8).

So here at least the point is not that a society based on Millian principles would be forced into the oppressive use of state power; rather, the idea is that precisely because it would be unwilling to employ such methods, such a society could not endure over time. By this, I assume Rawls means not that a Millian society would fall apart, descending into civil war, but rather that sects would arise that did not accept Mill's comprehensive doctrine. These sects would need to be coerced into abiding by the laws or the constitution; at best they could be expected to view the constitution as a *modus vivendi*.

---

[15] Gordon Davis and Blain Neufeld, "Political Liberalism, Civic Education, and Educational Choice," *Social Theory and Practice*, 33.1 (2007), 48–9, summarizing the view of Eamonn Callan, "Political Liberalism and Political Education," *Review of Politics*, 58.1 (1996), 5–33. See also Amy Gutmann, "Civic Education and Social Diversity," *Ethics*, 105.3 (1995), 557–79.

It is not clear that this is Rawls's considered position (the footnote cited above does not appear in the crucial paragraph of his last work, *Justice as Fairness: A Restatement*). If it is his considered view, it seems far more plausible than the earlier claims about the oppressive use of state power. But if Rawls is right about Mill – or more precisely, if he is right about the likely course of a society united around Millian principles – it is again necessary to ask: just how would a Rawlsian society differ? Under political liberalism, there would also be groups that remained outside the dominant overlapping consensus. They would also need to be persuaded to obey the law through some combination of coercion and calculations of mutual advantage. To evaluate Rawls's argument, we need to know who they are, and how they would differ from the people who would object to living in a Millian society.

Rawls says very little about which groups or individuals would remain outside his overlapping consensus. At one point he mentions fundamentalist religions and people who hold "certain non-religious (secular) doctrines, such as those of autocracy and dictatorship."[16] Elsewhere he refers to conceptions of the good "requiring the repression or degradation of certain persons on, say, racial or ethnic, or perfectionist grounds," strongly implying that people who hold such views would remain outside (*PL*, 196). Apart from his reference to religious sects that oppose the culture of the modern world, he also does not tell us which groups would find it impossible to support a constitution based on Millian principles. I want to suggest that the people who could not willingly support a Millian constitution are essentially the same ones who could not be part of a Rawlsian consensus. People who reject the modern world, people who refuse to endorse certain basic precepts about human equality, religious fundamentalists of various sorts, people who rely on religious (or political) authorities for their ideas about what to believe and how to live their lives, people who deny that reasonable men and women can disagree on moral and philosophical questions – these people would object to living in a Millian society with its emphasis on choice, diversity, experimentalism, skepticism, and toleration. But could they endorse "the fundamental ideas within which justice as fairness is worked out"? Could they endorse the egalitarian assumptions underlying the original position, the veil of ignorance, the commitment to equal liberty, the notion that we have a fundamental interest in forming and revising our conceptions of the good? Could they even accept the idea of society as a fair system of social cooperation, which underlies the entire theory? For the overwhelming majority, I believe the answer would be no. Here once again, Rawls is closer to Mill than he realizes.

---

[16] John Rawls, "The Idea of Public Reason Revisited (1997)," in *Collected Papers*, 613.

CHAPTER 6

Mill on consensual domination

Frank Lovett

In his essay *On Liberty*, John Stuart Mill does not discuss at any length the meaning of political liberty or freedom. "The only freedom which deserves the name," he is content to assert, "is that of pursuing our own good in our own way, so long as we do not attempt to deprive others of theirs" (*CW* XVIII, 26 [1, 12]). This is a clear statement of the *negative* conception of liberty – roughly speaking, the view that one is free simply to the extent that one is not interfered with by others. It is not surprising that Mill subscribed to this conception, given that its strongest proponents included both his mentor Jeremy Bentham, and Bentham's widely read contemporary William Paley. Nevertheless, it is important to keep in mind that the negative conception of liberty was at the time relatively new: it had been introduced first by Thomas Hobbes in the seventeenth century, and it arguably remained the minority view well into the eighteenth century.[1]

Recently, some have argued that the widespread adoption of the negative conception of liberty since Bentham and Paley has come at some cost – in particular, at the cost of obscuring an older, and in many ways more attractive, conception of political liberty or freedom as a sort of independence from arbitrary power or domination.[2] My discussion here will support this view. I will argue that Mill's more or less uncritical acceptance of the negative conception of liberty does him, at times, a disservice.

The author would like to thank Philip Pettit, Larry Temkin, Paul Litton, Jack Knight, and Andrew Rehfeld for their helpful comments on an earlier version of this chapter.

[1] Philip Pettit, *Republicanism: A Theory of Freedom and Government* (Oxford: Clarendon Press, 1997); Quentin Skinner, *Liberty Before Liberalism* (Cambridge: Cambridge University Press, 1998).

[2] In this connection, see especially Quentin Skinner, "The Idea of Negative Liberty," in Richard Rorty, J. B. Schneewind, and Quentin Skinner, eds., *Philosophy of History: Essays on the Historiography of Philosophy* (Cambridge: Cambridge University Press, 1984), 193–221; "The Paradoxes of Political Liberty," in David Miller, ed., *Liberty* (Oxford: Oxford University Press, 1991), 183–205; and *Liberty Before Liberalism* (Cambridge: Cambridge University Press, 1998); Pettit, *Republicanism*; and *A Theory of Freedom: From the Psychology to the Politics of Agency* (Oxford: Oxford University Press, 2001); and Maurizio Viroli, *Republicanism*, tr. Antony Shugaar (New York: Hill & Wang, 2002).

The particular difficulty I am interested in arises (apparently) only tangentially in *On Liberty*, and thus is not obvious on a casual reading. Suppose we accept the negative view of freedom as consisting simply in the absence of interference with one's choices. How far should this sphere of freedom extend? In one famous passage, Mill considers the question of whether the proper sphere of our negative freedoms should include the freedom to sell ourselves into slavery. Many libertarians have thought, at least in principle, that it should.[3] Mill, on the contrary, believed that it should not. He was by no means the first to argue this, but he was the first to try putting such an argument in strict negative liberty terms.[4] This, as we shall see, causes difficulties for him. Were the problem of voluntary slavery merely an isolated theoretical problem (few people, after all, volunteer to be slaves), these difficulties would not be very interesting. But in his later essay on *The Subjection of Women*, Mill must confront them more directly, and in doing so he is implicitly forced to set aside the negative liberty framework in order to make his point. A careful reading of both texts, therefore, provides insight into the disadvantages of embracing the negative conception of liberty.

I

Mill's argument against voluntary slavery appears in the fifth and last chapter of *On Liberty*, in the process of discussing a confusing tangle of questions relating to the social regulation of consensual agreements in general. That such questions arise at all, however, might seem puzzling. After all, is not the central aim of his essay precisely to argue, as Mill himself reiterates in the opening of chapter v, that "the individual is not accountable to society for his actions, in so far as these concern the interests of no person but himself" (*CW* xviii, 292 [v, 2])? Is it not obvious that if two persons, of their own free will, enter into a private agreement concerning only themselves, then (on Mill's own theory) society has no business interfering with them? What then is the issue here?

This confusion is due to a surprisingly common misunderstanding regarding the structure of Mill's argument in *On Liberty*. Mill is often thought to believe there exists some independently definable "private

---

[3] For example, Robert Nozick, *Anarchy, State, and Utopia* (New York: Basic Books, 1974), 331; although evasive, both Hillel Steiner, *An Essay on Rights* (Oxford: Blackwell, 1994), 231–6, and Jan Narveson, *The Libertarian Idea* (Calgary: Broadview Press, 2001), 66–8, apparently agree with him on this point.

[4] John Locke, for example, presents a sophisticated argument against voluntary slavery on natural law grounds. See John Locke, *Second Treatise of Government* (1690), ed. C. B. Macpherson (Indianapolis: Hackett Publishing, 1980), esp. sections 17, 23.

sphere" of human activity that, it turns out, is strictly self-regarding, in the sense that whatever a person does within this private sphere affects no one but herself. The argument is then thought to be, first, that private conduct cannot harm anyone but the actor herself; and second, because this is so, private conduct should not be regulated by formal law or social custom. Unfortunately, Mill often expresses his views in language that encourages this misunderstanding. He asserts, for example, that "the only part of the conduct of any one, for which he is amenable to society, is that which concerns others. In the part which merely concerns himself, his independence is, of right, absolute" (*CW* xviii, 224 [1, 9]). Somewhat later he explains that "there is a sphere of action in which society, as distinguished from the individual, has, if any, only an indirect interest; comprehending all that portion of a person's life and conduct which affects only himself" (*CW* xviii, 225 [1, 12]). These passages, while certainly open to multiple interpretations, at least on a casual reading seem to encourage the common misunderstanding. Relying on this reading of the argument, critics routinely assail Mill for failing to define rigorously a genuinely private sphere of individual conduct, for, strictly speaking, it is not clear that any such sphere exists at all. That some persons engage in what others regard as immoral sexual behavior, for example, even if only in private, may seriously offend the latter, thus affecting their well-being. Arguably, the members of a community as a whole might have a material interest in maintaining their shared moral norms: if so, then private conduct in violation of those norms might injure other community members, even if that conduct is itself harmless in the first instance.[5] No man, says the cliché, is an island.

Fortunately for Mill, this reading puts his argument precisely backwards.[6] Correctly understood, the notion of a self-regarding or private sphere of conduct is merely a by-product of his argument, not its basis. Mill's starting point is to wonder what sorts of legitimate reasons there might be for the social regulation of individual conduct. The answer, he claims, is that there is *only one* legitimate reason, *and no others*. Specifically, "the sole end for which mankind are warranted, individually or collectively, in interfering with the liberty of action of any of their number," he writes,

[5] This is the so-called "social disintegration thesis," as discussed for example in Robert P. George, *Making Men Moral: Civil Liberties and Public Morality* (Oxford: Oxford University Press, 1993). The classic critique of Mill along these lines can be found in Patrick Devlin, *The Enforcement of Morals* (London: Oxford University Press, 1965).

[6] The discussion here is partially indebted to D. G. Brown, "Mill on Liberty and Morality," *Philosophical Review*, 81 (1972), 133–58; and David Dyzenhaus, "John Stuart Mill and the Harm of Pornography," *Ethics*, 102 (1992), 534–51.

"is self-protection." Or, in other words, "the only purpose for which power can be rightfully exercised over any member of a civilized community, against his will, is *to prevent harm to others*. His own good," Mill adds for emphasis, "either physical or moral, is not a sufficient warrant" (*CW* xviii, 223 [1, 9], emphasis added). This doctrine is usually referred to as the "harm principle," though technically "prevention-of-harm-to-others principle" is more accurate.[7] According to the harm principle, it is no argument for a social regulation that it discourages immorality. But *if* it could be shown that some conduct (which also happens, let us suppose, to be immoral) caused a "distinct and assignable" harm to others, then *this* fact (and not the fact of its immorality as such) *would* be an argument for social regulation (*CW* xviii, 281 [iv, 10]).[8] Moreover, it would be *no* argument *against* social regulation (though there might, of course, be others) that the conduct in question happened to occur in private, on our everyday understanding of this term.[9] Mill's point is simply that harm prevention is the *only* legitimate reason for social regulation, and that the alleged morality or immorality of the conduct in question is neither here nor there.

It should immediately be clear that an implementation of the harm principle would create a sphere of conduct exempt from regulation on the grounds that it causes no distinct and assignable harms to others. This sphere of conduct, whatever it turns out to be – and Mill nowhere claims to have exhaustively determined it – we may term the "private sphere" in a somewhat technical sense. Conduct within the sphere is exempt from social regulation because it is harmless, not because it is (in some independently definable sense) private. Mill is thus not committed to any *a priori* claim concerning the shape or size of the private sphere; indeed, it is consistent with his argument, though unlikely, that the private sphere could turn out to be empty. Even assuming it is not, there is no reason to expect that the private sphere, so defined, will correspond precisely with that sphere of activities we ordinarily regard as "private" – though there is likely to be considerable overlap. (It likewise follows that some acts done "in public," again on our ordinary understanding of this term, might turn out to be

---

[7] "Harm-to-others" because harm to oneself does not warrant regulation, and "prevention" because regulation may in some cases anticipate harm and legitimately aim to prevent it from occurring. Mill maintains that regulating the sale of poisons, for example, is warranted on the grounds that it is likely to prevent future harms: "if a public authority … sees any one evidently preparing to commit a crime, they are not bound to look on inactive until the crime is committed, but may interfere to prevent it" (*CW* xviii, 294 [v, 5]).

[8] Cf. *CW* xviii, 282 (iv, 11), where the language is a "perceptible hurt to any assignable individual."

[9] Thus, if the "social disintegration thesis" (see n. 5 above) turns out to be empirically correct, then the conditions of legitimate regulation might be satisfied in some cases of alleged private immorality.

protected from regulation, on the grounds that they cause no distinct and assignable harm to others.)

We are now in a much better position to appreciate the tangle of problems discussed in the fifth chapter of *On Liberty*. These all relate to what, following Joel Feinberg, we might call "voluntary two-party harms."[10] This expression can be explained as follows: harms may be either self-inflicted, or else inflicted by or with the aid of others. Additionally, harms may be inflicted either with the consent of the harmed party, or without. If a person burns her own money (say, in a political demonstration), she harms herself voluntarily; if she unwittingly ingests berries that turn out to be poisonous, or stumbles off a precipice she did not see into a river, she harms herself involuntarily. Roughly speaking, what is often called *soft paternalism* seeks to avert only involuntary self-inflicted harms, whereas *hard paternalism* seeks to avert both involuntary and voluntary self-inflicted harms. Mill's foremost aim is to discredit hard paternalism. His position on soft paternalism is less clear, but we need not address that question here.[11]

These are all single-party cases. When one person punches another in the face, or fraudulently sells him dangerous goods, the former is directly or indirectly responsible for the latter's suffering an involuntary harm. These are two-party cases. Involuntary two-party harms are easily covered by the harm principle, which permits (provided there are no further countervailing considerations) the social regulation of such conduct.

Not so clear, however, is what to do in the case of *voluntary* two-party harms. Mill considers several cases in the opening pages of chapter v. For example, suppose that a fully informed person *B* voluntarily purchases goods from *A* that are defective, overpriced, or dangerous. On the one hand, *B* is harmed, and *A* contributes to the infliction of this harm, but on the other hand (supposing there is no deception or fraud involved), any risk entailed by the purchase was voluntarily assumed by *B*. Alternatively, suppose that *A* operates a gambling-house or pub where *B* wastes away his livelihood. Again *B* is harmed, and again *A* aids in the infliction of this harm. Nevertheless, the harm inflicted on *B* is inflicted with his (informed) consent. Note that there is no question of regulating *B*'s conduct in such cases by prohibiting drinking, gambling, or the assumption of risk: assuming for the sake of argument that *B* has no dependants, his actions harm only

[10] Joel Feinberg, *The Moral Limits of the Criminal Law*, vol. III: *Harm to Self* (Oxford: Oxford University Press, 1986).

[11] *CW* XVIII, 294 (v, 5) seems to support soft paternalism: "liberty consists in doing what one desires," he writes, and one "does not desire to fall into the river," for example.

himself, and therefore the harm principle precludes any social regulation.[12] The issue is strictly one of regulating *A*. On a straightforward application of the harm principle, it would seem there is at least a *prima facie* warrant for the social regulation of *A*'s conduct, so as to prevent harm to *B*. Mill does not, however, draw this conclusion. The sale of goods should generally be left to the free market, subject perhaps to labeling requirements and a few other minor restrictions; and, although he admits that "the case is one of those which lie on the exact boundary line between two principles," he ultimately concludes that the operation of private gambling-houses should be allowed (*CW* xviii, 296–7 [v, 8]).

Clearly, there is at work here some auxiliary principle modifying the application of the harm prevention doctrine. That Mill does intend there to be such limitations is evident when, for example, he notes that "it must by no means be supposed, because damage, or probability of damage, to the interests of others, can alone justify the interference of society, that therefore it always does justify such interference" (*CW* xviii, 292 [v, 3]). But what is the auxiliary principle in question? In an earlier statement of the harm principle, Mill writes that society should not regulate "that portion of a person's life and conduct which affects only himself, or if it also affects others, *only with their free, voluntary, and undeceived consent*" (*CW* xviii, 225 [i, 12], emphasis added). There are two possible interpretations of this statement. On the one hand, we might take him to mean that conduct is not harmful if it is (genuinely) consented to. This interpretation has the unfortunate result, however, that we cannot determine whether something constitutes a harm without first determining whether it is consented to or not, and this is not always easy to do. It seems simpler to say that a punch in the face is a harm, whether asked for or not. On the other hand, we simply might take Mill to mean that the harm principle should recognize an exception in cases of (genuine) consent. For the reason indicated, this seems the more sensible route, but either interpretation amounts to the same thing, practically speaking. The harm prevention doctrine must include some auxiliary principle along the lines of the traditional common law maxim *volenti non fit injuria* – what is agreed to does not constitute an injury (or, agreed-to injuries will be ignored as a matter of policy). In principle at least, if a person wishes to suffer a harm, or assume the risk of being harmed, at the hands of or with the aid of another, he or she should be

---

[12] When dependants are involved, the harm principle may permit social regulation according to *CW* xviii, 281 (iv, 10).

free to do so. Given Mill's overarching commitment to expanding the negative liberty of individuals, it is not surprising that he takes this view.

I I

Our introduction of the *volenti* maxim, however, leads directly to the voluntary slavery problem. Mill apparently realized this. Immediately after the discussion of voluntary two-party harms, he concedes that "in this and most other civilized countries … an engagement by which a person should sell himself, or allow himself to be sold, as a slave, would be null and void; neither enforced by law nor by opinion" (*CW* xviii, 299 [v, 11]). Strict libertarians aside, most have felt there must be something deeply wrong with slavery – voluntary or not. But if we accept the *volenti* maxim as a modification of the harm principle, together with the negative conception of liberty, it is not clear why we should.

This is where things get interesting. As is well known, Mill supports the judgment of law and opinion. From the point of view of the harm principle, then, voluntary slavery constitutes an exception to an exception: it is permissible to regulate conduct that it harms others, except when the harm is consented to, unless the consented-to harm is a contract for slavery. But how does Mill make the case for this exception to the exception? The argument opens as follows:

The reason for not interfering, unless for the sake of others, with a person's voluntary acts, is consideration for his liberty. His voluntary choice is evidence that what he so chooses is desirable, or at the least endurable, to him, and his good is on the whole best provided for by allowing him to take his own means of pursuing it.

In other words, we respect the choices that people make – even when those choices seem to us seriously harmful to their interests – because we place value on the enjoyment of individual liberty (understood here, we must presume by Mill's assertion at the opening of *On Liberty*, as the freedom to pursue one's own good in one's own way, as liberty in the negative sense). Fair enough. Mill continues:

But by selling himself for a slave, he abdicates his liberty; he forgoes any future use of it beyond that single act. He therefore defeats, in his own case, the very purpose which is the justification of allowing him to dispose of himself. He is no longer free; but is thenceforth in a position which has no longer the presumption in its favour, that would be afforded by his voluntarily remaining in it. The principle of freedom cannot require that he should be free not to be free. It is not freedom, to be allowed to alienate his freedom. (*CW* xviii, 299–300 [v, 11])

The argument here seems straightforward: it would be inconsistent with the normative principle underlying the *volenti* maxim to adhere to the latter so far as to undermine the former. In other words, since it is individual liberty that we are interested in promoting, it makes sense to discourage people from throwing their liberty away.[13]

It is easy to understand the attractiveness of this argument. It purports to avoid paternalistically second-guessing people's choices by showing that anyone who agrees to be a slave commits a sort of performative contradiction, undermining by that act the very principle that would otherwise render it legitimate. Jean-Jacques Rousseau may have intended to argue something similar when he wrote that "renouncing one's liberty is renouncing one's dignity as a man, the rights of humanity and even its duties ... Such a renunciation is incompatible with the nature of man. Taking away all liberty from his will is tantamount to removing all morality from his actions."[14] In other words, by renouncing one's freedom, one destroys the very human dignity or moral self-worth that might have supplied a basis for the right to do so. Voluntary slavery is (at least morally speaking) a contradiction at terms.[15]

Unfortunately, despite its attractiveness, Mill's argument does not go through. To begin with, it is worth observing that his argument relies on the assumption that the condition of slavery entails a severe reduction of liberty. Now on the negative conception of liberty as non-interference, this can be only a contingent truth. While slaves are, of course, usually subject to many unwelcome interferences, this is not necessarily a part of the condition of slavery as such. A benevolent or kindly master might interfere with his slaves relatively little, such that any reduction in their negative freedom turns out to be relatively small; indeed, if one happened to face particularly dismal alternatives, it might turn out that agreeing to be the slave of a kindly master would actually amount to a net *gain* in negative freedom.[16] It is far from obvious, in such cases, that voluntary slavery would constitute a performative contradiction. Let us, however, ignore this possibility, and assume that

---

[13] For an excellent extended discussion, see David Archard, "Freedom Not to Be Free: The Case of the Slavery Contract in J. S. Mill's *On Liberty*," *Philosophical Quarterly*, 40 (1990), 453–65.

[14] Jean-Jacques Rousseau, "The Social Contract" (1762), in Donald A. Cress, tr., *The Basic Political Writings* (Indianapolis: Hackett Publishing, 1987), 144–5.

[15] Alternatively, Rousseau might simply mean that the capacity to act morally is what gives human life its dignity and worth, and thus, since slavery destroys this, no reasonable person would agree to be a slave of his or her own free will. If so, however, Rousseau's argument is thereby vulnerable to a paternalism objection, whereas Mill's is not. I am grateful to Larry Temkin for pointing out this alternative interpretation of Rousseau.

[16] For further discussion, see Pettit, *Republicanism*, 63–4.

agreeing to be a slave would in fact entail a substantial reduction in one's negative freedom. In the usual course of things, this is a safe assumption, though as we shall see later, the "kindly master" problem in another guise poses a serious challenge for Mill.

Even granting the assumption, the problem is that many perfectly ordinary choices which Mill would certainly refuse to subject to social regulation entail reductions in a person's negative liberty. For example, when B signs an ordinary employment contract to work for A, this clearly reduces B's negative freedom; when B accepts a car loan from A, this clearly reduces B's negative freedom. Both constrain B subsequently to perform particular actions at particular times on pain of legal sanction, but B's conduct should not therefore be subject to social regulation on the grounds that "it is not freedom to be allowed to alienate his freedom."

Now perhaps Mill would reply that the freedom reductions entailed by such agreements are at least reversible or temporally limited in scope, whereas the slave contract is not. The peculiar objection to slavery might then seem to be the fact that it entails an *irreversible* reduction in one's negative freedom. But there are other cases. If B sells a valuable painting to A, he cannot simply reclaim the painting later on: his freedom to dispose of the painting is permanently alienated to A by the sale. Of course, this is a small reduction in one's negative freedom, compared with the extensive (by our prior assumption) reduction entailed by the condition of slavery. Perhaps the issue is instead (or in addition) that some freedom reductions are unacceptably large – that individuals should not be permitted, even by voluntary choice, to fall below some minimum threshold of negative liberty.[17] But deciding to have children is both a considerable and an irreversible reduction in one's negative freedom (even if, one hopes, this reduction is more than compensated for in other respects). Now suppose we add to this the decision to purchase a large house; then to accept a high-paying job with long hours to support the children and pay the mortgage; then to buy expensive cars so as to get from the house to the job; and so on, and on. A person might in many relatively small steps accumulate considerable freedom-reducing obligations, each perfectly reasonable and legitimate considered individually, to the point where he enjoys no more

---

[17] Feinberg, *Moral Limits of the Criminal Law*, vol. III: *Harm to Self*, chs. 18–19, argues that individual freedom should not be allowed to fall below some minimum threshold, and that since slavery would certainly cross that line, voluntary slavery should not be permitted. But he apparently does not notice the problem discussed next.

negative freedom than a slave. Henry David Thoreau believed many people do precisely this, without quite realizing it:

Our life is frittered away by detail … In the midst of this chopping sea of civilized life, such are the clouds and storms and quicksands and thousand-and-one items to be allowed for, that a man has to live, if he would not founder and go to the bottom and not make his port at all, by dead reckoning, and he must be a great calculator indeed who succeeds. Simplify, simplify. Instead of three meals a day, if it be necessary eat but one; instead of a hundred dishes, five; and reduce other things in proportion.[18]

If the problem with voluntary slavery is simply that the aggregate reduction in one's freedom from interference crosses some unacceptable threshold, why should all these smaller choices not also be socially regulated so as to prevent people from crossing it in many smaller steps? After all, it is far more probable that a person will unintentionally throw away his liberty in many small choices than in a single big one. Should people not be required to demonstrate publicly, before taking on each new freedom-reducing obliga-tion, that it will not (added to those already accepted) cross the threshold into *de facto* slavery? Clearly, even if it were feasible, such a program of detailed social regulation would be anathema to Mill.

Mill's argument would work, of course, on the assumption that some core set of individual freedoms are qualitatively (and not merely quanti-tatively) special, and therefore unalienable under any circumstances. Freedom-reducing choices would then be legitimate so long as they did not touch on this core. But the existence of unalienable freedoms is precisely what is at issue. The performative contradiction argument does not itself supply any grounds for regarding some freedoms and not others as alien-able. An independent argument to this effect would be needed, and Mill does not supply one. His commitment to the negative conception of liberty does him a disservice here. There seems to be something wrong with slavery as such, and Mill knows it. But its special wrongness cannot easily be explained in strict negative liberty terms. The slave of a reasonably benev-olent master might enjoy a greater degree of non-interference than others who, while not being slaves themselves, have nevertheless accumulated extensive and even irreversible freedom-reducing obligations. On the neg-ative conception of liberty, it seems, the former must be regarded as enjoying greater freedom. This does not seem right.

[18] Henry David Thoreau, "Walden; or, Life in the Woods," in Robert F. Sayre, ed., *A Week on the Concord and Merrimack Rivers; Walden, or, Life in the Woods; The Maine Woods; Cape Cod* (New York: Library of America, 1985), 395.

Voluntary slavery is largely a theoretical puzzle. Few people volunteer to be slaves, and in any case slave contracts are already condemned in both law and custom. But slavery is only one instance (albeit an extreme one) of domination, and so voluntary slavery is merely one example of the general problem of consensual domination. Other examples are not merely hypothetical, and present very real difficulties.

Some years later, in his essay on *The Subjection of Women*,[19] Mill again considers the problem of consensual domination, in a different context. "The existing social relations between the two sexes" in Mill's time were governed by "the legal subordination of one sex to the other." On the one hand, given the limitations on careers open to women, options outside marriage were few; this, together with the legal and social obstacles to divorce, rendered married women dependent on their husbands to a considerable degree. On the other hand, family law was designed so as to place few effective restrictions on the arbitrary power a husband could exercise over his spouse. In short, under the traditional regime of gender relations, married women arguably suffered under domination at the hands of their husbands. Mill firmly (and rightly) believed this situation "wrong in itself, and now one of the chief hindrances to human improvement" (*CW* XXI, 261 [1, 1]). But he also recognized that a great many prejudices stand in the way of this truth being recognized. Among the most serious of these is the prejudice that, in contrast with involuntary slavery, autocratic government, feudalism, and many other institutionalized forms of domination, "the rule of men over women differs from all these others in not being a rule of force: it is accepted voluntarily; women make no complaint, and are consenting parties to it" (*CW* XXI, 270 [1, 10]). In other words, the issue Mill confronts here is precisely the problem of whether domination should be permitted even when consensual; it is the same as the puzzle of voluntary slavery, but now applied to a very real problem.

Interestingly, Mill had already discussed marriage in *On Liberty*. Just after presenting his brief against voluntary slavery, he hesitates, suddenly recognizing that his arguments are "evidently of far wider application" than might at first be apparent. Rather than extend those arguments to additional cases, he concedes that "a limit is everywhere set to them by the necessities

---

[19] John Stuart Mill, *The Subjection of Women* (1869), in *The Collected Works of John Stuart Mill*, vol. XXI: *Essays on Equality, Law, and Education*, ed. John M. Robson, introduction by Stefan Collini (Toronto: University of Toronto Press, London: Routledge & Kegan Paul, 1984), 259–340.

of life, which continually require, not indeed that we should resign our freedom, but that we should consent to this and the other limitation of it." Agreeing to marriage – or, indeed, to any binding commitment – represents an abdication of one's negative freedom to some extent, as we have seen. Realistically speaking, we cannot, even in the interest of liberty, prohibit people from entering into such agreements. The best we can do, he thinks, is require "that engagements which involve personal relations of services, should never be legally binding beyond a limited duration of time," and that accordingly (once due consideration is given to the interests of any children), "the most important of these engagements, marriage ... should require nothing more than the declared will of either party to dissolve it" (*CW* xviii, 300 [v, 11]). In relations of marriage, then, the significant concern seems to be irrevocability. But for this fact, Mill evidently has no objection to the institution of marriage as such. Indeed, he goes to far as to advocate toleration of Mormon polygamy. "Far from being in any way countenanced by the principle of liberty," he writes, polygamous marriage

is a direct infraction of that principle, being a mere riveting of the chains of one-half of the community, and the emancipation of the other from reciprocity of obligation towards them. Still, it must be remembered that this relation is as much voluntary on the part of the women concerned in it, and who may be deemed the sufferers by it, as is the case with any other form of the marriage institution. (*CW* xviii, 290 [iv, 21])

Therefore, provided that women are permitted the freedom to leave their community if they so choose, he would not interfere with Mormon marriage customs. Excepting the peculiar and largely hypothetical case of voluntary slavery, then, Mill consistently maintains in *On Liberty* that consensual domination is permissible, or at least so long as the consent is genuine and not irrevocable.

Mill does not take this line in *The Subjection of Women*. According to his earlier position, the correct response to the unjust subordination of women in marriage would be simply to remove the legal and social obstacles to divorce. Naturally, he does not change his mind on the need for this reform, but he no longer regards this as sufficient. Against the claim that women are consenting parties to existing marital institutions, Mill now advances two arguments. The first is that women do *not* always consent, but that this fact is generally concealed. "All causes, social and natural," Mill points out, "combine to make it unlikely that women should be collectively rebellious to the power of men" – in particular, the fact that each married woman is placed directly under the unrestrained physical power of her husband, who can easily punish complaint with abuse (*CW* XXI, 271 [1, 11]). Thus most women who do complain, complain not of their husbands' power as such, but only of its excessive uses; and most do not complain at all.

While certainly correct, this first argument is less important for our purposes. His second argument is more so. It is hardly surprising, Mill says, that women generally consent to the domination entailed by marriage. First, "women are brought up from the very earliest years in the belief that … it is their nature, to live for others; to make complete abnegation of themselves, and to have no life but in their affections." Second, the married woman lives in "entire dependence on the husband, every privilege or pleasure she has being either his gift, or depending entirely on his will." Third, "all objects of social ambition, can in general be sought or obtained" by women only through marriage (*CW* XXI, 271–2 [1, 11]). In short, having so few alternatives, and those alternatives being what they are, it is perfectly reasonable for women to choose marriage, even if this means subjecting themselves to domination. Must it follow that this domination is not a bad thing? No. On the contrary, these considerations "afford not only no presumption in favour of this system of inequality of rights, but a strong one against it" (*CW* XXI, 272 [1, 12]). It is necessary to close all doors to women other than marriage precisely because, as things are, marriage itself entails subjection to the arbitrary will of another person (i.e., domination). As Mill says, those men who defend the traditional regime of gender relations

are afraid, not lest women should be unwilling to marry … but lest they should insist that marriage should be on equal conditions; lest all women of spirit and capacity should prefer doing almost anything else … rather than marry, when marrying is giving themselves to a master, and a master too of all their earthly possessions. And truly, if this consequence were necessarily incident to marriage, I think that the apprehension would be very well founded. (*CW* XXI, 281–2 [1, 25])

In other words, it is *because* there is something wrong with the subjection of women – even when consented to – that we should seek to ameliorate those circumstances compelling reasonable women to accept it of their own free will. Mill does not lack respect for the choices that women make: on the contrary, he advocates greater equality between the sexes precisely so that women need not voluntarily submit themselves to the injustice of marital domination. If what is freely consented to by a reasonable person does not (by that fact alone) count as an injury, we would demand no such reform.

Notice that, since Mill does not (as in the case of slavery) advocate abolishing marriage, he is not open to the charge of paternalism here.

Perhaps it *would* be a failure to respect women's choices if we prohibited the option of marriage, simply on the grounds that, as it stands, the condition entails domination. Indeed, not letting people do the best they can for themselves under hard and unfair circumstances merely adds insult to injury. But Mill does not suggest we do this. On the contrary, he aims to eliminate the necessity that a woman accept marriage on any terms by making sure that "all honourable employments" are "as freely open to her as to men." Once this is done, then "like a man when he chooses a profession, so, when a woman marries, it may in general be understood that she makes the choice of the management of a household, and the bringing up of a family, as the first call upon her exertions, during as many years of her life as may be required for the purpose" (*CW* xxi, 298 [ii, 16]). Now of course things did not quite work out this way. Far from becoming a mere occupation like any other, marriage has retained in social custom some of its obligatory status. Thus it has proved necessary, in the interests of gender equality, to transform the nature of marriage itself, a process still under way. That Mill did not foresee this eventuality is not, I think, an objection to his argument, or at least not with respect to its usefulness for our purposes here. What is significant is that, in his view, the subjection of women, like slavery, is wrong in itself, regardless of whether it is consented to or not.

Mill's conclusion here is the right one, but he cannot arrive at it starting from the negative conception of freedom as non-interference. Here the "kindly master" problem arises again, this time with greater force: it is by no means certain that a woman in the nineteenth century would increase the scope of her negative freedoms by refusing marriage. After all, conjugal feelings in "many men exclude, and in most greatly temper, the impulses and propensities which lead to tyranny" over their spouses, and so many married women might in fact be largely free from unwelcome interference. It would thus seem, on the negative conception of liberty as non-interference, that the case against the legal subordination of women is correspondingly weak. Mill, of course, rejects this view, as he must. Merely "because men in general do not inflict, nor women suffer, all the misery which could be inflicted and suffered if the full power of tyranny with which the man is legally invested were acted on," he complains,

the defenders of the existing form of institution think that all its iniquity is justified, and that any complaint is merely quarrelling with the evil which is the price paid for every great good. But the mitigations in practice, which are compatible with maintaining in full force this or any other kind of tyranny, instead of being any apology for despotism, only serve to prove what power human nature possesses of reacting against the vilest institutions. (*CW* xxi, 286 [ii, 2])

As in the case of slavery, there is something clearly wrong with the legal and social subordination of women as such – even when consented to, and even if we cannot explain that wrongness with reference to negative liberty.

When Mill goes on, in a later chapter, to present his positive arguments in favor of ending the legal and social subordination of women, he presents strictly instrumental utilitarian arguments. The education of children is distorted and corrupted by the inequality of their parents. Society will gain by doubling the pool of available talent. The happiness of women will increase. And so on. These are perfectly good arguments, so far as they go, but one cannot help feeling that something is missing. Were it to turn out that the sum total of happiness, once all possible factors are taken into consideration, would actually be served by continuing, not overturning, the legal and social subordination of women, should we change our minds? We should not. Certainly, we hope and (reasonably) expect equality to bring about greater overall happiness, but this cannot be the only reason we have struggled to achieve it.

Mill's uncritical adoption of the negative conception of liberty does him a disservice. Institutionalized domination, like slavery and the subjection of women in traditional family law and custom, is the negation of freedom if anything is, and this is not merely because we contingently expect that those subject to such domination will experience more unwelcome interferences with their choices than they otherwise would. It makes more sense to say that freedom consists in the absence of domination, and thus that we struggled to end slavery and achieve greater equality for women first and foremost in the interest of freedom. This was the usual view of political liberty or freedom before Bentham and Paley; had this conception been available to Mill, he might more easily have stated his arguments in such terms.

CHAPTER 7

Autonomy, tradition, and the enforcement of morality

Wendy Donner

INTRODUCTION

John Stuart Mill is committed to a utilitarian and liberal theory of human nature and the good. His theory of value is meshed with a liberal philosophy of education that is dedicated to encouraging a process of self-development.[1] Mill's utilitarianism and liberalism are also strongly influenced by the philosophical tradition of virtue ethics and politics. One sign of the link is Mill's advocacy of a kind of liberal education designed to develop the core intellectual and moral excellences in childhood. Mill's liberalism also champions democratic social and political institutions that have as one major goal to provide institutional support for life-long pursuits of these excellences.[2] Mill's many discussions of the educational processes of development and self-development can be seen as setting out a plan for inculcating these mental and moral virtues. The program of education in self-development aims to train human traits of reason, emotion, and sympathy as well as higher-order capacities of autonomy, individuality, sociality, and compassion. Mill is a liberal egalitarian, but he appreciates the Greeks and their virtue-ethical conception of a good human life as including essentially training in and habituation to these excellences.

Autonomy and individuality have pride of place in Mill's conception of human excellence. The two virtues are connected, for in Mill's theory one prime task of autonomy is to develop an individuality or identity that is authentic for each person. Mill professes liberal autonomy. Mill's liberal autonomy features the core abilities of self-determination, critical reflection,

[1] See Wendy Donner, *The Liberal Self: John Stuart Mill's Moral and Political Philosophy* (Ithaca: Cornell University Press, 1991), and "Mill's Utilitarianism," in John Skorupski, ed. *The Cambridge Companion to Mill* (Cambridge: Cambridge University Press, 1998), 255–92.
[2] For a more extensive treatment of these questions, see Wendy Donner, "John Stuart Mill on Education and Democracy," in *J. S. Mill's Political Thought: A Bicentennial Re-Assessment*, ed. Nadia Urbinati and Alex Zakaras (Cambridge: Cambridge University Press, 2007), 250–76.

and authenticity. It relies upon these talents for critical scrutiny and reflection upon options to choose conceptions of the good, life plans, core commitments, and character. Autonomy and individuality are connected skills. These capacities combine to enable agents to pursue lives and principled identities that are their own. Mill deems these talents to be so valuable that he claims that without them people lack character. "A person whose desires and impulses are his own – are the expression of his own nature, as it has been developed and modified by his own culture – is said to have a character"(*CW* XVIII, 264 [III, 5]). This could rightly be said to be the very essence of individuality. Without this, Mill says, there is no authentic character. Conformity to what is customary in society, just for the sake of custom, amounts to abandoning these crucial human excellences (and entitlements) and, in Mill's eyes, attacks the fundamentals of human well-being. Mill's impassioned argument for the indispensability of individuality in *On Liberty* is one of the most widely read and familiar pieces in the liberal pantheon. But this underscores the problem. Mill argues so eloquently for autonomy and individuality because he fears the constant threats from the counter-offensive forces of conformism. Conformity, in Mill's eyes, is the shadow side of the deep human desire for belonging and harmony with family and culture. It is because these needs and desires for connection and attachment run so deep in the human psyche that autonomy and individuality are frequently, he thinks, under threat. Authentic forms of belonging and attachment and connection are not threatened by healthy doses of autonomy and individuality. In their healthy forms, these are mutually reinforcing traits. But the shadow forms of belonging and attachment are masquerading as the real thing. Mill engaged in life-long battles with the human predilection for oppression and tyranny. His eloquent arguments for freedom and autonomy are designed not only to furnish positive arguments for their merits, but also to warn of those who try to undermine or diminish individuality and autonomy by appeals to questionable forms of belonging and attachment that corrode the human spirit. The encounter of autonomy and individuality with tradition is a rich backdrop against which to explore some of the most compelling questions of liberalism.

Mill himself provides an excellent case for study of these questions in his discussion of the proper application of the liberty principle in chapter IV of *On Liberty*. This case concerns the practice of polygamy within Mormon communities in Mill's day. The controversies surrounding this practice continue in the present, with ongoing investigations, especially of the treatment of women in the community. A striking current example is the Mormon community of Bountiful, British Columbia in Canada, which is a breakaway sect of Mormons.[3] No longer remote from the larger culture, Mormons in America and Canada live under the same laws as all other citizens. The mainstream Mormon group has long since ceased this practice and has outlawed polygamy, excommunicating any of its members who enter into new polygamous arrangements. The breakaway excommunicated group in Bountiful also are subject to Canadian law that outlaws polygamy, although there are longstanding complaints that the law is not enforced in this case. Mill characterizes the treatment of Mormons as persecution. He invokes the example as a notable test of the limits of the application of his liberty principle. At the time of his writing, Mormons had relocated their community to what was then a remote area of Utah, but today they exist as part of the wider cultures of the United States and Canada and are not separate societal cultures, in Will Kymlicka's terminology.[4] Why does Mill use the term "persecution"? He does so because in his time there were calls to send an expedition from Britain to Utah to force Mormons to end this practice.

My primary concern here is to examine Mill's liberal arguments for whether and under what conditions a female Mormon can correctly be seen as exercising autonomy when she participates in a polygamous marriage in which she is one of several wives. (It is never the case that one wife has several husbands.) Mill says that this case is vexing for him. Indeed, it is positively head-scratching. He characterizes the behavior of women in polygamous marriages as "voluntary" while admitting that the institution, "far from being in any way countenanced by the principle of liberty ... is a direct infraction of that principle, being a mere riveting of the chains of one-half of the community, and an emancipation of the other from reciprocity of obligation towards them" (CW xviii, 290 [iv, 21]). Yet, Mill continues, this marital relationship is as voluntary as any other sort of institution of marriage. Since the group has taken the drastic step of moving away, Mill concludes that it would be tyranny to try to stop them instituting and living by whatever laws they wish governing marriage within their community, as long as they do not attack other nations and they allow freedom of departure from the community – in other words, a right of exit for dissidents.

---

[3] This group is part of the Fundamentalist Church of Jesus Christ of Latter-day Saints (FLDS), a dissenting Mormon group which was excommunicated by the mainstream Mormon Church when members refused to stop the practice of polygamy, which is now outlawed by the mainstream Mormon Church (the LDS).

[4] Will Kymlicka, *Multicultural Citizenship: A Liberal Theory of Minority Rights* (Oxford: Clarendon Press, 1995). In Kymlicka's classification scheme, societal cultures are distinct from and should be treated differently from ethnic or religious groups. The former are distinct national cultures, while the latter are not distinct but are part of the larger dominant societal cultures. Canada, for example, has three societal cultures or nations, namely English, French, and Aboriginals.

Mill gazes at the Mormon group from the outside and at a distance. The case is jarring in its setting because, according to Mill, the express purpose of liberty is to defend each and every individual's right to autonomy and individuality within their social and cultural grouping. It is to defend the rights of rebels and eccentrics as well as those who are content to endorse, after reflection, the community's traditional ways. Viewing things from this vantage point, Mill argues that diversity and pluralism of life plans and situations are the spontaneous and natural result of self-development and individuality, and that therefore we should regard with deep suspicion any uniform and conformist outcomes. This is a major point of his argument for individuality in the second chapter of *On Liberty* (*CW* XVIII, 260–75 [III, 1–19]). Yet he does not think it is odd that Mormon young women all seem to accept polygamy, a distinctly disquieting marriage option. Mill regards the group stereotypically, as all having more or less the same preferences and "voluntary" choices, namely, polygamy or exit from the community. He scourges his own society for inducing conformity, yet the conformist patterns of Mormon marriages, he thinks, should be protected from persecution by liberal outsiders. He adds the qualifier that this form of marriage is as voluntary as a general choice as any other. Even if this were true in the nineteenth century (and this is doubtful), it is quite clearly false in present times. So the lens he looks through yields the expectation that most members of this group have similar marital preferences, whereas he excoriates his own society for having the same expectation. From a vantage point internal to the Mormon community, things might look different, when each person can be seen as an individual. In exploring this case Mill exhibits an apparent failure of empathy and sympathetic imagination. However, as I will argue, his theory actually provides the remedy and corrective for this lapse.

AUTONOMY, LIBERALISM, AND COMMUNITARIANISM

Fast-forwarding in time to the present, we can utilize the framework of the contemporary dialogue on liberalism and communitarianism to reflect upon Mill's example. Will Kymlicka's arguments for the rights of minority cultures within larger dominant liberal cultures provide a useful backdrop for this examination. Kymlicka's arguments explore the cases for both the rights of fully fledged minority societal cultures as well as for rights of ethnic and religious groups that are not separate nations. Kymlicka's principles furnish useful touchstones for Mill's case of a controversial religious group.

There are strong resonances between Kymlicka's and Mill's liberal commitments. Kymlicka endorses Mill's liberal argument for the right to autonomy. Mill's case for the right to self-determination revolves around the rights of competent adults to assess the meaning and value of their experiences for themselves. As Kymlicka puts it, we want to lead good lives, and this makes us reflect seriously about what in life is worth pursuing. Rational agents recognize their fallibility. They realize that they could be wrong in their current views about the good life, and they also recognize their essential interests in living a good life. Liberals hold that these interests have two preconditions. "One is that we lead our life from the inside, in accordance with our beliefs about what gives value to life; the other is that we be free to question those beliefs, to examine them in the light of whatever information, examples, and arguments our culture can provide."[5] We have an interest in forming and then examining and possibly revising our conception of the good. The societal culture thus provides the freedom and the resources for this reflection and questioning. It gives us the cultural materials needed to reach an awareness of different views of the good life, as well as the capacities required to reflect critically upon the presented options.

Any attempt to enforce from outside a particular conception of the good life undermines these essential liberal interests. Mill and Kymlicka also share the liberal view of the self as autonomous. On this view "individuals are considered free to question their participation in existing social practices, and opt out of them, should those practices no longer seem worth pursuing."[6] Liberals maintain that individuals therefore are not *defined* by any particular relationship, because they have autonomy and can question, endorse, or revise and reject particular attachments. While those relationships and attachments that we have committed ourselves to with awareness will tend to be enduring, still it will be healthy for us to carry on this questioning, of asking whether our life course is still worth pursuing and deserves our continuing commitment. The Buddhist principle of the impermanence of all things is a good companion precept for understanding this liberal perspective. If we try to hang on to pursuits, practices, relationships, and even self-perceptions after they have ceased to be worthy of our commitment, then they become sources of suffering rather than promoting good.

Mill's argument agrees with the spirit of Kymlicka's insistence that liberalism appreciates the necessity of a social context of choice to underwrite people's pursuit of a life in accord with their individuality. Mill is also always careful to balance the virtues of individuality and sociality, and to grant both

---

[5] Will Kymlicka, *Contemporary Political Philosophy: An Introduction*, 2nd edn. (Oxford: Oxford University Press, 2002), 216.
[6] Ibid., 221.

their place in his conception of human excellence. Mill says in *Utilitarianism* and other writings that sociality, fellow feeling, and the ability to cooperate and recognize the value of social enterprises are human excellences on a par with the other human virtues, including individuality. He frequently expounds upon the need for feelings of social unity and public spirit. Mill's individualism certainly does not lead him to discount the value and necessity of the social and cooperative capacities of human nature.

> The social state is at once so natural, so necessary, and so habitual to man, that, except in some unusual circumstances or by an effort of voluntary abstraction, he never conceives himself otherwise than as a member of a body ... They are also familiar with the fact of co-operating with others, and proposing to themselves a collective, not an individual interest, as the aim ... of their actions ... The good of others becomes to him a thing naturally and necessarily to be attended to. (*CW* x, 231–2 [iii, 9])

Mill also puts great stock in liberal forms of cultural belonging. He says that social stability requires a sense of cohesion among members of political society, but he emphatically rules out nationality "in the vulgar sense." He clarifies that "we mean a principle of sympathy, not of hostility; of union, not of separation" (*CW* viii, 923 [Bk. VI, x, 5]). Mill says that we have duties to cooperate with others in joint civic projects and to reciprocate legitimate expectations of love, affection, and friendship.

Mill and Kymlicka thus share some of liberalism's core concerns. They differ, I argue, in how they conceive of the social and cultural context that provides the support for individuality and the pursuit of identity. Kymlicka, perhaps unintentionally, turns the societal context into a framework that threatens to harden into a barrier, limiting the horizon of choice to one's own societal culture, the culture into which one is born. Mill's preferred context of choice is without such clear lines and limits, and fully supports those eccentrics and true originals who entirely reject the range of choices that happen to be currently on offer in their society. That is why his assessment of the Mormon community is so out of character.

Kymlicka is adamant about the requirement of a social context of a particular *kind* for a liberal good life. It cannot be just any social or cultural context, but rather it must be our own birth culture. Remove the context of our *own* birth culture, he says, and people are denied a Rawlsian primary good.[7] Kymlicka, as a liberal, does not agree with communitarian claims of the "politics of the common good."[8] He surely intends the societal culture

---

[7] A Rawlsian primary good is "a good which people need, regardless of their particular way of life." Kymlicka, *Multicultural Citizenship*, 214 n. 11.
[8] Kymlicka, *Contemporary Political Philosophy*, 220.

to be an enabler for self-determination and freedom. He argues that this is liberalism's commitment. But the result of his argument may not be what he intends, but rather may produce unintended consequences which throw into question his chain of argument, and reveal its weaknesses.[9] Individualism and freedom, autonomy and individuality, are bound up with and dependent upon membership in a societal culture, says Kymlicka, one with a shared history, language, values, norms, and practices. The society furnishes the information, models, education, and conditions needed to formulate a judgment and perspective about different options and plans for the good life. The society arrays the range of options as live ones, as real prospects. The result is that active participation in a cultural context is necessary since it is this context that furnishes meaningful and vivid options and choices for viable life plans and paths.

The pitfalls of this line of thought are obvious. First, why limit this to our birth culture? Second, any currently available range of options of life paths has limits, and Mill, *contra* Kymlicka, seeks to remove horizons set by birth cultures on imaginative possibilities for good lives – that is one main intention of his argument for individuality and originality in *On Liberty*. Even a few decades ago, the supposed options for a young woman in a Western democracy were to marry a doctor or a lawyer rather than to become one herself. As a graduate student in philosophy at a Canadian university in the 1970s, I was aware that one of my professors, an eminent scholar, held the view that women were not suited to study philosophy. And until quite recently, antisemitism produced quotas limiting Jewish admissions to medical and law schools in Canada and the United States. The question then is: what is to stop this range of options from transforming into a horizon-limiting obstacle, setting certain options firmly in stone, discouraging struggles to overcome racist and sexist barriers, and becoming Mill's feared scenario of the "hurtful compression" of "the small number of moulds which society provides in order to save its members the trouble of forming their own character" (*CW* XVIII, 267–8 [III, 11])?

Even though Mill and Kymlicka disagree about the nature of the social context of choice to support autonomy, neither of their liberal senses of community and belonging is carried to the lengths that communitarian thinkers take them. For one thing, Mill would dispute that we have an

[9] I pursue this claim in more depth in "Is Cultural Membership a Good? Kymlicka and Ignatieff on the Virtues and Perils of Belonging," in William Aiken and John Haldane, eds., *Philosophy and its Public Role: Essays in Ethics, Politics, Society and Culture* (Exeter: Imprint Academic, 2004), 84–101.

obligation to belong, in Charles Taylor's communitarian language.[10] Mill would have sharp words for Taylor's claim that in certain liberal societies with collective goals, such as Quebec, "political society is not neutral between those who value remaining true to the culture of our ancestors and those who might want to cut loose in the name of some individual goal of self-development."[11] Mill's sharp words would say that we do not have a duty to live according to others' expectations of preserving a culture of a particular form (and Taylor believes Quebecois have such a duty[12]) particularly when those expectations amount to coercion to live out our lives according to the desires and wants of others.

The hazards of insufficient attention to the proper balance between individuality and attachment to traditional community are apparent. Even for a communitarian like Taylor, who carves out a space for autonomy within a society with collective goals, the balance can tip dangerously against those who want to "cut loose" for the sake of their self-development. This becomes acutely painful in cases of parental or community expectations about young adults' choices in marriage or work. And it is not to be underestimated just how frequently young adults' choices to fall in love and marry outside of their community of birth are viewed as betrayals, with painful repercussions. The coercion to marry within the community is often served up as a means of preserving traditional ways or cultural practices that bond. A prominent pattern is to perceive a need for the youthful generation of the community to follow the traditional norms and practices, and to curb their individual desires and preferences and allow parents or community to decide their destiny, to control major life decisions such as whom they marry. It is a recipe for a volatile encounter between tradition on the one hand and autonomy and individuality on the other. The current practice of arranged marriage among some cultural and religious communities is less extreme, although more common, than the practice of polygamy. The practice of arranged marriage can perhaps serve as a more realistic example to test the limits of liberalism, for those who view polygamy as too far outside the pale to merit serious consideration. This brings to the foreground some compelling questions in contemporary ethics and politics. We can ask whether the traditional way of life of the community functions as an empowering context for its members or whether it circumscribes and

---

[10] Charles Taylor, "Atomism," in Shlomo Avineri and Avner de-Shalit, eds., *Communitarianism and Individualism* (Oxford: Oxford University Press, 1992), 29–50.

[11] Charles Taylor, "The Politics of Recognition," in Amy Gutmann, ed., *Multiculturalism: Examining the Politics of Recognition* (Princeton: Princeton University Press, 1994), 58.

[12] Ibid., 58–60.

restricts, channeling their plans in directions amenable to the community but insensitive to the harms of quelling their individuality.

Amartya Sen sounds the warning about faulty reasoning that can "tie people up in knots of their own making." He is talking about coercion that can underwrite group pressure to comply with tradition. Sen says that

the importance of cultural freedom, central to the dignity of all people, must be distinguished from the celebration and championing of every form of cultural inheritance, irrespective of whether the people involved would choose those particular practices given the opportunity of critical scrutiny, and given an adequate knowledge of other options and of the choices that actually exist in the society in which they live. The demands of cultural freedom, include, among other priorities, the task of resisting the automatic endorsement of past traditions, when people see reason for changing their ways of living.[13]

The argument comes face to face with the tension between people's commitment to a group or community and their desire or need to acquire and pursue an identity of their own, within or without that community. Ties of belonging fuel some of the most powerful human emotions, but they can easily turn into a sense of alienation or even of suffocation. If people feel like aliens within a birth community or family, they may seek their kin and kindred spirits outside these confines. The drive for authenticity can and often does propel people beyond their initial community. They relocate from their community of origin to a found community of choice, in Marilyn Friedman's terminology.[14]

MILL'S RESPONSE

Mill's reflections on the example of polygamy, I argue, do not reveal a weakness of his theory. Rather, this example illustrates the importance of distinguishing his carefully constructed theoretical structure from the examples he offers of its application. The examples may well be outdated, and it is manifestly uncharitable to judge the theory by reading back from outdated examples. A more current and less extreme example than polygamy, and one that is very much in the center of discussion about multiculturalism and the limits of toleration, is the practice of arranged marriage within several ethnic and religious communities in Western democracies. Moreover,

---

[13] Amartya Sen, "Two Confusions, and Counting," *The Globe and Mail*, August 23, 2006.
[14] See Marilyn Friedman, "Feminism and Modern Friendship: Dislocating the Community," in Shlomo Avineri and Avner de-Shalit, eds., *Communitarianism and Individualism* (Oxford: Oxford University Press, 1992), 101–19.

Mill's example, I argue, even allowing for its datedness, reveals weakness in his *application* of his theory, a failure of his sympathetic and empathic imagination in adopting the stance of viewing an entire group stereotypically rather than as a group of distinct individuals.

The contentious example is from *On Liberty*, and the same essay presents the corrective response of Mill's theory to the example. In effect, he answers himself and corrects his own error. He paints a clear portrait of the rejoinder to excessive ties or bonds of community. He responds to his own example when he attacks excessive parental control over children as requiring the protection of the rights of children, if necessary, by state intervention to guard their autonomy and individuality from parental and (by extension) community tyranny.

In *The Subjection of Women*, Mill wisely distinguishes between liberty of individuality and autonomy, on the one hand, and power over others or the power of the tyrant to dominate others. The latter is a source only of degradation and corruption of the despot, in Mill's eyes. This distinction between liberty and power runs as a clear line throughout his philosophical system, allowing him to promote the liberal freedoms while condemning oppressive power over others. In *On Liberty* he invokes this same distinction between liberty and despotic power to attack marital tyranny, as a kind of example where "liberty is often granted where it should be withheld." The state must respect the liberty of each person in self-regarding matters, and equally must "maintain a vigilant control over his exercise of any power which it allows him to possess over others." The family ought to be a prime sphere for watchful vigilance, but sadly this is not the case, and instead of friendship and equal rights of spouses, the reality is despotism of husbands over wives. The state fails even more to fulfill its duties to protect the rights of children. Children suffer under patriarchal control of fathers just as wives do. Foremost in Mill's mind is children's right to an education, which, according to his philosophy of education, must include the right to be educated in the capacities required for the exercise of autonomy and individuality. "Is it not almost a self-evident axiom, that the State should require and compel the education, up to a certain standard, of every human being who is born its citizen?" (*CW* XVIII, 301 [v, 12]). Parents owe it to children to secure their education. It is a "moral crime" to fail to provide an education along with other basic essentials of well-being. Mill has no hesitation in saying that the state should step in to force compliance if parents fail in their duties, since the state also has a clear duty to ensure education for all its members. Mill was far ahead of his time in advocating and campaigning for the right to universal education. He is more out of step with the contemporary climate in arguing that parents should fully control the form of the education. Mill believed that state education would work against diversity in education, and so he argued that state education should be but one experiment among many. Mill could have heeded the results of his own home schooling by his father, since he observed its flawed results through keen self-scrutiny, and wrote about it in his *Autobiography*.[15] He was trained to be the lineage holder of Benthamite utilitarianism and suffered severe depression in the aftermath of his education, fully controlled by his father who exhibited limited understanding of the importance of "internal culture" or cultivation of the feelings (*CW* I, 147 [v, 14]).

Mill's proposals for diversity of forms of education are underwritten by his device of ensuring educational standards of excellence through uniform public examinations at all levels. This would make "a certain minimum of general knowledge, virtually compulsory." Mill is anxious about circumstances of undue influence of the state over opinions. To counter this, under his program the exams would test only factual knowledge. He says that "the examinations on religion, politics, or other disputed topics, should not turn on the truth or falsehood of opinions, but on the matter of fact that such and such an opinion is held, on such grounds, by such authors, or schools, or churches" (*CW* XVIII, 303 [v, 14]). The concerns Mill expresses here are unbalanced, for he is more worried about excessive state power and not sufficiently about parental neglect. According to his professed principles, his concern should extend equally to any who attempt to gain power over others. Society may manifest the tyranny of the majority and exert coercion to conform, but the family can also function as a school for training in the patriarchal vices. In *The Subjection of Women*, for example, Mill devotes considerable attention to the capacity of the family to function as a school for training boys to be despots. His aim, of course, is to establish that it should not and does not have to be so. The family has the equal potential to be a training ground for emancipation, if children are educated to appreciate that "the true virtue of human beings is fitness to live together as equals."[16]

In Mill's system, children not only have a right to an education; they have a right to an education of a certain kind. If they are to be well placed to function autonomously as adults, and to lead authentic lives of their own,

[15] John Stuart Mill, *Autobiography* (1873), in *The Collected Works of John Stuart Mill*, vol. I: *Autobiography and Literary Essays*, ed. John M. Robson and Jack Stillinger, introduction by Lord Robbins (Toronto: University of Toronto Press; London: Routledge & Kegan Paul, 1981), 137–91 (ch. v).
[16] John Stuart Mill, *The Subjection of Women* (1869), in *The Collected Works of John Stuart Mill*, vol. XXI: *Essays on Equality, Law, and Education*, ed. John M. Robson, introduction by Stefan Collini (Toronto: University of Toronto Press; London: Routledge & Kegan Paul, 1984), 294 (II, 12).

children must be nurtured in childhood education to have the capacities necessary for exercising autonomy as adults. The upshot is that children have a right-in-trust to be autonomous when they reach adulthood, or, in other words, they have a right to an open future, as Joel Feinberg puts it.[17] Their rights are violated if their childhood education and socialization are constricted so that certain options are effectively closed off as live options in adulthood. In matters of religion, politics, and ethics, it is clear that Mill's philosophy does not grant parents the right to arrange things so as to determine their children's future plans, even though they have legitimate hopes that their children will freely choose to carry on their traditions in adulthood. The entire weight of Mill's argument in the chapters on freedom of expression and individuality in *On Liberty* can be brought to bear to establish this as the logical outcome of his argument that people have rights to individuality and autonomy in adulthood. From the vantage point of these arguments, people's rights are violated if their childhood education cuts them off from living contact with alternative visions of life, and thwarts their individuality as adults. This is equally the case whether the children are part of the larger dominant culture or part of a smaller ethnic or religious group within the society. Mill's theory does not allow for any differentiation in rights to autonomy on such grounds.

Kymlicka presents the danger arising from the fears of traditionalists that their group will be weakened by mass exits of members:

They fear that if their members are informed about other ways of life, and are given the cognitive and emotional capacities to understand and evaluate them, many will choose to reject their inherited way of life, and thereby undermine the group. To prevent this, fundamentalist or isolationist groups often wish to raise and educate their children in such a way as to minimize the opportunities for children to develop or exercise the capacity for rational revisability … Their goal is to ensure that their members are indeed "embedded" in the group, unable to conceive of leaving it or to succeed outside of it.[18]

This is what frequently happens in closed religious or ethnic communities such as the breakaway Mormon group. Mill's core commitments face a

---

[17] Joel Feinberg succinctly expresses the core of this. "When sophisticated autonomy rights are attributed to children who are clearly not yet capable of exercising them, their names refer to rights that are to be saved for the child until he is an adult, but which can be violated in advance, so to speak, before the child is even in a position to exercise them. Violations guarantee now that when the child is an autonomous adult, certain key options will already be closed to him. While he is still a child, he has the right to have these future options kept open until he is a fully formed self-determining agent capable of deciding among them." Joel Feinberg, "The Child's Right to an Open Future," in J. Howie, ed. *Ethical Principles for Social Policy* (Carbondale: Southern Illinois University Press, 1983), 98.

[18] Kymlicka, *Contemporary Political Philosophy*, 228.

blunt showdown with parents and communities who wish to close off their children's rights to open futures. In Mill's system, rights correlate with duties and are effectively guaranteed by society. When children reach adulthood and are capable of self-determination, they will be well placed to reflect critically and with a degree of critical awareness of and detachment from the norms and customs of their society, in order to choose and endorse forms of life plans that are an authentic expression of their own individuality, identity, and character – not of those around them.

Vulnerable minority groups may, as Kymlicka argues,[19] have grounds for special protection against persecution and discrimination, but this must proceed, in Mill's framework, on the clear understanding that the rights of individuals are foundational. Kymlicka's distinction between internal restrictions and external protections is very helpful at this juncture in asking how we can separate out the legitimate from the illegitimate. Kymlicka notes many liberals' mistrust of demands of special protection for the traditional practices of minority cultures, observing that this can provide a venue for trampling on individual rights of some members. Kymlicka argues that this line of argument conflates two distinct kinds of collective rights. He claims that liberals should support external protections of minority ethnic and cultural groups. These are claims of the group as a whole against the larger culture, in which the group "may seek to protect its distinct existence and identity by limiting the impact of the decisions of the larger society".[20] This is designed to protect the group as a whole from external destabilizing forces, including discrimination. This is what Mill primarily has in mind when he seeks to prevent persecution of Mormons by external groups. Kymlicka separates this out from internal restrictions, which, he notes, do undoubtedly clash with fundamental liberal principles. The internal kind "is intended to protect the group from the destabilizing impact of *internal dissent* (e.g. the decision of individual members not to follow traditional practices or customs)."[21] This kind of right seeks to employ the notion of solidarity or group integrity to restrict the liberty of internal dissenters and rebels. It is what critics argue is involved in traditional cultural and religious groups whose practices are patriarchal and involve the oppression of women and their restrictions in sexist gender roles. Kymlicka concludes that external protections are legitimate to support group identity, but liberals "should reject internal restrictions which limit the right of group members to question and revise traditional authorities and practices."[22]

---

[19] Kymlicka, *Multicultural Citizenship*, 34–48.   [20] Ibid., 36.   [21] Ibid., 35.   [22] Ibid., 37.

This distinction is indeed helpful, but it is not strong enough to do the work Kymlicka asks of it. Kymlicka's analysis suggests that it is possible to separate out clearly the external protection of the community from persecution, from the protection of the internal rights of community members to dissent. If this were so, then Mill's aim of shielding Mormon marriage from discrimination or persecution would gain more legitimacy. However, the worry is that critics may be right in thinking that external protections of collective rights may simply serve to prop up the power of the dominant group within the traditional community to oppress dissidents. In such a case, it can be argued that "persecution" of the community can be interpreted as others invoking reasonable sanctions to protect the vulnerable who prefer marriage to one husband over either polygamy or exit. Viewing the community as homogeneous also distorts the view. The community is composed of individuals, but at the same time it is composed of groups differentiated along power lines. There is no clear boundary between these internal and external rights and protections. In the absence of a clear boundary, the protection of internal rights of members must take precedence for a liberal theorist like Mill.

Mill's stance does not commit him to overlooking the dialogical elements of identity construction, or ignoring the importance of advice, counsel, desires, preferences, and influences of significant others, and the social conventions that may reflect the accumulated wisdom, rather than the biases, of experience. However, it does require the trained capacity to prevent the influences from turning into determinants of choices. Mill's mantra is "persuasion, not coercion." Autonomous people are influenced but not determined by significant others, whose views they take seriously. Communitarian Charles Taylor argues that "we define our identity always in dialogue with, sometimes in struggle against, the things our significant others want to see in us. Even after we outgrow some of these others – our parents for instance – and they disappear from our lives, the conversation with them continues within us as long as we live."[23] This statement contains a portion of the truth, in Millian many-sidedness terms, but it does not have the biting upshot that Taylor intends. Liberalism can agree with this. What distinguishes autonomous, self-developed people from conformists is what they do with this process of interaction and dialogue. Do they accept the stories about them and their fate that these interlocutors tell, or do they set up their own narratives about their lives after reflection on and scrutiny of the stories and roles these significant others present? Deferentially accepting

[23] Charles Taylor, "The Politics of Recognition," 32–3.

others' stories and family dramas is an invitation to oppression and in-
authenticity. Susan Moller Okin sharply critiques the communitarian pen-
chant for telling other people about the range and limits of their life tales,
when she interrogates Alasdair MacIntyre's presentation of storylines in her
feminist critique, "Whose Traditions? Which Understandings?"[24] Okin has
little sympathy for what she regards as the communitarian yearning for
patriarchal traditional privilege. MacIntyre argues that children's education
must proceed by immersion in the narratives and myths of their cultural
traditions, so that they can discover the plot of their own life narrative.
MacIntyre describes these as stories "about wicked stepmothers, lost children,
good but misguided kings, wolves that suckle twin boys, youngest sons who
receive no inheritance but must make their own way in the world." He argues
that in the absence of such stories that educate children in "the cast of
characters … in the drama into which they have been born and what the
ways of the world are," children will be reduced to being "unscripted, anxious
stutterers."[25] Okin replies that MacIntyre's stories are thoroughly sexist and
"permeated by the patriarchal power structure within which they evolved."[26]
More authentic women's stories would have a rather different focus. This is
very true. But the more fundamental Millian point surely is that other
people's stories are other people's stories, and likely involve their own
projections and fantasies. Autonomous adults put other people's stories on
the bookshelf and, while respecting the hopes and reasonable expectations of
significant others, immerse themselves in their own tales, or perhaps even
reach an awakened awareness that their own life, authentically lived moment
to moment, is better than any storyline.

   If it is asked who would choose polygamy when all of the proper
conditions and safeguards are in place, including vivid awareness of the
range of family and partnership options available to autonomous, equal, and
self-respecting women, the answer may be "Precious few." This is not an
option likely to thrive when children are educated for freedom, and when
polygamy relies for its survival on control, oppression, and even abuse and
violence against young women and girls of the community. Mill's framework has little space for artificially propping up traditional cultural practices
that do not survive the critical scrutiny of its own members – that is, the
vulnerable members as well as the dominant members of the group. On the

---

[24] Susan Moller Okin, "Whose Traditions? Which Understandings?," in Susan Moller Okin, *Justice,
   Gender, and the Family* (New York: Basic Books, 1989), 41–73.
[25] Alasdair MacIntyre, *After Virtue* (Notre Dame: University of Notre Dame Press, 1981), 201.
[26] Okin, "Whose Traditions? Which Understandings?," 58.

other hand, many practices that hold together traditional communities seem automatically suspect to members of the larger dominant liberal culture. So Mill's concerns about persecuting minority groups can be regarded as supplying a caution against general refusal to accept that women may *ever* legitimately and authentically engage in traditional practices such as arranged marriage. Mill's built-in conditions for proper education in autonomy could also go awry if the outcomes are all the same in the opposite direction. Expected or predictable patterns of outcomes or results of choices of any sort, given the multifarious array of human creativity in life paths, should be suspect.[27]

Mill's awareness of human epistemic fallibility serves as a caution against thinking we can predict the predilections of even those whom we feel we know well. Their destiny may surprise and amaze in completely unanticipated ways. Mill's paean to eccentricity signals his astute comprehension of the mysterious ways that lives unfold. He probably did not anticipate that he would fall in love with a married woman, and so he was catapulted into the frame of mind of one who is forced to improvise and deviate from what was expected of him in his marital life. Choices of life paths that seem to be restrictive or bizarre to others, such as the choice to enter a monastic life, Christian or Buddhist, can indeed be authenticated as legitimately autonomous if the conditions of education for freedom and rational, critical reflection and endorsement or ratification are met. It is not beyond the pale to anticipate that some women may endorse a marriage arranged by their parents, for reasons of religious faith or loyalty, among others. To expect that none at all will do so is to fall prey to the same error of failure of

---

[27] The debate about the politics of recognition is another stage on which these practices play out. Anthony Appiah considers Mill to be a friend and theoretical companion, and shares Mill's worries about the demands of communities to conform to shared values. Appiah's canvas is the debate about individual identity and collective identity that occupies a central place in the liberalism–communitarianism dialogues. Appiah's worries zero in on the host of collective identities – Quebecois, Mormon, Hindu, Jewish, black, gay – that struggle for recognition and against discrimination in liberal national cultures. This includes the demand for recognition of these collective identities. "It is because someone is authentically Jewish or gay that we deny them something in requiring them to hide this fact, to pass for something that they are not." K. Anthony Appiah, "Identity, Authenticity, Survival: Multicultural Societies and Social Reproduction," in Amy Gutmann, ed., *Multiculturalism: Examining the Politics of Recognition* (Princeton: Princeton University Press, 1994), 149. In this context, requiring individual Mormons or Hindus to forgo the marriage practices that bind the group together in shared practices and a sense of their common good and shared destiny amounts to asking them to pass for what they are not. These groups are already struggling against demeaning images of themselves in the dominant culture, and this amounts to the persecution that Mill points out. But Appiah also points to the double-edged sword, the razor's edge, which group demands for solidarity in the face of discrimination can become. "There will be proper ways of being black and gay, there will be expectations to be met, demands will be made. It is at this point that someone who takes autonomy seriously will ask whether we have not replaced one kind of tyranny with another" (ibid., 162–3).

imagination. Mill's core point is that we should be wary of thinking we are prescient and that we can anticipate the legitimate authentic dreams of others. Even when we think we know people well as intimates, we can be startled by where they end up, and how their lives unfold in sometimes extraordinarily unexpected ways. This can be tragic, as in the case of a beloved sibling who becomes a homeless street person or drug-dealer. Or it can be inspiring, as in the case of a trailblazer like Elisabeth Kübler-Ross. Kübler-Ross, born a triplet in Switzerland, became a pioneer researcher on death and dying (and later near-death and afterlife experiences). She dreamed from early childhood of becoming a physician. Her father dictated that she would work for him as his secretary until she became a nice housewife.[28] She rebelled and rejected her father's demands, persisting at great personal cost until she achieved a life of her own design. She describes her eccentric life:

I could never, not in my wildest dreams – and they were pretty wild – have predicted one day winding up the world-famous author of *On Death and Dying*, a book whose exploration of life's final passage threw me into the center of a medical and theological controversy. Nor could I have imagined that afterward I would spend the rest of my life explaining that death does not exist.[29]

Whatever one thinks about the near-death and afterlife research to which she devoted the latter part of her life (and despite Mill's own scorn for transcendental metaphysics), she is indisputably a true original. And it is also very evident that the fruits of her courageous pioneer work on the dying process have had immeasurable benefits and cracked open the death-denying cultural attitudes that caused such suffering by routinely preventing terminally ill people from even talking about their impending death. She provides a blue-chip example of Mill's claim that encouraging individuality allows for the opportunity of cultural innovation and progress. Kübler-Ross's research and activism helped to create the hospice movement and the revolution in treatment of dying people, so that now it is virtually unheard of to deny dying patients the dignity of communicating with others about their approaching death. Kubler-Ross is the exemplar of whom Mill speaks, opening new cultural pathways and breaking down outdated molds.

Mill's guidelines for evaluating the traditional ways of a society follow the same pattern of argument. He draws the general distinction between relying

[28] Elisabeth Kübler-Ross, *The Wheel of Life: A Memoir of Living and Dying* (New York: Scribner, 1997), 22.
[29] Ibid., 15.

upon the wisdom of accumulated human experience, which he lauds, and habitually and uncritically conforming to custom that is stultifying and impedes cultural improvement, which he condemns. In *Utilitarianism*, for example, he heaps scorn upon critics of utilitarianism who put the objection that the theory requires agents to calculate afresh the tendencies of actions each time they make a moral decision. This objection is rebuffed and Mill states as obvious that agents rely upon the accumulated wisdom of experience that "murder and theft are injurious to human happiness." But moral rules, like any other precepts of practical art, or particular conceptions of the good, "admit of indefinite improvement, and, in a progressive state of the human mind, their improvement is perpetually going on" (*CW* x, 224 [II, 23]).[30] His argument in *On Liberty* follows the pattern also. In this essay he says that it is absurd to proceed in life as though previous human experience had taught us nothing about whether one form of action or living is preferable to another. And so children should be educated to know about the accumulated wisdom of their culture, and to have a proper degree of deference to this. And yet, "it is the privilege and proper condition of a human being, arrived at the maturity of his faculties, to use and interpret experience in his own way" (*CW* XVIII, 262 [III, 3]). Moreover, even those cultural practices which merit continuation need to be reflected upon and ratified and endorsed, if they are to be held as living convictions rather than as dead dogmas. As well, nonconformist individuals, such as Kübler-Ross, are needed to experiment with new practices in order to see which ones are worthy of acceptance as customs. In this way, the momentum of social progress is maintained and new and better customs worthy of general acceptance are discovered, thanks to highly original innovators. The debt owed to innovators is large, for progress depends upon their unwillingness to accept the customary. Mill says that

the despotism of custom is everywhere the standing hindrance to human advancement, being in unceasing antagonism to that disposition to aim at something better than customary, which is called, according to circumstances, the spirit of liberty, or that of progress or improvement … The progressive principle … is antagonistic to the sway of Custom, involving at least emancipation from that yoke; and the contest between the two constitutes the chief interest of the history of mankind. (*CW* XVIII, 272 [III, 17])

[30] John Stuart Mill, *Utilitarianism* (1861), in *The Collected Works of John Stuart Mill*, vol. x: *Essays on Ethics, Religion and Society*, ed. John M. Robson (Toronto: University of Toronto Press; London: Routledge & Kegan Paul, 1969), 224.

Book VI of *A System of Logic* is an extensive study of the moral arts and sciences, and a central question of this study asks what are the driving forces of social progress and improvement. Mill holds to methodological individualism in his philosophy of social science. He looks to uncover the one element that is the primary driver for social progress and improvement. He argues there that the predominant cause of social progress and improvement is "the state of the speculative faculties of mankind" and that "speculation, intellectual activity, the pursuit of truth" are "the engines that propel improvement in social affairs."[31] If traditions are wise, then they are part of this movement.

Moreover, Mill rejects the claim of cultural traditionalists and conservatives that once an excellent set of traditions and cultural practices is discovered, human well-being is best promoted by conserving it without further scrutiny and experimentation. He compares the state of progress of Europe and China and finds the condition of the latter lamentable. His Eurocentrism is on display, yet his discussion lucidly illustrates his framework. The historical example of China, he says, is a cautionary tale of the effects of cultural stagnation. China had the good fortune historically to have rulers who were sages and philosophers, and who designed excellent practices and customs. But there it stopped, and the culture has been stationary ever since. Chinese society since has been successfully impeding further human progress and has managed to eliminate individuality and produce uniformity of thought and conduct. European society has avoided the stationary character and has progressed because of its extreme diversity and pluralism of character and culture. The lesson is clear, in Mill's mind. Cultural practices and traditions that encourage respect for freedom and dignity, that propel human well-being and progress, and that are freely accepted by members of the society are worthy of protection. Conformity to custom and tradition just as custom impedes human progress and well-being and deserves opposition, not support, from liberals.

THE ART OF LIFE AND THE ENFORCEMENT OF MORALITY

These questions about the relationship of autonomy and tradition are closely connected to questions about whether traditions in the form of general shared moral doctrines or conceptions of the good should be

[31] John Stuart Mill, *A System of Logic Ratiocinative and Inductive* (1843; 8th edn. 1871), vols. VII–VIII of *The Collected Works of John Stuart Mill*, ed. John M. Robson, introduction by R. F. McRae (Toronto: University of Toronto Press; London: Routledge & Kegan Paul, 1973), vol. VIII, 926 (Bk. VI, X, 7).

enforced. I will argue that much of what the advocates of shared doctrines or values have in mind as candidates for enforcement falls outside the domain of morality within Mill's system, and so cannot possibly be enforced *as* morality. And since nothing *outside of* morality can be coerced within Mill's schema of the Art of Life, they are not candidates for enforcement within his philosophy.[32]

The Hart–Devlin debate was the starting point for these questions.[33] However, there has been a sea change in thinking since the 1960s, when Patrick Devlin could, in all seriousness, assert that reasonable people in an entire Western democratic society could share a set of moral doctrines and values, and that society was under threat of disintegration if it did not enforce a common moral code. Foremost in Devlin's mind was his argument that this required the criminalization, for example, of homosexuality and abortion, since both kinds of conduct violated, in his view, the shared Christian moral code of England. However, progress has overtaken those who seek to enforce their favored tastes upon others or to prohibit their disgusts in matters of sexual preference, since rights to freedom of sexual orientation are now constitutionally protected in Western democracies. These societies have progressed beyond Patrick Devlin's framework of society based upon Christian values to views of societies holding diverse and pluralistic doctrines in areas of religion, sexual preference, and lifestyle. Devlin's views were controversial and unconvincing to many even at that time. But this debate has been overtaken by the debates of the politics of difference and the politics of recognition, as well as the ascendancy of John Rawls's political liberalism, which all move in the same direction as Mill does in propounding diversity and pluralism. Discussions of shared views of the common good now tend to take place only in the context of the bonds of sub-groups within a state, such as cultural, ethnic, or religious groups.

John Rawls's framework of political liberalism has sharpened focus on the salient point that liberal political theory in the context of Western democratic societies must not only accommodate difference, but must also accept that difference is essentially ingrained into public democratic culture, and that, *contra* Devlin, it is unreasonable to expect it to be otherwise. This is what Rawls means by the claim that democratic societies are characterized by the fact of reasonable pluralism. The diversity and pluralism of

---

[32] I developed these ideas in depth in "John Stuart Mill and Virtue Ethics," delivered as a Keynote Lecture at the John Stuart Mill Bicentennial Conference, 1806–2006, University College London, April 5–7, 2008.

[33] Patrick Devlin, *The Enforcement of Morals* (London: Oxford University Press, 1965); H. L. A. Hart, *Law, Liberty and Morality* (Stanford: Stanford University Press, 1963).

reasonable moral and religious doctrines are "not a mere historical condition
that may soon pass away" but "a permanent feature of the public culture of
democracy."[34] This fact of reasonable pluralism, therefore, is not appropriately regarded as "an unfortunate condition of human life," but is rather to
be appreciated as "the inevitable outcome of free human reason." The result
is the understanding that the only way to maintain the illusion that there is
but one reasonable shared doctrine of morality or religion is to call on the
machinery of "oppressive use of state power."[35] Free human reason naturally
and inevitably results in diversity and individuality, and only oppression
and tyranny can suppress this spontaneous pluralism. According to Rawls, a
well-ordered society is one in which every citizen accepts the basic *political*
principles of justice. Mill agrees; in the *Logic* he sets down the stabilizing
features that bind a society together. Liberals Rawls and Mill agree that
these unifying features that bind society are shared political and democratic
principles and values, and not the matters of private morality that Devlin
invokes as binding factors. Mill says that the feelings of unity, allegiance,
and loyalty in modern democracies are attached to the principles of freedom
and political and social equality.

Devlin unselfconsciously proposes that of course the arbiters of moral
correctness (whom Mill would label the "moral police") are white Christian
heterosexual and homophobic men. Writing in the era a short time before
rights to sexual preference and orientation and women's rights to reproductive control over their own bodies were to be enshrined in constitutional
charters of rights, Devlin proposed that social stability mandated the treatment of homosexuality and abortion as crimes. He says that in England

the Christian institution of marriage has become the basis of family life and so part
of the structure of our society … a non-Christian is bound by it, not because it is
part of Christianity, but because, rightly or wrongly, it has been adopted by the
society in which he lives … if he wants to live in the house, he must accept it as built
in the way in which it is.[36]

According to Devlin, "a common morality is part of the bondage. The
bondage is part of the price of society; and mankind, which needs society,
must pay its price."[37] Devlin's arbitrator is the standard of the reasonable
man, who, he admits, "is not to be confused with the rational man," because
he does not usually arrive at his views by reasoning, but largely by feelings,
especially feelings of disgust or approval. He was well known, in Devlin's

[34] John Rawls, *Political Liberalism* (New York: Columbia University Press, 1993), 36.   [35] Ibid., 37.
[36] Devlin, *The Enforcement of Morals*, 9.   [37] Ibid., 10.

England, as the man in the street, or the "man on the Clapham omnibus."[38] It is the moral code of common sense, what every "right-minded" man would accept.

Devlin's argument that society's doctrine of morality should be enforced to ensure social cohesion and prevent disintegration has been refuted by the thriving reality of social diversity and pluralism of modern democracies. But it is worth some further scrutiny to illustrate just how resistant Mill's system is to the notion that morality should be enforced, when morality is conceived broadly so as to include matters like sexual preference, as Devlin maintains. Mill certainly does believe that rules of moral obligation should be enforced, and that breaches of moral obligations should be subject to sanctions and punishment. But Mill conceives of this domain of moral obligation much more narrowly than does Devlin. Indeed, it is one of Mill's missions to contain the zeal of those whom he labels "moralists by profession," who seek to expand the realm of morality to include many examples of what Mill would classify as matters of virtue or of individual freedom.

Morality, the subject that Mill examines in *Utilitarianism*, inhabits only an allotted part of the Art of Life. The principle of utility is the foundation of *all* of the many practical arts of human nature and society. The principle says that "the promotion of happiness is the ultimate principle of Teleology" (*CW* VIII, 951 [Bk. VI, XII, 7]). The principle of utility is the foundation of morality, but it is equally the grounding of the other areas of the Art of Life, as well as the numerous other practical moral arts that Mill explores in Book VI of the *Logic*. He says that there is a "body of doctrine, which is properly the Art of Life, in its three departments, Morality, Prudence or Policy, and Aesthetics; the Right, the Expedient, and the Beautiful or Noble, in human conduct and works" (*CW* VIII, 949 [Bk. VI, XII, 6]). The principle of utility is a principle of the good, and to interpret it as being a principle of right rather than as the principle that provides the foundation of morality is to court misunderstanding. Many questionable interpretations of Mill arise out of simple misunderstanding of the difference between Morality and Virtue, two separate compartments of the Art of Life. Viewed through the lens of the Art of Life, utilitarianism is most accurately depicted, in Mill's eyes, as a "theory of life on which this theory of morality is grounded" (*CW* X, 210 [II, 2]). This comment can certainly mystify unless it is understood in the light of his expectation that readers of *Utilitarianism* would draw the link to his examination of the Art of Life in the *Logic*.

---

[38] Ibid., 15.

In *Utilitarianism*, Mill explains how the sphere of Morality is to be marked off from the rest of the Art of Life and the other moral arts. He separates out the place of Morality within the Art of Life from "the remaining provinces of Expediency and Worthiness" (*CW* x, 247 [v, 15]). He says:

> We do not call anything wrong, unless we mean to imply that a person ought to be punished in some way or other for doing it ... This seems to be the real turning point of the distinction between morality and simple expediency. It is a part of the notion of Duty in every one of its forms, that a person may rightfully be compelled to fulfil it ... There are other things ... which we wish that people should do, which we like or admire them for doing, perhaps dislike or despise them for not doing, but yet admit that they are not bound to do it; it is not a case of moral obligation ... we say that it would be right to do so and so, or merely that it would be desirable or laudable, according as we would wish to see the person whom it concerns, compelled, or only persuaded and exhorted, to act in that manner. (*CW* x, 246 [v, 14])

This is a familiar quotation. It cordons off morality's legitimate domain from the territories of the other provinces of life. But the rules governing this demarcation are not always appreciated. Nor is it always understood that Mill seeks not only to define but also to set firm jurisdictional limits on morality.

In this light the liberty principle can be seen to function not simply to protect a sphere of liberty, although it certainly does that, but also to clarify the limits beyond which morality has no business intruding. Morality is not, in Mill's view, the overseer of the large swaths of human life that "moralists by profession" would like to see put under its authority. The domains of virtue and liberty are companion areas of the Art of Life, and actions within these domains have entitlements to be guided by their own principles, and to be free of the coercion that is legitimate only in the domain of moral obligation. They have their own ways of promoting happiness and well-being, and Mill maintains that overall human happiness is best promoted if actions in these domains are allowed to follow their own principles and are unfettered by coercion. Coercion outside of this sphere of morality acts to short-circuit self-development, and to undercut the spontaneity of individuality and the virtues. Since the right to self-development is a foundational right in Mill's system, such undercutting and short-circuiting are serious violations. Liberty and virtue are best promoted by encouragement rather than by force. Morality's authority is primarily to protect the most vital interests of people. It is a mistake to think that if virtue is a good thing, then attempting to coerce people to be more virtuous is justified or appropriate. If coercion is restricted to the narrow range of moral obligations, society will reap the benefits of its liberality, as far as Mill is concerned.

Demanding no more than this, society, in any tolerable circumstances, obtains much more; for the natural activity of human nature, shut out from all noxious directions, will expand itself in useful ones … there is an unlimited range of moral worth, up to the most exalted heroism, which should be fostered by every positive encouragement, though not converted into an obligation. (*CW* x, 339 [Part II, 14])

As well, Mill is very clear in his argument that it is not a vital human interest to be protected from feelings of offense or disgust, which Devlin takes to be standard reactions of the "man on the Clapham omnibus." Mill's liberty principle says that "the only purpose for which power can be rightfully exercised over any member of a civilized community, against his will, is to prevent harm to others" (*CW* XVIII, 223 [I, 9]). Mill's liberty principle is a principle of justice within his philosophy, protecting rights. Rights are socially guaranteed within his moral philosophy, and thus located in a protected zone. Harm to others is cashed out in terms of violation of vital interests of others, and not in terms of less weighty matters. Mill does not consider feelings of disgust or offense weighty, and so such feelings cannot be the basis for challenging a right to liberty. Mill dismisses offended feelings as insignificant in comparison with the importance of protecting core elements of identity and individuality.

There are many who consider as an injury to themselves any conduct which they have a distaste for, and resent it as an outrage to their feelings; as a religious bigot … has been known to retort that they disregard his feelings, by persisting in their abominable worship or creed. But there is no parity between the feeling of a person for his own opinion, and the feeling of another who is offended at his holding it. (*CW* XVIII, 283 [IV, 12])

He amplifies his concern about dangers to autonomy and individuality arising from the zealous public that "invests its own preferences with the character of moral laws … it is not difficult to show … that to extend the bounds of what may be called moral police, until it encroaches on the most unquestionably legitimate liberty of the individual, is one of the most universal of human propensities" (*CW* XVIII, 284 [IV, 13]). Few features are closer to the heart of human identity and individuality than religious faith or sexual orientation. In these areas, with the understanding that this expression of identity, "if it also affects others, [does so] only with their free, voluntary, and undeceived consent and participation" (*CW* XVIII, 225 [I, 12]), the liberty principle protects the freedom of sexual expression of gays and lesbians from homophobic bigotry. Mill's response is to protect that which is most worthy of protection and firmly suggest that feelings of offense or disgust should be addressed through reflective self-scrutiny as to the source of the afflictive attitudes of malice.

Mill's assessment of Auguste Comte and Jeremy Bentham as advocates of an overactive role for morality clarifies his own position. In *August Comte and Positivism* Mill pillories Comte for his moral zealotry. Mill complains that Comte is a "morality-intoxicated man" who wants to turn every practical question into a moral question (*CW* x, 336 [Part II, 9]). Comte shares the Calvinist mistake of believing that

whatever is not a duty is a sin. It does not perceive that between the region of duty and that of sin, there is an intermediate space, the region of positive worthiness. It is not good that persons should be bound, by other people's opinion, to do everything that they would deserve praise for doing. There is a standard of altruism to which all should be required to come up, and a degree beyond it which is not obligatory, but meritorious. It is incumbent on every one to restrain the pursuit of his personal objects within the limits consistent with the essential interests of others. What those limits are, it is the province of ethical science to determine; and to keep all individuals and aggregations of individuals within them, is the proper office of punishment and of moral blame. If in addition to fulfilling this obligation, persons make the good of others a direct object of disinterested exertions, postponing or sacrificing to it even innocent personal indulgences, they deserve gratitude and honour, and are fit objects of moral praise. So long as they are in no way compelled to this conduct by any external pressure, there cannot be too much of it; but a necessary condition is its spontaneity ... The object should be to stimulate services to humanity by their natural rewards; not to render the pursuit of our own good in any other manner impossible, by visiting it with the reproaches of other and of our own conscience. The proper office of those sanctions is to enforce upon every one, the conduct necessary to give all other persons their fair chance: conduct which chiefly consists in not doing them harm, and not impeding them in anything which without harming others does good to themselves ... Through this principle the domain of moral duty, in an improving society, is always widening. When what once was uncommon virtue becomes common virtue, it comes to be numbered among obligations, while a degree exceeding what has grown common, remains simply meritorious. (*CW* x, 337–8 [Part II, 12])

Mill's fellow utilitarian, Jeremy Bentham, Mill argues, also grants too much authority to morality. Bentham's

one-sidedness, belongs to him not as a utilitarian, but as a moralist by profession, and in common with almost all professed moralists, whether religious or philosophical: it is that of treating the *moral* view of actions and characters, which is unquestionably the first and most important mode of looking at them, as if it were the sole one: whereas it is only one of three, by all of which our sentiments towards the human being may be, ought to be, and without entirely crushing our own nature cannot but be, materially influenced. Every human action has three aspects: its *moral* aspect, or that of its *right* and *wrong*; its *aesthetic* aspect, or that of its *beauty*; its *sympathetic* aspect, or that of its *loveableness*. The first addresses itself to our reason and conscience; the second to our imagination; the third to our human fellow-feeling. According to the first, we approve or disapprove; according to the second, we admire or despise according to the third, we love, pity, or dislike. The morality of an action depends on its foreseeable consequences; its beauty, and its loveableness, or the reverse, depend on the qualities which it is evidence of … It is not possible for any sophistry to confound these three modes of viewing an action; but it is very possible to adhere to one of them exclusively, and lose sight of the rest. Sentimentality consists in setting the last two of the three above the first; the error of moralists in general, and of Bentham, is to sink the two latter entirely. This is pre-eminently the case with Bentham: he both wrote and felt as if the moral standard ought not only to be paramount (which it ought), but to be alone; as if it ought to be the sole master of all our actions, and even of all our sentiments. (*CW* x, 112–13)

The domain of morality is concerned with the arena of rules of duty or obligation. Mill defines moral duty in *Utilitarianism* in terms of moral rules whose violation calls for coercive moral sanctions, compulsion, and punishment. From this analysis it follows that not all acts that fail to maximize or even to promote the good are morally wrong. Many actions are outside of this domain of actions that do not maximize the good and yet are not morally wrong. So the range of moral duties in Mill's moral philosophy is narrower than is often maintained (by Devlin, for example). But those duties in Mill's system are quite stringent. As Alan Fuchs puts it, "when our moral obligations are satisfied, or when (as will usually be the case) they do not even apply to the question in hand, the other practices of the art of life such as the Expedient and the Noble may hold sway and directly lead us to the summum bonum of the greatest happiness."[39] Mill has a doctrine of Virtue that complements his theory of Morality. The governing principles of the domain of virtue make room for encouragement of meritorious and honorable behavior. Mill devotes many writings to exploring how the mental and moral virtues can be encouraged and cultivated in numerous public and private domains.[40] In adopting the stance that virtues are best cultivated by encouragement rather than coercion, he agrees with other virtue ethics traditions, including the Buddhist tradition, that regard virtuous attitudes like compassion and loving-kindness as natural aspects of human nature that are amenable to cultivation and training. But the governing principles of the domain of morality that appeal to the application of sanctions and coercion are inefficacious in the sphere of life of virtue and liberty. Mutual encouragement and engagement using persuasion and

---

[39] Alan Fuchs, "Mill's Theory of Morally Correct Action," in Henry West, ed., *The Blackwell Guide to Mill's Utilitarianism* (Oxford: Blackwell, 2005), 139–58.
[40] See Donner, "John Stuart Mill on Education and Democracy."

furnishing models for emulation are the permissible tools and means. Mill values interactive dialogue and exchanges on these matters. He says: "Human beings owe to each other help to distinguish the better from the worse, and encouragement to choose the former and avoid the latter. They should be forever stimulating each other to increased exercise of their higher faculties" (*CW* xviii, 277 [iv, 4]). While Mill's theory urges reciprocal engagement with others, the game rules for promoting virtue and self-development are firmly in place to avert infringing liberty-protecting boundaries. Autonomy and individuality are thus shielded from attempts by "moralists by profession" illicitly to enlarge the mandate and domain of morality to encroach upon the spheres of liberty and virtue in Mill's conception of the Art of Life.

CHAPTER 8

Mill and multiculturalism

Jeremy Waldron

I

Accommodating cultural diversity is not quite the same as religious toleration, and neither of them is the same as recognizing a principle of
individual liberty so far as ethics and lifestyle are concerned. But there are
important commonalities between them and, just as it would not be
surprising to find that someone who espoused a principle of liberty for
lifestyles would also espouse a regime of religious toleration, so we should
not be surprised to find a defender of individual liberty saying things that
could be adduced in support of a principle of cultural diversity.

This certainly seems to be the case with John Stuart Mill. There is a lot in
common between the concerns about religious toleration that John Locke
wrote about in the 1680s and the concerns about individuality that Mill
wrote about almost two centuries later in *On Liberty*: both thinkers emphasize the importance of sincerity in the life-structuring choices that people
make and both condemn the attempt to produce genuine faith or ethical
conviction by coercion as counterproductive. Nor is it hard to see continu-
ity between Mill's concerns in *On Liberty* and the concerns of those who
argue in the late twentieth and early twenty-first centuries for a diverse
society with a citizenry of disparate ethnic and national origins, a society in
which many cultures are embraced, in which people are respected for their
cultural identity, in which both the state and the members of its ethnic and
national majority (if there is one) go out of their way to tolerate and
accommodate practices that are quite different from their own. As far as I
know, Mill does not use the term "culture" in its modern sense, but some
version of the multiculturalism idea is present in his work. Whether it is a
matter of lifestyle, religion, or culture, one would expect Mill to be sympathetic to individual claims for tolerance and accommodation and hostile
to demands on the part of the majority that everyone should conform to the
socially dominant view. Mill's work celebrates diversity, and we are entitled

to think therefore that the spirit of *On Liberty* is as hospitable to cultural diversity as it is to diversity in religion and diversity in personal ethics.

Accordingly, when Mill writes in chapter III of *On Liberty* against the idea that one size fits all, when he writes against social majorities who "cannot comprehend why [their] ways should not be good enough for everybody" (*CW* XVIII, 261 [III, 2]), and when he urges people to choose their own path in life and allow others to choose theirs, we expect him to apply this to each individual's cultural predilections as well as to the personal "plan of life" (*CW* XVIII, 262 [III, 4]) that is the chapter's ostensible subject. We might hesitate to extend the argument if we thought Mill was urging each individual to invent an entirely original way of life for himself. Then adherence to a given culture would not be on a par with the pursuit of a novel lifestyle. But this is not what Mill believed: he said that "it would be absurd to pretend that people ought to live as if nothing whatever had been known in the world before they came into it" (*CW* XVIII, 262 [III, 3]).[1] The crucial thing is not the provenance of the lifestyle but the element of autonomous choice:[2] "it is the privilege and proper condition of a human being, arrived at the maturity of his faculties, to use and interpret experience in his own way. It is for him to find out what part of recorded experience is properly applicable to his own circumstances and character" (*CW* XVIII, 262 [III, 3]). In this spirit, an individual may end up choosing a way of life congenial to the majority, and, if it is genuine choice, Mill has no objection. But equally, he may choose to follow some other "part of recorded experience," for example the path laid out by a minority culture, and if he does, then this choice must be respected also.

We can put the same point using the language of authenticity. Mill espouses a sort of romantic ideal, in which each person is called upon to respond authentically to a sort of inner vocation.[3] He says that each individual life is like a tree,[4] "which requires to grow and develop itself on all sides, according to the tendency of the inward forces which make it a living thing" (*CW* XVIII, 263 [III, 4]). The doctrine of authenticity points two ways.[5] On the one hand, authenticity is a responsibility incumbent on

---

[1] See also the discussion of Mill and Rawls on this point in Will Kymlicka, *Liberalism, Community, and Culture* (Oxford: Clarendon Press, 1989), 177.

[2] Cf. Joseph Raz, *The Morality of Freedom* (Oxford: Clarendon Press, 1986), ch. 14.

[3] There is an excellent account of this in Nancy L. Rosenblum, *Another Liberalism: Romanticism and the Reconstruction of Liberal Thought* (Cambridge, MA: Harvard University Press, 1987).

[4] The arboreal metaphor is also used to characterize the position of his opponents: "Many persons, no doubt, sincerely think that human beings thus cramped and dwarfed, are as their Maker designed them to be; just as many have thought that trees are a much finer thing when clipped into pollards" (*CW* XVIII, 265 [III, 8]).

[5] See Charles Taylor, *The Ethics of Authenticity* (Cambridge, MA: Harvard University Press, 1991).

each person to live and grow in the way that is appropriate for him. On the other hand, all of us have a responsibility to recognize what is required for the authentic self-development of each person, not on the basis that "one size fits all," but paying actual attention to what is required for the life that each other person is trying to live. Sometimes that may require an exquisite attention to the details of an individual's idiosyncratic lifestyle. Other times, however, what it may mainly require is sensitivity to a type of lifestyle that is already well established. It all depends on what the individuals in question have chosen.

The case that Mill is committed as much to cultural diversity as to diversity of idiosyncratic individual lifestyles can also be supported on social grounds as well as on grounds of the recognition and respect due to particular individuals. What Mill dreads in a society is deadening uniformity. And what he celebrates is the process by which social life becomes "rich, diversified, and animating" (*CW* xviii, 266 [iii, 9]). A stationary society is the product of homogeneity and conformism. Progress depends on the sort of "remarkable diversity of character and culture" that he thought had characterized Europe up to his time:

Individuals, classes, nations, have been extremely unlike one another: they have struck out a great variety of paths, each leading to something valuable; and although at every period those who travelled in different paths have been intolerant of one another, and each would have thought it an excellent thing if all the rest could have been compelled to travel his road, their attempts to thwart each other's development have rarely had any permanent success, and each has in time endured to receive the good which the others have offered. (*CW* xviii, 274 [iii, 18])

The progress Mill celebrates stems not just from the interaction of diverse individuals, but also from what he refers to in chapter ii of *On Liberty* as "the rough process of a struggle between combatants fighting under hostile banners" (*CW* xviii, 254 [ii, 36]). The parties may be ideologies or religious sects or they may be diverse cultures.[6] What is important is that they be represented in active intellectual engagement. And, he adds, it is *minority* beliefs which are particularly important in this process, for as minorities they represent, for the time being, "the neglected interests, the side of human well-being which is in danger of obtaining less than its share" (*CW* xviii, 254 [ii, 36]) in the rough struggle of ideas.

With argument of this kind, then, it is not difficult to create the impression that Mill – the great apostle of individuality – would also be a

---

[6] The example Mill uses is the contribution of the secular side of Greek and Roman cultures to the deficiencies in Christian ethics (*CW* xviii, 255 [ii, 37]).

friend to multiculturalism, to cultural diversity, to cultural accommodations, and to the ethics and politics of cultural identity.

On the other hand, there are strands in Mill's social and political thought
that are a good deal less hospitable to these ideals; there are concerns in his
thinking about social, cultural, and individual life that might generate some
misgivings about modern identity politics as a mode of cultural engagement
in a diverse society. I am going to devote the rest of this chapter to an
exploration of these misgivings – not because I want to show that Mill was
or would have been hostile to multiculturalism, but because I think Mill's
work has important things to say about the variety of ways in which cultural
allegiances are practiced and experienced by individuals. Some modes of
cultural allegiance may have exactly the effects that Mill is looking for in a
society that is "rich, diversified, and animating" (CW xviii, 266 [iii, 9]). But
there may be other ways of holding and parading one's cultural identity that
make as much of a contribution to the deadening of society as the hegemony of a single view.

II

One danger signal, one ground for concern about Mill's relation to multiculturalism, stems from what he says elsewhere in his political philosophy
about multinational societies. It is not very promising. In the chapter of his
book *Considerations on Representative Government*[7] devoted to nationality,
Mill ventures the startling opinion that "there is a *prima facie* case for
uniting all the members of [a given] nationality under the same government, and a government to themselves apart" (CW xix, 547 [xvi, 2]), and
that "it is in general a necessary condition of free institutions that the
boundaries of governments should coincide in the main with those of
nationalities" (CW xix, 548 [xvi, 4]). Unless there is a sharp distinction
between culture and nationality, this is not a promising foundation for
celebrating the idea of a multicultural society.

Fortunately, there is – at least at the beginning of Mill's discussion – a
distinction between culture and nationality. "Nationality" Mill defines as
the uniting of a portion of mankind "by common sympathies which do not
exist between them and any others – which make them co-operate with each

---

[7] John Stuart Mill, *Considerations on Representative Government* (1861), in *The Collected Works of John
Stuart Mill*, vol. xix: *Essays on Politics and Society*, Part II, ed. John M. Robson, introduction by
Alexander Brady (Toronto: University of Toronto Press; London: Routledge & Kegan Paul, 1977),
371–577.

other more willingly than with other people, desire to be under the same government, and desire that it should be government by themselves, or a portion of themselves, exclusively" (*CW* XIX, 546 [XVI, 1]). Nationality, in this sense, is a very thin concept. The sentiments that define it may in a particular case be associated with culture and ethnicity or they may be associated with something else – "identity of race and descent," "community of language," "community of religion," geography, and most of all the possession of a common history, "collective pride and humiliation, pleasure and regret, connected with the same incidents in the past" (*CW* XIX, 546 [XVI, 1]). We might imagine, then, a society which *we* would call multicultural but which Mill would call mononational, because all the inhabitants (even those from different cultural backgrounds) are sufficiently sympathetic to one another to desire to be together in one single society. Maybe francophone Quebecois and Anglo-Canadians committed to living in modern Quebec are in this situation: they trust one another maybe more than they trust people committed to living in Ontario, even though they belong to somewhat different linguistic and cultural communities. Indeed, if we stick with the very thin definition he begins with, then, as Mill himself observes, the "prima facie" position mentioned above says no more than that "the question of government ought to be decided by the governed" (*CW* XIX, 547 [XVI, 2]). It's a matter of self-determination. Anglophone and francophone inhabitants of Quebec should decide whether they want to form a political community with one another, and if they have a settled disposition to do so, because they trust and like one another, then that is all that is needed, on Mill's thin account, to constitute them as a single nationality.

However, not all the arguments Mill adduces for this mononational position are predicated on such a thin definition of nationality. Some have to do with the issue of language differences among the components of a multinational society.[8] Mill thinks that language differences (which I guess we should group with cultural differences) make it very hard to sustain the common sympathies and common identity definitive of democracy:[9]

Especially if they read and speak different languages, the united public opinion necessary to the working of representative government can not exist. The influences which form opinions and decide political acts are different in the different

---

[8] There is a good discussion in Will Kymlicka, *Multicultural Citizenship: A Liberal Theory of Minority Rights* (Oxford: Clarendon Press, 1995), ch. 4.
[9] For an excellent account of Mill's views on democracy, see Nadia Urbinati, *Mill on Democracy: From the Athenian Polis to Representative Government* (Chicago: University of Chicago Press, 2002).

sections of the country ... The same books, newspapers, pamphlets, speeches, do not reach them. One section does not know what opinions or what instigations are circulating in another. (*CW* XIX, 547 [XVI, 2])

If a multicultural society is multilingual to any considerable extent – with many people talking and reading primarily in different languages – then Mill is pessimistic about the prospects for their political union.

Can a multiculturalist take any comfort from the fact that Mill said that the case "for uniting all the members of [a given] nationality under the same government, and a government to themselves apart" (*CW* XIX, 547 [XVI, 2]) is just a *prima facie* case? Mill made much of this, for he said that "several considerations are liable to conflict in practice" with the general principle of a one-nation state (*CW* XIX, 548 [XVI, 4]). One such consideration is that disparate national populations may be so intermingled that "it is not practicable for them to be under separate governments," and they have no choice "but to make a virtue of necessity, and reconcile themselves to living together under equal rights and laws" (*CW* XIX, 549 [XVI, 4]).

But Mill also implies that there is a moral case to be made for a multi-national state in these circumstances, a case based on ideas that I suspect will not be welcome to defenders of a multicultural polity:

Experience proves that it is possible for one nationality to merge and be absorbed in another; and when it was originally an inferior and more backward portion of the human race, the absorption is greatly to its advantage. Nobody can suppose that it is not more beneficial to a Breton, or a Basque of French Navarre, to be brought into the current of the ideas and feelings of a highly civilized and cultivated people – to be a member of the French nationality, admitted on equal terms to all the privileges of French citizenship, sharing the advantages of French protection, and the dignity and prestige of French power – than to sulk on his own rocks, the half-savage relic of past times, revolving in his own little mental orbit, without partici-pation or interest in the general movement of the world. (*CW* XIX, 549 [XVI, 4])

In other words, Mill does not imagine a multinational society, at its best, as a showcase for clearly delineated diversity. He imagines that a backward people will benefit from something like assimilation (*CW* XIX, 550 [XVI, 9]). Or perhaps there will be a gradual blending and mixture of culture and ideas.

Whatever really tends to the admixture of nationalities, and the blending of their attributes and peculiarities in a common union, is a benefit to the human race ... The united people, like a crossed breed of animals (but in a still greater degree, because the influences in operation are moral as well as physical), inherits the special aptitudes and excellences of all its progenitors, protected by the admixture from being exaggerated into the neighbouring vices. (*CW* XIX, 549–50 [XVI, 6])

This need not involve the actual disappearance of the minority group in the blended whole, but it will be close. It is a process that will work "not by extinguishing types, of which … sufficient examples are sure to remain, but by softening their extreme forms, and filling up the intervals between them" (*CW* XIX, 549 [XVI, 5]).

That, for Mill is the best case. That it really does not answer to the modern ideal of a diverse multicultural society is apparent from Mill's description of one of the ways it can be frustrated. If the distinct national and ethnic groups are equal in numbers and/or power, then each is likely to resist assimilation:

each cultivates with party obstinacy its distinctive peculiarities; obsolete customs, and even declining languages, are revived, to deepen the separation; each deems itself tyrannized over if any authority is exercised within itself by functionaries of a rival race; and whatever is given to one of the conflicting nationalities is considered to be taken from all the rest. (*CW* XIX, 551 [XVI, 10])

In this case, Mill's pessimistic view is that all the original disadvantages of a multinational polity come back into view.

III

"Each cultivates with party obstinacy its distinctive peculiarities; obsolete customs, and even declining languages, are revived, to deepen the separation" (*CW* XIX, 551 [XVI, 10]) – this, for Mill, is the worst sort of way in which different nations, cultures, or ethnicities might coexist. But it is not entirely an inaccurate way of characterizing the modern politics of cultural identity, though it is certainly an unkind way of characterizing it. In this section and the next, I want to consider how we should evaluate some aspects of the identity politics endemic to modern multicultural societies in light of Mill's concerns.

In *On Liberty*, Mill celebrates diversity. But it is not just any sort of diversity. He looks forward to a situation in which rival ethics, cultures, and creeds interact aggressively with one another, taking risks in open confrontation and debate, each putting forward in interaction with others the best defense it can make of its distinctive beliefs and definitive customs. But he views with horror the prospect that sects might separate themselves and their beliefs so much from any intellectual challenge that they never engage with one another, never take the risk of confronting one another's ideas.

We know this mainly from the criticisms he makes of the spirit in which socially dominant beliefs – the views of the majority – tend to be held. They are commonly held in ways that establish dissent as unthinkable, and consequently those who hold them never have the opportunity of defending them to themselves or others. As a result, the holders of the dominant opinion lose touch with the true grounds on which it used to be held. The majority view is held as "an hereditary creed ... received passively, not actively" (*CW* xviii, 248 [ii, 27]). Each person "assents undoubtingly" to the dominant position, though he has no idea of its grounds "and could not make a tenable defence of it against the most superficial objections" (*CW* xviii, 244 [ii, 22]). In these circumstances, says Mill, "there is a progressive tendency to forget all of the belief except the formularies" (*CW* xviii, 248 [ii, 27]).

> The creed remains as it were outside the mind, encrusting and petrifying it against all other influences ... manifesting its power by not suffering any fresh and living conviction to get in, but itself doing nothing for the mind or heart, except standing sentinel over them to keep them vacant. (*CW* xviii, 248 [ii, 27])

Even if the opinion is true, Mill concludes, "truth, thus held, is but one superstition the more, accidentally clinging to the words which enunciate a truth" (*CW* xviii, 244 [ii, 22]).

Mill makes this case with regard to the dominant views of the majority. And no doubt the complacency that comes with dominance enhances the probability that this sort of stance will be taken. Still, there is no reason to suppose that he is talking about a vice peculiar to majoritarian positions. Though Mill says that minority views are much more often put to their mettle by having to defend themselves, it is easy to imagine that in an atmosphere of general solicitude for their survival, they too may become as insulated from confrontation and from genuine intellectual engagement as a majority position. On this scenario, each separate sect becomes ossified in the way Mill feared. Each becomes a merely "hereditary creed," and in each case there is a tendency among its adherents to "forget all of the belief except the formularies" (*CW* xviii, 248 [ii, 27]). In each case, those who hold the view hold it as a hollow form of words; in each case, "instead of a vivid conception and a living belief, there remain only a few phrases retained by rote" (*CW* xviii, 247 [ii, 26]).

The danger is not just theoretical. In modern diverse multicultural societies, it is often thought to be an offense to a cultural community to ask hard questions about its customs, to challenge them, or confront them with alternatives in a way that requires them to defend themselves. It is thought that since, in confrontations like these, the minority view will necessarily lose, those who care for a minority culture must protect it from this sort of interaction, insulate it from any demand that it give an account of itself as one way of doing things among others, and define a place for it in society and politics that does not constantly put it on the defensive in this way.

To a large extent, the politics of cultural identity provides such insulation.[10] When an individual "identifies" with a culture, he presents its constitutive norms and beliefs and the way of life that the culture defines as part of his identity, part of who he is. With this identification, any challenge to the culture is a challenge *to him*, and the respect that is demanded for his identity is equated with respect for the culture itself. To put it to its mettle, to insist that it must give a proper defense of itself or give way, is tantamount to an assault *on him* or to a demand that *he* give an account of *his* right to exist (as the person he is). Traditional liberalism has always distinguished between the inviolability of persons and the vulnerability of their beliefs; persons are inviolable against attack, but beliefs may always be argued with, and objected to, and demolished if they cannot support themselves in intellectual engagement. To be sure, an individual is inviolable in holding his beliefs: *he* may not be attacked for the sake of attacking a belief of his thought to be false or pernicious. But the belief itself is fair game for attack. Unfortunately the politics of identity tends to blur these distinctions and extend the protection that is usually given to individuals to the beliefs with which they identify, so that not just the holding of the beliefs, but the beliefs themselves, come under the umbrella of inviolability.

Mill himself was not familiar with a politics of the kind that I have described, though he did devote some discussion at the end of chapter II of *On Liberty* to the "morality of public discussion," commenting on the demand by many defenders of the status quo that the tone of any attack on received beliefs should be moderate. He noted that "unmeasured vituperation" tends to be employed more on the side of the prevailing opinion than on the side of dissident minority beliefs, and he insisted that it was this intemperance that most needed restraint (*CW* XVIII, 259 [II, 44]). However, he did also observe that there is a sense in which any attack on anyone's views is likely to be perceived as offensive to the person if the view is put under real pressure:

If the test be offence to those whose opinion is attacked, I think experience testifies that this offence is given whenever the attack is telling and powerful, and that every

[10] I have developed this argument at length in Jeremy Waldron, "Cultural Identity and Civic Responsibility," in Will Kymlicka and Wayne Norman, eds., *Citizenship in Diverse Societies* (Oxford: Oxford University Press, 2000), 155–74.

opponent who pushes them hard, and whom they find it difficult to answer, appears to them, if he shows any strong feeling on the subject, an intemperate opponent. (*CW* xviii, 258 [ii, 44])

In general, Mill is suspicious of any *per se* connection between an attack on opinion and an offense to its holder. The key is to avoid "malignity, bigotry or intolerance of feeling" (*CW* xviii, 259 [ii, 44]) on the one hand, but also lack of candor and intellectual evasion on the other. One wants people to respect one another, but not to commit themselves so fanatically to the avoidance of offense that nothing ever gets discussed, nothing ever gets considered.

If we get ourselves into a position where people tiptoe around each other's identities and sensitivities, then we are heading for social and intellectual stagnation.

Where there is a tacit convention that principles are not to be disputed ... we cannot hope to find that generally high scale of mental activity which has made some periods of history so remarkable. Never when controversy avoided the subjects which are large and important enough to kindle enthusiasm, was the mind of a people stirred up from its foundations, and the impulse given which raised even persons of the most ordinary intellect to something of the dignity of thinking beings. (*CW* xviii, 243 [ii, 20])

Once again, the crucial thing is to see how the very concerns that Mill applies to criticize the cramped mental atmosphere of society's domination by a single majority view apply also to a critique of a society dominated by the ultra-sensitive politics of identity. For there, too, as much as in the cowed majoritarian society, most people "dare not follow out any bold, vigorous, independent train of thought, lest it should land them in something which would admit of being considered irreligious or immoral" (*CW* xviii, 242 [ii, 20]). The only difference is that the criteria of being "irreligious or immoral" (or culturally inauthentic) are given now by an array of disparate cultural groups and by an overarching ethos intended to deflect or dissuade us from any genuine engagement between them.

I think it is important, finally, to tie these concerns back to the prospects for a multinational society that Mill considered in his book on *Representative Government*. As we saw, he believed the only chance for success in a multinational polity involved a willingness on the part of various national cultures to engage with one another, even at the risk of losing their distinctive identity, because the alternative was either mutual antipathy and incomprehension or a retreat on the part of one or both of the protagonists to the role of "sulk[ing] on his own rocks" (*CW* xix, 549 [xvi, 5]). In other words, as so often in *On Liberty*, Mill's general characterization of the ethics of intellectual engagement has an important political dimension, associated with what he saw as the exigencies of both civil peace and social progress.

I V

There is another point associated with the politics of cultural identity that should also arouse concern from the perspective of the arguments in *On Liberty*. This has to do with the mode in which cultural beliefs and practices are espoused by those who identify with them. It has to do with the ethics of personal belief.

The position Mill defends is one in which those who are convinced of a given view or convinced that a given practice is right or good should be prepared not only to live by it but to defend it, whenever it comes under attack. Their defense of it should not be *self*-defense (not a defense of their own identity), but a clear statement of the reasons that support the belief or practice, and a rebuttal (if rebuttal is possible) to any objections put forward against it. But in the politics of cultural identity, this is not how views are held or practices adopted. They are not adopted for the reasons that purport to make sense of them but because these are the beliefs and practices associated with one's culture or one's way of life. One does not say, "I adopt this practice or hold to this belief, for this or that reason, which I am now prepared to argue for." Instead one says, "I adopt this practice or hold to this belief, because this is the practice and belief of my culture, the customary heritage of my people."[11]

Now it is well known that Mill reserved great scorn for those who held to a practice or belief simply because it was customary. "He who does anything because it is the custom, makes no choice" (*CW* xviii, 262 [iii, 3]). Letting "the world, or his own portion of it, choose his plan of life for him, [he] has no need of any other faculty than the ape-like one of imitation" (*CW* xviii, 262 [iii, 4]). Once again his most scathing comments are reserved for those who conform in this mode to a dominant majority view. But there is every reason to apply the comments also to those who let their culture (their own little portion of the world) choose their practices and their beliefs for them. So it would be a mistake, for example, to read the following famous passage from *On Liberty* as though it applied only to the conventionalities of bourgeois life:

[11] See ibid., 168–71.

Not only in what concerns others, but in what concerns only themselves, the individual, or the family, do not ask themselves – what do I prefer? or, what would suit my character and disposition? or, what would allow the best and highest in me to have fair play, and enable it to grow and thrive? They ask themselves, what is suitable to my position? what is usually done by persons of my station and pecuniary circumstances? or (worse still) what is usually done by persons of a station and circumstances superior to mine? I do not mean that they choose what is customary, in preference to what suits their own inclination. It does not occur to them to have any inclination, except for what is customary. Thus the mind itself is bowed to the yoke: even in what people do for pleasure, conformity is the first thing thought of; they live in crowds. (CW xviii, 264–5 [iii, 6])

The critique is quite general. It expresses concern about anyone who fails honestly and candidly to consider the reasons for the beliefs and practices they adopt – either the social reasons that make those beliefs and practices right and sensible for anyone to adopt or the self-regarding reasons that make the beliefs and practices particularly appropriate for them. Consideration and choice – that is what is necessary, not customary choice, not "lik[ing] in crowds."

I suppose a defender of identity politics could respond by insisting on the voluntaristic aspect of modern cultural identity. One does not simply follow custom; one *chooses* to identify oneself with the customs of a particular culture, because one likes the idea of this culture's being one's own. But it is an odd idea of choice, separated as it is from the sort of reasoned consid- erations to which (on Mill's account) choice properly responds. My point here turns partly upon the way we look at culture. For the most part, a culture is not in the first instance an individual lifestyle. It is something social and it presents itself in the first instance as a repository of social wisdom. A given culture is the heritage of a particular people's attempts to come to terms with serious problems of social life. It comprises a particular way of dealing with issues like the relations between the sexes, the rearing of children, the organization of an economy, the transmission of knowledge, the punishment of offenses, and in general the vicissitudes that affect all the stages of human life and relationships from conception to the disposition of corpses, and from the deepest love to the most vengeful antipathies. So when we refer to a culture, we are referring not just to a sort of individual hobby, or to a set of dances, costumes, recipes, and incantations that one might indulge in as a recreation, but to a distinct set of practices and beliefs that have been settled upon as solutions to the serious problems of human life in society. Considering the choice of a culture, then, ought to be a way of engaging with the customs in question that brings to the fore the social reasons that may be adduced to support them on their merits.

Now, some of what Mill says indicates a strong antipathy to the very idea of custom: "The progressive principle … is antagonistic to the sway of Custom" (*CW* XVIII, 272 [III, 17]). But in much of *On Liberty*, his view is more nuanced. Though "the despotism of custom is everywhere the standing hindrance to human advancement," still we need to remember that

the spirit of improvement is not always a spirit of liberty, for it may aim at forcing improvements on an unwilling people; and the spirit of liberty, in so far as it resists such attempts, may ally itself locally and temporarily with the opponents of improvement; but the only unfailing and permanent source of improvement is liberty, since by it there are as many possible independent centres of improvement as there are individuals. (*CW* XVIII, 272 [III, 17])

For Mill, in the end, the celebration of consideration and choice is partly a matter of determining what is fit to be a custom or "to be converted into customs" (*CW* XVIII, 269 [III, 14]). Custom is not self-justifying: it must struggle with alternatives, including both other customary and non-customary alternatives, each defended "with equal talent and energy," so that truth has a chance to emerge either through direct intellectual debate or "by the rough process of a struggle between combatants fighting under hostile banners" (*CW* XVIII, 254 [II, 36]). But this cannot happen if people adopt their cultural positions essentially in the mode of individual posture, rather than political argument, or if people adopt some belief or practice not because they think it right – an opinion they would be willing to defend or be argued out of – but because they like the look of it or like the look of themselves arrayed in its appurtenances.

Even if we were to take seriously the idea that a social culture could be understood as an individual identity, there would be the further question of whether the sort of "choice" typical of cultural politics responds appropriately to the considerations at stake in this sort of self-defining decision. I said at the beginning of this chapter that Mill does not dismiss out of hand the idea that an individual can draw his identity or lifestyle authentically from what is posited by an existing culture. "It would be absurd to pretend that people ought to live as if nothing whatever had been known in the world before they came into it." Still, Mill added, each person has an individual responsibility to scrutinize the customs that seem attractive to him and to "find out what part of recorded experience is properly applicable to his own circumstances and character" (*CW* XVIII, 262 [III, 3]). We should not think of the choice of individual ethics and lifestyles as a matter of buying an identity off the shelf, as it were, in a cultural supermarket: "There is no reason that all human existences should be constructed on some one, or some small number of patterns" (*CW* XVIII, 270 [III, 14]).

The traditions and customs of other people are, to a certain extent, evidence of what their experience has taught them … but, in the first place, their experience may be too narrow; or they may not have interpreted it rightly. Secondly, their interpretation of experience may be correct but unsuitable to him. Customs are made for customary circumstances, and customary characters: and his circumstances or his character may be uncustomary. Thirdly, though the customs be both good as customs, and suitable to him, yet to conform to custom, merely as custom, does not educate or develop in him any of the qualities which are the distinctive endowment of a human being. (*CW* xviii, 262 [iii, 3])

Differences among individuals, differences in the conditions of their development and fulfillment, outstrip what any number of ready-made cultural alternatives can offer.

v

In recent discussions of multiculturalism, some writers have drawn our attention to the way in which cultures can be oppressive to their own internal minorities, to women, or to dissidents and those whose lifestyle deviates from the cultural norm. After all, when we talk about a particular culture, we are talking (within that culture) of people who are as different from one another as you and I are. Different members of the culture will have different levels of allegiance or ambivalence in respect of the cultural values that are, on a simple-minded view, supposed to constitute their identity. Some will have been hurt by their culture, some will have been exalted by it; some will be campaigning for change within the culture or reaching out to other cultures. A culture's religious customs may belie the presence of dissident sects or converts to outside religions; a culture's family norms may be oppressive to women; its sexual mores may be unfair to or violent toward homosexual members of the culture; and so on. As Leslie Green has pointed out, "without respect for internal minorities, a liberal society risks becoming a mosaic of tyrannies; colourful, perhaps, but hardly free."[12]

These points have been made most forcefully with regard to the position of women. Traditional cultures often subordinate women and control their lives and activities very closely. In a powerful body of work, the late Susan Moller Okin argued that

the sphere of personal, sexual, and reproductive life provides a central focus of most cultures … Religious or cultural groups are often particularly concerned with

---

[12] Leslie Green, "Internal Minorities and Their Rights," in Will Kymlicka, ed., *The Rights of Minority Cultures* (Oxford: Oxford University Press, 1995), 270.

"personal law" – the laws of marriage, divorce, child custody, division and control of family property, and inheritance. As a rule, then, the defense of "cultural practices" is likely to have much greater impact on the lives of women and girls than those of men and boys, since far more of women's time and energy goes into preserving and maintaining the personal, familial, and reproductive side of life. Obviously culture is not only about domestic arrangements, but they do provide a major focus of most contemporary cultures. Home is, after all, where much of culture is practiced, preserved, and transmitted to the young. In turn, the distribution of responsibilities and power at home has a major impact on who can participate in and influence the more public parts of the cultural life, where rules and regulations about both public and private life are made.[13]

Accordingly, Okin argues that when cultural diversity is being pursued as a policy, "special care must be taken to look at within-group inequalities … especially … inequalities between the sexes, since they are likely to be less public, and less easily discernible."[14]

One would expect John Stuart Mill to be particularly alert to this issue. If there is any support in his work for cultural diversity, it is as an aspect of *individual* liberty, and he would be uncomfortable about any application of his theory which permitted oppression in the name of a tolerated culture, sect, or creed. If someone is pleading for the liberty to live a style of life incompatible with the customs and prejudices of "his" culture, one would expect Mill to be as favorable to that individual dissident as he is to his equivalent rebelling against the hegemony of majority faith or majority custom. Support for dissidents and internal minorities against their culture is thus not an exception to Mill's general support for cultural and ethical diversity; it is a direct application of it.

There might be a question, I suppose, of whether in this situation Mill's position would be affected by a qualification he *does* impose – namely, that the principle of individual liberty is not applicable to those "backward states of society in which the race itself may be considered as in its nonage" (*CW* XVIII, 224 [1, 10]). I think, though, that this is better read as an exception to the anti-paternalistic aspect of Mill's principle, rather than as a license of "backward" cultural communities to exercise unchecked repression over their own members. It may not be particularly palatable for us to read Mill as arguing in favor of something like imperialism – "Despotism is a legitimate mode of government in dealing with barbarians, provided the

---

[13] Susan Moller Okin, "Is Multiculturalism Bad for Women?," at http://www.bostonreview.net/ BR22.5/okin.html. Okin's argument is also available in book form: *Is Multiculturalism Bad for Women?* (Princeton: Princeton University Press, 1999).
[14] Ibid.

end be their improvement, and the means justified by actually effecting that end" (*CW* XVIII, 224 [I, 10]) – but that is how I think this qualification should be understood.

The other exception he admits in this passage, however, is not so easily disposed of. Mill says that his doctrine is "meant to apply only to human beings in the maturity of their faculties" (*CW* XVIII, 224 [I, 10]), not to children or young persons below the age of majority. A weak interpretation of this proviso means that parents and the state can act "paternalistically" toward children. A stronger interpretation would mean, however, that children are fair game for indoctrination at the hands of their parents or their parents' culture until they come of age. There is some evidence that this is what Mill meant: in chapter IV of *On Liberty* he said that society has absolute rights over a person all through his childhood. "The existing generation is master both of the training and the entire circumstances of the generation to come" (*CW* XVIII, 282 [IV, 11]); if they emerge as adults acting in ways that society judges irrational, society has only itself to blame. Yet he also conceives of parents' rights and duties in this regard in terms of an ideal standard of rational education, rather than just indoctrination in the local mores (*CW* XVIII, 301–4 [v, 12–14]). The issue remains an important one for a multicultural society;[15] it is an issue on which Mill's arguments throw considerable light but on which his own final position is not altogether clear.

Certainly, if someone uses his ascendancy in a particular cultural community to harm others, there is no doubt that *On Liberty* provides a powerful argument for intervention. Indeed, Mill would assert that the clarity of the case he makes for liberty helps us understand (in a way that people did not previously understand) why intervention is justifiable in cases like these: "owing to the absence of any recognized general principles, liberty is often granted where it should be withheld, as well as withheld where it should be granted" (*CW* XVIII, 301 [v, 12]). Sometimes the celebration of cultural diversity is associated with a demand for cultural accommodation, in the sense of providing exceptions of one sort or another to otherwise generally applicable provisions of the criminal law. Where the aim of such provisions is simply to uphold public order or promote various diffuse public goods, a case can perhaps be made for cultural accommodations. But to the extent that the aim of the criminal law is to prevent harm to assignable individuals, there is no case that can be made – at least on the

---

[15] See *Wisconsin* v. *Yoder* 406 U.S. 205 (1972). See also Stephen Macedo, *Diversity and Distrust: Civic Education in a Multicultural Democracy* (Cambridge, MA: Harvard University Press, 2000).

principles defended in *On Liberty* – for exempting anybody from its requirements simply on the ground that inflicting these harms is regarded as
permissible or reasonable in their culture.[16]

Something similar could be said about the specific feminist concerns
about multiculturalism voiced by Susan Moller Okin.[17] If someone uses his
cultural freedom or the support that a multicultural society gives to his
authority in some minority community to oppress women, there are plenty
of resources in Mill's account to oppose this: "The State, while it respects
the liberty of each in what specially regards himself, is bound to maintain a
vigilant control over his exercise of any power which it allows him to possess
over others." Mill observes that this particularly affects what he calls "the
almost despotic power of husbands over wives" (*CW* XVIII, 301 [v, 12]), and
it would equally affect the sort of cultural oppression of women that we have
been talking about.

But what if people *choose* to identify with such a culture? Or what if they
have a real option of exit and fail to exercise it? Do we not have to say that
society should tolerate any abuse or oppression people have chosen to
subject themselves to? I am not so sure. Even in the case of cultures with
which people voluntarily identify, Mill's toleration would have its limits. An
argument for intervention in these cases might proceed by analogy with his
remarks at the end of the book to the effect that the principle of liberty does
not permit an individual to sell himself into slavery.[18]

By selling himself for a slave, he abdicates his liberty; he forgoes any future use of it,
beyond that single act. He therefore defeats, in his own case, the very purpose
which is the justification of allowing him to dispose of himself … The principle of
freedom cannot require that he should be free not to be free. (*CW* XVIII, 299–300
[v, 11])

On the other hand, we must be careful not to use this doctrine of non-
self-enslavement too enthusiastically to license intervention under *On
Liberty*'s banner in any or all cases in which we think a culture is oppressive.
Mill himself was wary of what we might call humanitarian intervention on
libertarian grounds. The case that elicited his caution was the case of
Mormon polygamy. The Mormons, he notes, were openly persecuted in
the eastern United States. And even after they were "chased into a solitary

[16] See also Jeremy Waldron, "One Law for All: The Logic of Cultural Accommodation," *Washington and Lee Law Review*, 59 (2002), 29–30.
[17] See the extracts from "Is Multiculturalism Bad for Women?" quoted above.
[18] For a discussion of Mill's complex and perhaps inconsistent view on this subject, see C. L. Ten, *Mill on Liberty* (Oxford: Clarendon Press, 1980), 117–23.

recess in the midst of a desert," many have proclaimed a right "to send an expedition against them, and compel them by force to conform to the opinions of other people" on the issue of polygamy (*CW* xviii, 290 [iv, 21]). Now Mill accepted that polygamy was not protected by the principle of liberty:

No one has a deeper disapprobation than I have of this Mormon institution … far from being in any way countenanced by the principle of liberty, it is a direct infraction of that principle, being a mere riveting of the chains of one half of the community, and an emancipation of the other from reciprocity of obligation towards them. (*CW* xviii, 290 [iv, 21])

But he was not in favor of intervention, at least so long as no request for intervention came from the victims of polygamy.

So long as the sufferers by the bad law do not invoke assistance from other communities, I cannot admit that persons entirely unconnected with them ought to step in and require that a condition of things with which all who are directly interested appear to be satisfied, should be put an end to because it is a scandal to persons some thousands of miles distant, who have no part or concern in it. Let them send missionaries, if they please, to preach against it. (*CW* xviii, 291 [iv, 21])

Part of what is involved here is the element of distance. Mill's remarks on the Mormons have the flavor almost of an argument from sovereignty, rather than liberty.[19] Given that the polygamists

have left the countries to which their doctrines were unacceptable, and established themselves in a remote corner of the earth … it is difficult to see on what principles but those of tyranny they can be prevented from living there under what laws they please, provided they commit no aggression on other nations, and allow perfect freedom of departure to those who are dissatisfied with their ways. (*CW* xviii, 290–1 [iv, 21])

So it is not clear how this (ambivalent) tolerance would transfer into a crowded multicultural society where similar (and similarly oppressive) customs might present themselves. Maybe we would be entitled to repress even voluntary polygamy in our midst, though we cannot do so at a distance.

Even so, Mill's comments on polygamy should give pause to those who claim that intervention is in principle acceptable when either the practice is (like slavery) too oppressive to be consented to or there is some other reason to doubt the reality of voluntary consent. Mill said of the Mormon wives:

---

[19] See also the discussion of Mill's hesitancy about interventionism in other circumstances, in Michael Walzer, "Mill's 'A Few Words on Non-Intervention' – A Commentary," in Nadia Urbinati and Alex Zakaras, eds., *J. S. Mill's Political Thought: A Bicentennial Reassessment* (Cambridge: Cambridge University Press, 2007), 347–56.

This relation is as much voluntary on the part of the women concerned in it, and who may be deemed the sufferers by it, as is the case with any other form of the marriage institution; and however surprising this fact may appear, it has its explanation in the common ideas and customs of the world, which teaching women to think marriage the one thing needful, make it intelligible that many a woman should prefer being one of several wives, to not being a wife at all. (*CW* XVIII, 290 [IV, 21])

And though there are plenty of notes of caution and alarm in this character-ization of its voluntariness, Mill does not jump precipitously to the con-clusion that intervention is all right, whenever we can raise a question mark over the element of choice. His position is more cautious and more complicated than that.[20]

V I

It is probably a good idea to end on that unsatisfactory note. I do not want to pretend that the application of Mill's views to the issue of cultural diversity is always clear or straightforward. What he says about many practical issues is nuanced and hesitant;[21] and we should not be surprised if this is true of multiculturalism also.

I have argued that although one can apply much of what Mill wrote about individual lifestyle to cultural choices as well, still we ought to be very careful about equating the two. A person's lifestyle is in some sense an inherently individual thing, at least as Mill urged us to think about it; but a culture is a social thing and so it partakes of all the dangers that apply to forms of life that a society imposes on its members. Many critics of multi-culturalism express concerns about the pursuit of diversity for its own sake and about the character of identity politics. I have tried to show there is plenty in Mill's argument in *On Liberty* which might vindicate those concerns. Mill did not value diversity for its own sake.[22] He valued it as a means to progress and therefore he did not use his principles of liberty to

[20] For an interesting reading of Mill on Mormon polygamy, and the suggestion that a Mormon woman's acceptance of polygamy exhibits autonomy but not freedom, see Richard J. Arneson, "Mill versus Paternalism," *Ethics*, 90 (1980), 476–7.

[21] Consider, for example, his views on those who procure and encourage immoral conduct (*CW* XVIII, 296–7 [V, 8]) and on the use of taxation to discourage vice (*CW* XVIII, 297–8 [V, 9]). I have recently discussed the complicated and surprising view he takes of state efforts to control sexually transmitted diseases, in Jeremy Waldron, "Mill on the Contagious Diseases Acts," in Nadia Urbinati and Alex Zakaras, eds., *J. S. Mill's Political Thought: A Bicentennial Reassessment* (Cambridge: Cambridge University Press, 2007), 11–42.

[22] See also Kwame Anthony Appiah, *The Ethics of Identity* (Princeton: Princeton University Press, 2005), 114–54.

support each and every sect or view or culture, irrespective of the mode in which it was held and inculcated among its members or in which it engaged with other views. Some modes in which cultures might be practiced might be as bad as the absence of diversity, so far as genuine ethical engagement was concerned. Indeed, they may be bad for the very same reasons that majoritarian social and ethical hegemony is bad in a monocultural society. That is the main argument I have tried to make.

To make it, I have no doubt exaggerated certain aspects of the politics of cultural identity: the self-conscious posturing associated with it, the discarding of the reasons that might support the views and practices that one adopts as one's heritage, and their replacement by rather more fatuous reasons of individual cultural self-presentation; and the use of "identity" to build a layer of insulation around each practice and belief, characterizing any criticism of it as a personal attack upon the individual who identifies with it. No doubt, there are many different types of cultural identification, and the version I have given is something of a caricature.[23] But the caricature is useful in highlighting a tendency in diversity politics and the politics of cultural identity which is completely at odds with the spirit of Mill's enterprise. Inasmuch as that tendency is present in a multicultural society, it is worth pointing out that it goes against the grain of Mill's arguments in *On Liberty*, even though, like Mill's arguments, it can be presented superficially as an affirmation of diversity and a call for mutual respect.

---

[23] See, e.g., the criticisms of the author by Will Kymlicka, *Politics in the Vernacular: Nationalism, Multiculturalism, and Citizenship* (Oxford: Oxford University Press, 2001), 211–12.

CHAPTER 9

Mill, liberty, and (genetic) "experiments in living"

Justine Burley

INTRODUCTION

Few cases have arisen in the contemporary policy domain that John Stuart Mill, were he alive today, would likely deem "harder" than the case of human reproductive cloning. In this chapter, I explore the question of whether Mill's views on liberty – its justifications and limits – would support or condemn recourse by private individuals to reproductive cloning technology.[1] Should people be left free to conduct this kind of (genetic) "experiment in living"?[2] As we shall see, even though cloning was not a known theoretical possibility in Mill's time, his writings have plenty that is instructive to offer on the topic.

Mill's curiosity about the moral and legal debate over cloning would have been piqued, or so one imagines, by the fact that almost everyone – scientists, citizens, and governments – has come down against it.[3] Putting aside speculations about Mill's own attitude to the cloning debate, it merits emphasis

---

I am very grateful to Alan Colman, Charles A. Erin, and C. L. Ten for comments on earlier drafts of this chapter.

[1] Cloning is asexual reproduction. "Reproductive cloning technology" here refers to the technique of somatic cell nuclear transfer (SCNT). In the course of natural human reproduction, a haploid sperm cell fertilizes a haploid oocyte (egg) to form a diploid zygote which then undergoes cleavage to become a blastocyst. The blastocyst implants in the uterus and ultimately may develop to birth. In SCNT, the diploid nucleus of an adult donor cell is introduced into an enucleated egg, which, after artificial activation, divides into a cloned (nuclear transfer) blastocyst. Following transfer into surrogate mothers, some of these blastocysts will develop to birth.

At the time of writing, twelve mammalian species have been cloned using SCNT. All attempts to clone primates, the closest genetic cousins of humans, have failed. No success with human reproductive cloning has been substantiated in fact, and, so far as this author knows, the procedure remains only a theoretical possibility.

[2] This is a Millian phrase used throughout J. S. Mill's *On Liberty*.

[3] Many of the pioneers of mammalian reproductive cloning research object to its application in humans. For examples, see Ian Wilmut, "The Age of Biological Control," in Justine Burley, ed., *The Genetic Revolution and Human Rights* (Oxford: Oxford University Press, 1999), ch. 2; and, more recently, Rudolf Jaenisch, "Human Cloning – The Science and Ethics of Nuclear Transplantation," *New England Journal of Medicine*, 351.27 (2004), 2787–91.

that virtually all contributors to it, if they trouble with theory at all, have variously referenced notions of liberty or utility.[4] Yet most of those who claim that their positions are backed either by liberalism or by utilitarianism, and, on occasion, by both at once, have not troubled much to spell out the theoretical basis of their arguments.[5] Others still have proceeded as if they are wholly ignorant of rather glaring inconsistencies in their reasoning.[6]

Mill furnishes a coherent, theoretically rich context in which to explore the moral permissibility of reproductive cloning. In his own times, Mill's thought constituted a new kind of utilitarian radicalism. It retains certain elements of the classical school, but embodies, in addition, a more subtle understanding of human nature which emphasizes the capacity of individuals to develop "higher" moral and aesthetic sentiments and how their development is linked to the complexion of reigning political institutions.[7] The core distinguishing feature of Mill's utilitarian thought is that free expression, choice, and action are indispensable to utility promotion.

Opponents of reproductive cloning predict that its practice would entail a myriad of harms, including violations of security of the person, fettering individual autonomy, and undermining conventional morality, established custom, and shared impersonal values. On all of these aspects of social and moral life, Mill adopted a firm stance. In addition, the case raises the issue of the duties of actual and prospective parents, a topic about which Mill had strong philosophical opinions. It also requires due consideration of human nature, and the values of justice, freedom, and utility – key ingredients of Mill's philosophical oeuvre. One is tempted to say, indeed, that the case of cloning was "made" for Mill.

For up-to-date overviews of global legislation on reproductive cloning see Gail H. Javitt, Kristen Suthers, and Kathy Hudson, "Cloning: A Policy Analysis," Genetics and Public Policy Center (rev. June 2006), available at: www.DNApolicy.org; The "Database of Global Policies on Human Cloning and Germ-Line Engineering," available at www.glphr.org/genetic/genetic.htm

[4] Unsurprisingly, perhaps, many scientists who have entered the debate over human cloning, and who are untutored in the niceties of philosophical disputation, fall into this category.

[5] Even one of the most prominent academics in the human cloning debate, John Harris, fails to make clear in any detail the theoretical foundations of his arguments or the links between them. In many pieces, he appears to be arguing his case as a liberal (see, e.g., John Harris, "Clones, Genes, and Human Rights," in Justine Burley, ed., The Genetic Revolution and Human Rights (New York: Oxford University Press, 1999), 61–94; and his On Cloning (London: Routledge & Kegan Paul, 2004), but in others, he advances arguments with a decidedly consequentialist flavor. See, e.g., his "Procreative Beneficence: Why We Should Select the Best Children," Bioethics, 15 (2001), 413–26.

[6] This is most apparent when the harms predicted for human reproductive cloning are not discussed in relation to the outcomes of natural procreation, and when the right to reproductive freedom is not thought about in relation to protecting the interests of actual children.

[7] See Jonathan Riley's "Introduction" to John Stuart Mill, Principles of Political Economy, and Chapters on Socialism (Oxford: Oxford University Press, 1998), xiv–xv.

The following inquiry traverses sprawling territory. In Section I, I endeavor to tease out the features of Mill's ethical and political writings that are applicable to the ensuing discussion. In section II, I tackle David Benatar's anti-natalism argument. On this view, non-existence is preferable to existence because the former involves no pain whereas the latter involves significant pain and suffering.[8] This may strike some as a rather *outré* starting point to our investigation of reproductive cloning and harm in the context of Mill's thought. However, if we cannot adduce an adequate rejoinder to Benatar, there will be little point in pressing on with our inquiry. If Benatar is right, and it is true that it is better never to exist, then that will be true irrespective of how one might come into existence. There are several Millian rejoinders to Benatar's position which give us reason to doubt its cogency. In section III, by reference to Mill, I focus discussion on individual-affecting harms that cloning would likely entail if attempted in humans, namely, the infliction of egregious physical welfare deficits on cloned children. Here I discuss a consistency argument advanced by Harris and Savulescu, according to which there is no morally meaningful difference between natural reproduction and cloning in that both are "creation lotteries."[9] I argue that they have overstated their case. This discussion reveals, as Jonathan Glover[10] has insisted, that there remains much difficult work to be carried out in defining the scope and weight of the right to reproductive freedom. Mill's writings provide guidance on how reproductive freedom might be demarcated in keeping with liberal notions of security of the person. There is ample textual evidence in Mill's essay *On Liberty* of a presumption in favor of reproductive freedom. Mill, however, as I shall demonstrate, would not endorse risk-taking by prospective parents in all those cases where serious damage to the body or mind of future children was a strong possibility. In section IV, I examine different formulations of the objection that cloning would adversely impact on the autonomy

---

[8] David Benatar, *Better Never to Have Been: The Harm of Coming into Existence* (Oxford: Oxford University Press, 2006). See also his "Why It Is Better Never to Come into Existence," in David Benatar, ed., *Life, Death and Meaning* (Lanham, MD: Rowman and Littlefield, 2004), 155–68, and his "Why it is Better Never to Come into Existence," *American Philosophical Quarterly*, 34.3 (1997), 345–55. I first came across an argument of this kind when reading the BPhil thesis of a fellow Oxford University graduate student, Seana Valentine Shiffrin. Her further developed views may be found in her "Wrongful Life, Procreative Responsibility, and the Significance of Harm," *Legal Theory*, 5 (1999), 117–48.

[9] John Harris and Julian Savulescu, "The Creation Lottery: Final Lessons from Natural Reproduction: Why Those Who Accept Natural Reproduction Should Accept Cloning and Other Frankenstein Reproductive Technologies," *Cambridge Quarterly of Healthcare Ethics*, 13 (2004), 90–5.

[10] Jonathan Glover, *Choosing Children* (Oxford: Oxford University Press, 2006).

of children. Søren Holm,[11] Matthew Clayton,[12] and Onora O'Neill[13] all claim that choosing a person's genetic makeup would have autonomy-compromising effects which are serious enough to warrant a ban on cloning. Using Mill, I demonstrate that the supporting argumentation for this claim is not robust. In the closing section of this chapter, section V, I marshal Mill's views on liberty to rebut the notion, eloquently expressed by Leon Kass,[14] that artificial methods of procreation, including reproductive cloning, undermine both customary morality and certain important shared human values. Mill offers a compelling counter-argument to the idea that changes to customary practices which might precipitate a shift in our moral parameters should be legally proscribed.

I LIBERTY, INDIVIDUALITY, AND UTILITY[15]

Mill's project in his essay *On Liberty* (*CW* XVIII, 217–18 [1, 2]) is to define the limits of the coercive power which the state and society may legitimately wield in democracies. Mill was deeply concerned about, and sought curbs on, the power of the majority. He reasoned that, if left unchecked, what he called the "the tyranny of the majority" (*CW* XVIII, 219 [1, 4]) would compromise individual self-creation and, by extension, human happiness and social progress. According to Mill, no state or society may justifiably interfere with the conduct of mature, rational agents in areas of conduct which concern only or primarily their interests. He introduced a principle to circumscribe both legal and other forms of such interference. In its fullest,

[11] Søren Holm, "A Life in the Shadow: One Reason Why We Should Not Clone Humans," *Cambridge Quarterly of Healthcare Ethics*, 7.2 (1998), 160–2.

[12] Matthew Clayton, "Individual Autonomy and Genetic Choice," in Justine Burley and John Harris, eds., *A Companion to Genethics* (Oxford: Blackwell, 2002), 191–205.

[13] Onora O'Neill, *Autonomy and Trust in Bioethics* (Cambridge: Cambridge University Press, 2002).

[14] Leon Kass, "The Wisdom of Repugnance," *The New Republic*, June 2, 1997, 17–26.

[15] I do not propose to offer any novel interpretation of Mill's moral and political philosophy in this section. Space does not permit that venture. Moreover, it would be impossible to defend in adequate detail the interpretation that I do offer and, at the same time, address the question that motivates my inquiry. I confine myself, therefore, to elucidating an interpretation of only those features of Mill's writings which are relevant to the question at hand. I offer further refinements to my interpretation, which finds points of agreement with the so-called revisionists among Mill scholars (most particularly, with John Gray), in subsequent sections. I do not ignore the fact that there are important differences between these scholars, who include C. L. Ten, *Mill on Liberty* (Oxford: Oxford University Press, 1980); John Gray, *Mill's On Liberty: A Defence* (London: Routledge & Kegan Paul, 1983); Jonathan Riley, *Liberal Utilitarianism* (Cambridge: Cambridge University Press, 1988); Roger Crisp, *Mill on Utilitarianism* (London: Routledge and Kegan Paul, 1997). A paragon of pre-revisionist critical works on Mill is James Fitzjames Stephen, *Liberty, Equality, Fraternity*, ed. R. J. White (Cambridge: Cambridge University Press, 1967). For elucidation of the intellectual divisions between revisionist and pre-revisionist interpretive schools, see John Gray, "John S. Mill, Traditional and Revisionist Interpretations," *Literature of Liberty*, 2 (1979), 7–37.

That principle is, that the sole end for which mankind are warranted, individually or collectively in interfering with the liberty of action of any of their number, is self-protection. That the only purpose for which power can be rightfully exercised over any member of a civilized community, against his will, is to prevent harm to others. His own good, either physical or moral, is not a sufficient warrant. He cannot rightfully be compelled to do or forbear because it will be better for him to do so, because it will make him happier, because, in the opinions of others, to do so would be wise, or even right. These are good reasons for remonstrating with him, or reasoning with him, or persuading him, or entreating him, but not for compelling him, or visiting him with any evil, in case he do otherwise. To justify that, the conduct from which it is desired to deter him, must be calculated to produce evil to some one else. The only part of the conduct of any one, for which he is amenable to society, is that which concerns others. In the part which merely concerns himself, his independence is, of right, absolute. Over himself, over his own body and mind, the individual is sovereign. (*CW* XVIII, 223–4 [1, 9])[16]

The above-quoted liberty (or harm) principle sets the bounds of state and societal intervention in individuals' lives. It is important for the argumentation in ensuing sections that we elaborate on its meaning and intended applications.

The distinction that Mill invokes between conduct which "merely concerns" the individual and that which concerns others has been recast by Mill scholars in the terms "self-regarding" and "other-regarding" actions. To illustrate this distinction Mill writes:

No person ought to be punished simply for being drunk; but a soldier or a policeman should be punished for being drunk on duty. Whenever, in short, there is a definite damage, or a definite risk of damage, either to an individual or to the public, the case is taken out of the province of liberty, and placed in that of morality or law. (*CW* XVIII, 282 [IV, 10])

Self-regarding conduct typically involves either no effects on others, or effects which, even if adverse in some ways, are not directly adverse with respect to their vital interests. The principal vital interests of individuals are security of the person and security of property. These vital interests ground moral rights, and, as I explain later on below, their protection is a necessary condition of utility promotion. Self-regarding conduct may not be interfered with, even when such interference would be to the benefit of the individual himself. The main exception to this rule is any case involving clear and present danger where the balance of evidence indicates that a person risks harm because he is not in full possession of his faculties at the

---

[16] That Mill describes this as "one very simple principle" is perhaps a testament to his cleverness.

time or does not have pertinent facts to hand. Hence if we see a man attempting to cross a bridge that we know is unsafe, and surmise he is unaware of the impending danger, we are justified in forcibly restraining his passage (*CW* xviii, 294 [v, 5]).

Other-regarding actions are those with adverse effects on other individuals' vital interests or on the *fundamental* shared values of a society. Physical assault, theft, and dereliction of duty in cases where the vital interests of others are actually violated or threatened, invite punitive sanctions or other coercive measures, when, that is, such measures are feasible and/or expedient. The emphasis that Mill places on granting freedom of expression, choice, and action to adults so long as no other-regarding harm obtains is intimately connected with his brand of utilitarianism. Further elucidation of Mill's conception of liberty is required if we are to make sense of this relationship.

Underpinning Mill's ideas about individual liberty is a theory of human nature. Mill gives little weight to the "species-nature" of man[17] as the following passage from his essay *Nature*[18] makes plain:

Allowing everything to be an instinct which anybody has ever asserted to be one, it remains true that nearly every respectable attribute of humanity is the result not of instinct, but of a victory over instinct; and that there is hardly anything valuable in the natural man except capacities – *a whole world of possibilities, all of them dependent upon eminently artificial discipline for being realised.* (*CW* x, 393, emphasis added)

For Mill, human nature is not static, but infinitely modifiable.[19] Mill regards all human beings as engaged in a never-ending process of self-creation through the exercise of their critical faculties, and the associated performance of actions. Individuality is a form of self-creation, and is lauded as a means by which individual well-being and human progress are furthered.

As it is useful that while mankind are imperfect there should be differences in opinions, so it is that there should be different experiments of living; that free scope should be given to varieties of character, short of injury to others; and that the worth of different modes of life should be proved practically, when any one thinks fit to try them. It is desirable, in short, that in things which do not primarily concern others, individuality should assert itself. Where, not the person's own character, but

[17] Gray, *Mill's* On Liberty, 85.
[18] John Stuart Mill, *Nature*, in *The Collected Works of John Stuart Mill*, vol. x: *Essays on Ethics, Religion, and Society*, ed. John M. Robson, introduction by F. E. L. Priestley (Toronto: University of Toronto Press; London: Routledge & Kegan Paul, 1985), 373–402.
[19] In *On Liberty*, Mill appears also to suggest that humans possess an essence of which liberty will enable the expression: "Human nature is not a machine to be built after a model, and set to do exactly the work prescribed for it, but a tree, which requires to grow and develop itself on all sides, *according to the tendency of the inward forces which make it a living thing*" (*CW* xviii, 263 [iii, 4], emphasis added).

the traditions or customs of other people are the rule of conduct, there is wanting one of the *principal ingredients of human happiness, and quite the chief ingredient of individual and social progress.* (*CW* XVIII, 260–1 [III, 1], emphasis added)

The importance of individuality to utility promotion should not be under-estimated. Mill writes in *On Liberty* that he regards "utility as the ultimate appeal on all ethical questions," but he says that "it must be utility in the largest sense, grounded on the permanent interests of man as a progressive being" (*CW* XVIII, 224 [II, 11]). Although Mill posits utility as the ultimate standard, he does not recommend that it be directly aimed for. For Mill, liberty is a necessary condition of happiness because it secures the vital interests. This in turn facilitates free thought and choice, which are con-stitutive of happiness. Utility is promoted by leaving individuals free to form, revise, reflect on, and act out their respective conceptions of what a meaningful life is, provided that no one else is thereby harmed.

In *Utilitarianism*,[20] in describing the "creed" which accepts utilitarianism, Mill says: "Utility, or the Greatest Happiness Principle, holds that actions are right in proportion as they tend to promote happiness, wrong as they tend to produce the reverse of happiness. By happiness is intended pleasure, and the absence of pain; by unhappiness, pain, and the privation of pleasure." He qualifies this statement by adding: "To give a clear view of the moral standard set up by the theory, much more requires to be said; in particular, what things it includes in the ideas of pain and pleasure; and to what extent this is left an open question" (*CW* X, 210 [II, 2]). What Mill is pointing to here is a distinctive notion of pleasure: "It is quite compatible with the principle of utility to recognise the fact, that some *kinds* of pleasure are more desirable and more valuable than others" (*CW* X, 211 [II, 4]). Mill's utilitarian theory distinguishes between "higher pleasures" (those which can be attained only by using the reflective faculties) and lower pleasures (states of body or mind which require no or little rational reflection for their attainment).

Now it is an unquestionable fact that those who are equally acquainted with, and equally capable of appreciating and enjoying, both, do give a most marked preference to the manner of existence which employs their higher faculties. Few human creatures would consent to be changed into any of the lower animals, for a promise of the fullest allowance of a beast's pleasures; no intelligent human being would consent to be a fool, no instructed person would be an ignoramus, no person of feeling and conscience would be selfish and base, even though they should be

---

[20] John Stuart Mill, *Utilitarianism*, in *The Collected Works of John Stuart Mill*, vol. x: *Essays on Ethics, Religion, and Society* (Toronto: University of Toronto Press; London: Routledge & Kegan Paul, 1969), 203–59.

persuaded that the fool, the dunce, or the rascal is better satisfied with his lot than
they are with theirs. (*CW* x, 211 [11, 6])

Thus Mill parts company with his utilitarian predecessors both by emphasizing the quality (as opposed to quantity) of pleasures, and by insisting that
the higher pleasures can be produced only when political institutions are
shaped so as to make possible lives which are freely chosen and freely lived.

Armed with an interpretation of Mill's thought, according to which
liberty is a means to and a composite of utility, it will be helpful at this
stage to remind the reader of the central question of our inquiry. That
question is: do Mill's views on liberty – its justification and limits – support
or condemn recourse by private individuals to reproductive cloning technology? It might be thought, upon review of our sketch of the key features
of Mill's theory, that the question has been ill-framed. It is indisputable that
when people have children, others' interests are affected. But such is the case
with respect to many things that individuals do. The crucial issues to be
resolved are: what kinds of effects, and on whom? The specific task before us
therefore is to determine whether or not cloning is rightly regarded as
harmful, who or what is being harmed, how severe the harm is, and,
given answers to the preceding, whether the state and society should
adopt a liberty-constraining stance on reproductive cloning or leave people
free to conduct genetic experiments in living.

II BEING AND NOTHINGNESS: WHY NON-EXISTENCE IS NOT PREFERABLE TO EXISTENCE

In his handsome new book *Better Never to Have Been*,[21] David Benatar
contends that it is immoral to have children. He supports this central
contention by defending two sub-claims: an asymmetry claim about pain
and pleasure in the context of non-existence, and a claim about how
harmful actual existence is for all sentient creatures.[22] From Mill, we shall
draw interesting counter-replies to both of these.

According to Benatar, whereas there is symmetry between:
1. the presence of pain is bad; and
2. the presence of pleasure is good,

---

[21] See above, n. 8.
[22] When Benatar says that "all sentient creatures are always harmed by being brought into existence"
(*Better Never to Have Been*, 28–9), he is not saying that sentient creatures are necessarily harmed; in
hypothetical examples in which it is posited (*contra* fact) that a life contains only good, Benatar is
agnostic as to whether non-existence or existence is preferable.

there is an asymmetry between:

3. the absence of pain is good, even if that good is not enjoyed by anyone; and
4. the absence of pleasure is not bad unless there is somebody for whom this absence is a deprivation.[23]

The claim is represented diagrammatically:

Scenario A (X exists)	Scenario B (X never exists)
1. Presence of pain (bad)	3. Absence of pain (good)
2. Presence of pleasure (good)	4. Absence of pleasure (not bad)

Three supporting reasons are adduced to back this asymmetry claim. First, we do not think that there is a duty to bring happy people into existence, but we do think that we have a duty to avoid bringing children into the world who will suffer. Second, sometimes people seek to avoid bringing a child into the world on the basis that existence would run contrary to a child's interests. Third, we sometimes make retrospective judgments about why it was bad for certain children to have been brought into existence. Benatar argues that it would be wrong to weigh up the presence of (1) pleasures, with (2) pain, as a comparison of the desirability of existence and never existing, because the correct comparison to be made is that between existence and non-existence – the left- and right-hand sides of the diagram above.[24] In making this comparison himself, Benatar states that there are benefits both to existing and to not existing: it is a good that actual people enjoy pleasure, and also that pains are avoided through non-existence. But, and importantly, he stresses that it is also the case that there is nothing bad about not coming into existence, yet there is something bad about coming into existence. Therefore, Benatar tells us, all things being considered, non-existence is preferable to existence.[25]

The asymmetry between (3) and (4) that Benatar posits is misleading. Any scenario of non-existence is most accurately described by the term "nothingness" or the numerical value 0, and not by the evaluative terms "good" or "not bad." Second, when we talk about it being wrong to bring people into the world under certain circumstances, when people actually seek to avoid

---

[23] Here I closely follow Benatar's own exposition of his asymmetry claim in Benatar, "Why It is Better Never to Come into Existence" (2004), 156.
[24] Ibid., 160.   [25] Ibid.

bringing a child into the world because they think that existing would run contrary to his interests, and when people make retrospective judgments that the lives of some children are regrettable ones, it is a comparison between nothingness and being in a state of wretched suffering that they are making. The determination that X's life is, was or would not be worth living equates with the judgment: "Existence for X is worse than nothingness; its worth is minus 0." Consider the following scenario A, in which (1) X has, let us say, Tay-Sachs, and (2) X has an average amount of pleasure; and scenario B, in which (3) is a state of nothingness, and (4) a state of nothingness.

Scenario A (X exists)	Scenario B (non-existence)
1. Presence of pain – e.g., Tay-Sachs –1000 (bad)	3. Absence of pain 0
2. Presence of pleasure 100 (good)	4. Absence of pleasure 0

To determine whether existence for X in scenario A(1) is better than non-existence (3, 4) we make a judgment as to the worth of X's life. If X is in a state of dire, irreversible suffering, we accord a negative value to it. In my example of an individual afflicted by Tay-Sachs, the value that might be given is –1000.[26] We then compare that value to 0, i.e., a state of nothingness. In short, non-existence is preferable to existence when (1) existence for X with pain is –0.[27]

People will of course disagree about which values best represent various pain states. Bentham devoted a lifetime trying to schematize pleasures and pains of different intensity, without making convincing progress. Mill himself says: "Neither pains nor pleasures are homogeneous, and pain is always heterogeneous with pleasure" (*CW* x, 213 [II, 8]). The ascription of such values can be merely subjective, but it need not necessarily be so. It is plain that some value accounts are more cogent than others. What makes them relatively persuasive is not principally that people more or less agree on one; rather, it is the force of independent, non-(directly)welfarist arguments which can be adduced to support them.

Mill's is a "primary goods" or "objective list" account of the good, two components of which are the possession of, and ability to exercise, certain capacities. If an actual individual lacks the capacities required for self-creation

---

[26] Any figure could be chosen provided it reflected the badness of living in this state relative to 0.

[27] And, relatedly, existence is preferable to non-existence when, (2) for X, pleasure plus pain equals a positive number.

or is so wrought with pain that he could not possibly employ these capacities, then his life may not be worth living. The same holds true of possible persons who would not possess or ever be able to utilize these capacities. I elaborate on this point in discussion of Benatar's second supporting claim for his contention that non-existence is preferable to existence: existence involves morally significant suffering for all sentient beings.

Benatar seeks to persuade us that against whatever account of human welfare one adopts – a hedonistic, desire-fulfilment, or objective list account – it can be successfully argued that human life is filled with dreadful pain and suffering. Mill, I think, would concede the general point. Mill, like Benatar, observed that the world is filled with misery. "Unquestionably it is possible to do without happiness; it is done involuntarily by nineteen-twentieths of mankind, even in those parts of our present world which are least deep in barbarism" (*CW* x, 217 [II, 15]). Mill wrote elegantly about the degradations of poverty, along with many other human calamities. In addition, he wrote prolifically about the kind of political institutions that might ameliorate the human condition. We also know that Mill, although from a somewhat privileged background, was no stranger to personal suffering, having himself endured a catastrophic mental crisis when a young man.[28] However, as we have noted several times now already, Mill has a different understanding of the greatest-happiness principle than his utilitarian predecessors. Consider Mill's oft-quoted phrase: "It is better to be a human being dissatisfied than a pig satisfied; better to be Socrates dissatisfied than a fool satisfied" (*CW* x, 212 [II, 6]). This passage, together with others exposited above, suggests that the complete absence of suffering may not be as preferable as Benatar assumes – indeed, for Mill, its presence can be indicative of an advantageous state of affairs.

A being of higher faculties requires more to make him happy, is capable probably of more acute suffering, and certainly accessible to it at more points, than one of an inferior type; but in spite of these liabilities, he can never really wish to sink into what he feels to be a lower grade of existence. (*CW* x, 212 [II, 6])

By "lower grade of existence," Mill has in mind the Epicurean or Benthamite creeds of pleasure and pain. In contrast, Mill's theory of utilitarianism gives prominence to the quality of pleasures. The higher pleasures consist in the free exercise of thought, imagination, and choice. They can be produced even when accompanied by suffering. A person can

[28] John Stuart Mill, *Autobiography*, in *The Collected Works of John Stuart Mill*, vol. I: *Autobiography and Literary Essays*, ed. John M. Robson and Jack Stillinger, introduction by Lord Robbins (Toronto: University of Toronto Press; London: Routledge & Kegan Paul, 1981), 1–290; see especially 137–92.

be a utility-maximizer, in other words, even when brute pain obtains, though whether this is true, and the extent to which it will be true, will depend on how severe the raw pain suffered is.

In a world in which there is so much to interest, so much to enjoy, and so much also to correct and improve, every one who has this moderate amount of moral and intellectual requisites is capable of an existence which may be called enviable; and unless such a person, through bad laws, or subjection to the will of others, is denied the liberty to use the sources of happiness within his reach, he will not fail to find this enviable existence, if he escape the positive evils of life, the great sources of physical and mental suffering – such as indigence, disease, and the unkindness, worthlessness, or premature loss of objects of affection. The main stress of the problem lies, therefore, in the contest with these calamities, from which it is a rare good fortune entirely to escape; which, as things now are, cannot be obviated, and often cannot be in any material degree mitigated. (*CW* x, 216 [II, 14])

Mill addresses the "stress of the problem" by affirming that human nature is not fixed, and that mankind holds within its power the tools to improve both his own lot and that of all.

Yet no one whose opinion deserves a moment's consideration can doubt that most of the great positive evils of the world are in themselves removable, and will, if human affairs continue to improve, be in the end reduced within narrow limits. Poverty, in any sense implying suffering, may be completely extinguished by the wisdom of society, combined with the good sense and providence of individuals. Even that most intractable of enemies, disease, may be indefinitely reduced in dimensions by good physical and moral education, and proper control of noxious influences; while the progress of science holds out a promise for the future of still more direct conquests over this detestable foe. And every advance in that direction relieves us from some, not only of the chances which cut short our own lives, but, what concerns us still more, which deprive us of those in whom our happiness is wrapt up. As for vicissitudes of fortune, and other disappointments connected with worldly circumstances, these are principally the effect either of gross imprudence, of ill-regulated desires, or of bad or imperfect social institutions. (*CW* x, 216 [II, 14])

Although Mill argued that the sources of human suffering are all "in a great degree, many of them almost entirely, conquerable by human care and effort," he acknowledges that "their removal is grievously slow – [and] though a long succession of generations will perish in the breach before the conquest is completed, and this world becomes all that, if will and knowledge were not wanting, it might easily be made." But he emphatically maintains that "every mind sufficiently intelligent and generous to bear a part, however small and unconspicuous, in the endeavour, will draw a noble enjoyment from the contest itself, which he would not for any bribe in the form of selfish indulgence consent to be without" (*CW* x, 217 [II, 14]). Mill's appeal to the

Aristotelian notion of a skillful performance is inextricably linked to his conception of utility promotion: actual participation in finding solutions to man's problems is, in itself, utility-maximizing. Mill believes that the reflective choices individuals make between the time they are born and the time they die, and the experiments in living that they conduct, will not only enhance their personal happiness but improve the lot of humankind.

Benatar concludes his defense of the two claims – the asymmetry claim, and the "human existence is rotten" claim – by drawing out their main implication: anti-natalism. It is immoral to have children. The consequence of pursuing an anti-natalist policy is the extinction of *Homo sapiens*. Compare this with Mill's alternative, a world moving haltingly toward an improved state. Mill's philosophical opinions are neither uncontroversial nor free of internal inconsistency. Nevertheless, in marshaling Mill, one is confident of endorsing a superior *moral* approach. Benatar would have us remove all human suffering in one fell swoop through an anti-procreation pact that would bring an end to all human suffering once the demise of the human race had occurred.[29] Does Benatar further advocate that it would be morally preferable to despatch *every* living creature on earth (save bacteria, perhaps), because all of them too suffer while alive, and they too die (death being an "intrinsic tragedy" in Benatar's words)? Then the world would contain no suffering at all, and should, according to Benatar, be a "better" place than it is now. My concluding point here, following Mill, is simply that some aspects of existence matter more than the presence of pain and suffering.[30]

Having argued that non-existence is not necessarily preferable to existence and therefore that Benatar's anti-natalist view is not compelling, we turn now to evaluate whether or not limits can justifiably be imposed on people who want to use cloning by somatic cell nuclear transfer (SCNT) to bring children into the world.

III MILL, REPRODUCTIVE FREEDOM, AND INDIVIDUAL-AFFECTING HARMS

Mill held strong opinions on the begetting[31] and parenting of children. He reflected on the harm to some individuals of being brought into existence, and on harms to pre-existing members of society that might be caused by an

---

[29] Benatar, "Why It is Better Never to Come into Existence" (2004), 167.
[30] Not always, and not for everyone, but enough.
[31] Mill indeed was arrested in his youth for distributing contraceptive advice to passers-by on the street. Pedro Schwartz, *The New Political Economy of J. S. Mill* (London: Weidenfeld & Nicholson, 1972), pp. 245–54, cited in Benatar, *Better Never to Have Been*, 113.

increase in population. Mill was, in addition, morally outraged by the widespread ill-treatment of children, in particular the failure of parents to meet the educational needs of their offspring. Of such negligence, Mill complained:

It still remains unrecognised, that to bring a child into existence without a fair prospect of being able, not only to provide food for its body, but instruction and training for its mind, is a moral crime, both against the unfortunate offspring and against society; and that if the parent does not fulfil this obligation, the State ought to see it fulfilled, at the charge, as far as possible, of the parent. (*CW* XVIII, 302 [v, 12])

And further:

Yet current ideas of liberty, which bend so easily to real infringements of the freedom of the individual in things which concern only himself, would repel the attempt to put any restraint upon his inclinations when the consequence of their indulgence is a life or lives of wretchedness and depravity to the offspring, with manifold evils to those sufficiently within reach to be in anyway affected by their actions. (*CW* XVIII, 304 [v, 15])

As should by now be plain, Mill also held strong views about individual liberty, and there is, to be sure, a presumption in favor of reproductive freeom in Mill's writings: "Over himself, over his own body and mind, the individual is sovereign" (*CW* XVIII, 224 [I, 9]). It now will be established what Mill's response would be to the objection that human SCNT would place all clones at risk of egregious physical and mental welfare deficits.

The experience of SCNT in animal models has given rise to fears about the safety of applying it in humans. It is well documented that SCNT is extremely inefficient: the success rate of the transfer procedure itself is very low; and it involves significant loss of life at the embryonic and fetal stages. SCNT is also associated with the development of prenatal and postnatal abnormalities, a good proportion of which do not arise until the late stages of pregnancy or feature in the context of sexual reproduction. Furthermore, it has been argued, on the basis of careful experimentation, that no human clone could possess a normal genome.[32] By circumventing the processes of gametogenesis and fertilization, SCNT prevents the proper reprogramming and imprinting of the clone's genome – prerequisites for the embryo's development into a normal organism.[33] Bearing in mind these facts about

---

[32] Jaenisch, "Human Cloning."

[33] There are two main reasons why mammals cloned using SCNT suffer from abnormalities: faulty reprogramming, and gene imprinting. In natural reproduction, the union of the sperm and the egg at fertilization brings together the two sets of male and female chromosomes with their respective complement of genes. During development, cell numbers increase and different (somatic) cell types

SCNT in animal models, I want now to evaluate the claim that cloning is not morally worse than natural procreation.

Certain philosophers (including me) have made much of the parity between natural procreation and reproductive cloning with respect to both the loss of early human lives, and the possibility of severe abnormalities occurring in the process.[34] Acceptance of natural procreation, we have said, implies acceptance of reproductive cloning. In a recent formulation of this point, Harris and Savulescu argue:

> For those who accept natural reproduction, however, there is no objection to reproductive cloning on grounds of inefficiency or lack of safety. Even if attempts at reproductive cloning involve many embryos that will perish in early embryonic development and others that go on to be grossly deformed human beings, this is no different than natural reproduction. They are both relevantly similar creation lotteries.[35]

A creation lottery is defined as "the creation of a population of embryos for the purpose of creating a new human being."[36] It is, I think, quite right to say that both are "relevantly similar" creation lotteries, and also that if one accepts a natural reproduction creation lottery, one cannot then object to

emerge. But all cells inherit the same complete set of genes that were possessed by the fertilized egg. However, the particular set of genes that are *expressed* in a given cell nucleus varies enormously between different cell types. (The mechanisms that lead to this selective expression are termed epigenetic.)

In the case of SCNT, when the nucleus from a specialized cell type (e.g., a skin cell) is transferred to an enucleated egg a radical reprogramming of gene expression needs to take place quickly if development is to proceed normally and a "cloned" animal is to emerge. In the early embryo, many of the genes that are "on" in the skin cell nucleus have to be turned off. At this stage, the genes that need to be switched "on" are the embryonic genes (dormant in the skin cell nucleus of a fully formed adult). Scientists have determined that in *every case* of a cloned animal (that has been examined in detail), this reprogramming is aberrant. It would seem that compensatory mechanisms can intervene to deal with a modest degree of faulty reprogramming, which accounts for why some cloned animals have developed to term.

The second reason that SCNT is inefficient and that cloned mammals suffer from abnormalities is a consequence of the different history behind the union of parental genomes in SCNT and in sexual reproduction. There are a small number of genes whose expression during a crucial stage of fetal development does not depend on which cell type they are in but on which parent they were inherited from. For example, some imprinted genes inherited from the male parent are off in the early fetus while the same gene from the female parent is on, and vice versa for other imprinted genes. If this imprinted pattern of expression is altered, abnormal fetal development can occur. Although the correct imprinting pattern is present in somatic cell nuclei, this pattern can be altered by the cell culture that occurs as a prelude to SCNT. It is also disrupted in a major way when the somatic cell nucleus is exposed to the egg cytoplasm. In normal fertilization, the maternal genes in the egg are protected from major biochemical modification; this protection is not available to the incoming male sperm or to the male- or female-derived genes that are delivered with the somatic cell nucleus.

[34] Justine Burley and John Harris, "Human Cloning and Child Welfare," *Journal of Medical Ethics*, 25 (1999), 108–13.

[35] Harris and Savulescu, "The Creation Lottery," 92.   [36] Ibid., 90.

cloning on the grounds of embryo loss and the incidence of deformity *per se*.
A high rate of embryo loss is a feature of natural reproduction.[37] And serious
mental and physical abnormalities do occur. But, as the authors note in
passing, themselves, there are different possible creation lotteries. Some
lotteries have relatively favorable odds: certain creation lotteries afford
"bigger and better wins" than do others. Does this matter morally? I
think it does, and so too, I judge, would Mill. He would reject the
consistency argument pushed by Harris and Savulescu above, to wit: natural
procreation involves the risk of serious disability as does cloning; therefore,
if we accept that the former is morally permissible, we are committed to
accepting the latter. Mill would place weight on the relative risks of the two
methods of reproduction when there was significant risk that a certain level
of welfare could not be attained.

The fact itself, of causing the existence of a human being, is one of the most
responsible actions in the range of human life. To undertake this responsibility – to
bestow a life which may be either a curse or a blessing – unless the being on whom it
is to be bestowed will have at least the ordinary chances of a desirable existence, is a
crime against that being. (*CW* xviii, 304 [v, 15])

I read Mill's phrase "ordinary chances of a desirable existence" to mean
"threshold of well-being" and to reference an objective-list account of the
good, composed, in part, of the possession by individuals of certain capacities and the ability to exercise these. Given the vast disparities in wealth that
existed in Mill's time, not to mention the lack of available efficacious
medical care, the threshold that Mill had in mind is best understood as
being quite low. That said, the facts surveyed above about SCNT indicate
that both the loss of very early human lives and the incidence of genetic and
epigenetic-based abnormalities would likely be much higher, of a greater
magnitude, and of a different character in a reproductive cloning creation
lottery. Cloning would present, in short, a relatively high risk of bringing
people into the world who did not have lives worth living. This is not
factually the case with natural procreation. We can therefore provisionally
conclude that Mill would object to cloning for as long as it takes to bring
SCNT safety levels up to the "ordinary" standards of natural reproduction.
This is not, of course, an objection in principle to reproductive cloning.

---

[37] C. Boklage, "Survival Probability of Human Conceptions from Fertilization to Term," *International
Journal of Fertility*, 35 (1990), 75–94. See also H. Leridon, *Human Fertility: The Basic Components*
(Chicago: University of Chicago Press, 1977).

And it is obvious that "ordinary" is not a static concept in a world in which rapid developments are being made in the biosciences.[38]

Harris does note in his book *On Cloning*[39] that safety and efficiency all come down to a matter of degree. But, although he acknowledges that high failure rates or the relatively high incidence of abnormalities might constitute a good reason not to use reproductive cloning as a technology of choice, he also says that "for those who can only have the children they seek through assisted reproduction this might not be a sufficiently powerfully moral reason either for these would-be parents to forgo cloning nor for society to prevent them the freedom to access the technology if they choose."[40]

It would appear, then, that Harris believes that the scope of reproductive liberty is such as to permit the begetting children through SCNT irrespective of the likely outcome of severe mental and physical welfare deficits. Harris is not alone in maintaining that reproductive freedom should be vigilantly safeguarded. Many fear that any state intrusion in this area of our lives would entail disastrous consequences.[41] Mill himself was only too aware of the "great evil" of adding to governmental power (*CW* xviii, 306 [v, 20]). In addition, from certain passages in *On Liberty* it might plausibly be inferred that Mill would regard as an unavoidable evil any harms inflicted on someone in the process of bringing him into existence.

In the first place, it must by no means be supposed, because damage, or probability of damage, to the interests of others, can alone justify the interference of society, that therefore it always does justify such interference. In many cases, an individual, in pursuing a legitimate object, necessarily and therefore legitimately causes pain or loss to others, or intercepts a good which they had a reasonable hope of obtaining. Such oppositions of interest between individuals often arise from bad social institutions, but are unavoidable while those institutions last; and *some would be unavoidable under any institutions*. (*CW* xviii, 292 [v, 3]), emphasis added)[42]

---

[38] Determining where the benchmark for "ordinary" standards should be set is a thorny problem, and is beyond the scope of the present inquiry.

[39] See above, n. 5.   [40] Harris, *On Cloning*, 111.

[41] For examples, see Ronald Dworkin, *Life's Dominion: An Argument about Abortion and Euthanasia* (New York: Knopf, 1993); John Robertson, *Children of Choice: Freedom and the New Reproductive Technologies* (Princeton: Princeton University Press, 1994); Allen Buchanan *et al.*, *From Chance to Choice* (Cambridge: Cambridge University Press, 2002).

[42] This passage in *On Liberty* is drawn from a discussion about free trade, and how, in that context, when the gains one makes preclude another from making the same or similar gains, no violation of liberty occurs.

It is also the case that Mill was aware that even when curtailing individual liberty is in theory warranted, it might be futile and/or produce worse outcomes.

In all things which regard the external relations of the individual, he is *de jure* amenable to those whose interests are concerned, and if need be, to society as their protector. There are often good reasons for not holding him to the responsibility: but these reasons must arise from the special expediencies of the case: either because it is a kind of case in which he is on the whole likely to act better, when left to his own discretion, than when controlled in any way in which society have it in their power to control him: or because the attempt to exercise control would produce other evils, greater than those which it would prevent. When such reasons as these preclude the enforcement of responsibility, the concern of the agent himself should step into the vacant judgment seat, and protect those interests of others which have no external protection: judging himself all the more rigidly, because the case does not admit of his being made accountable to the judgment of his fellow-creatures. (*CW* xviii, 225 [i, ii])

Nevertheless Mill was quite clear that the government could permissibly impose limits on reproductive freedom, under limited circumstances. Providing that it was legally expedient, Mill states that he would endorse such constraints.

The laws which, in many countries on the Continent, forbid marriage unless the parties can show that they have the means of supporting a family do not exceed the legitimate powers of the State: and whether such laws be expedient or not (a question mainly dependent on local circumstances and feelings), they are not objectionable as violations of liberty. Such laws are interferences of the State to prohibit a mischievous act – an act injurious to others, which ought to be a subject of reprobation, and social stigma, even when it is not deemed expedient to super-add legal punishment. (*CW* xviii, 304 [v, 15])

Mill's writings on existing children and potential people suggest that he would not regard the parameters of reproductive freedom as encompassing cloning so long as there was a high probability of its resulting in severe physical damage. The prediction by scientists that human cloning would entail serious harm obtains with respect to all instances of it. Moreover, access to SCNT, from a logistical standpoint, could quite easily be denied. The situation as regards natural procreation is qualitatively different. There is an incidence of serious physical deficits in individuals who are conceived through natural means, but it is relatively low. Furthermore, the occurrence of such disabilities can, using a variety of health-screening methods, some-times be pinpointed in advance. Finally, whereas it is expedient legally to control access to SCNT, this is far from being true of natural procreation.

IV CLONING AND PERSON-AFFECTING
HARMS: AUTONOMY

I shall now proceed to address the argument that a ban on cloning is warranted because the selection of a child's genes made possible by SCNT would involve unacceptable violations of individual autonomy.[43] Although Mill did not employ the term "autonomy" in his essay *On Liberty*, the fact that he championed the liberty principle, and concomitantly individuality, is evidence enough that the promotion of individual autonomy was of central importance to him. As noted above, the intended subjects of the liberty principle are rational agents. Children constitute a special case. They do not yet possess fully developed capacities for critical reflection, but have the potential for such. It is thus essential for Mill that children receive some instruction.

Hardly any one indeed will deny that it is one of the most sacred duties of the parents (or, as law and usage now stand, the father), after summoning a human being into the world, to give to that being an education fitting him to perform his part well in life towards others and towards himself. (*CW* xviii, 301–2 [v, 12])

Would Mill deem the limitations on autonomy that cloning would allegedly involve to be analogous to the harms suffered by children who are not provided with any education?

The claim that cloning would involve the autonomy of children has been advanced by a number of thinkers, and has taken a variety of different forms.[44]

1. Autonomy is a precondition of being treated in certain ways. A clone's autonomy would be unacceptably reduced because the genes which constitute it are manipulated or chosen on the basis of a parent's conception of the good.[45]
2. A clone's autonomy would be compromised through the parental selection of its genes because it would live its life in the shadow of the genetic donor. Its autonomous development would be impeded by the knowledge of what the genetic donor was like when he/she was alive and/or by others' expectations of what the clone will or should be like.[46]

---

[43] Henceforward, I proceed as if cloning in humans were safe from the standpoint of physical welfare.

[44] The two formulations of the claim that I go on to consider are fictionalized in Eva Hoffman's novel *The Secret* (London: Secker & Warburg, 2001), reviewed by Justine Burley, "Exactly the Same but Different," *Nature*, 417 (2002), 224–5.

[45] Clayton, "Individual Autonomy and Genetic Choice," appeals to Raz's idea of "conditions of independence"; Joseph Raz, *The Morality of Freedom* (Oxford: Clarendon Press, 1986), 377–8.

[46] Hølm, "A Life in the Shadow"; Kass, "The Wisdom of Repugnance"; O'Neil, *Autonomy and Trust in Bioethics*; Martha C. Nussbaum, "Little C," in Martha C. Nussbaum and C. R. Sunstein, eds., *Clones and Clones: Facts and Fantasies about Human Cloning* (New York: Norton, 1998), 338–46.

We can extrapolate from Mill's dim view of state education some support for the autonomy-based objection to cloning currently under review.

All that has been said of the importance of individuality of character, and diversity in opinion and modes of conduct, involves, as of the same unspeakable importance, diversity of education. A general State education is a mere contrivance for moulding people to be exactly like one another: and as the mould in which it casts them is that which pleases the predominant power in the government, whether this be a monarch, a priesthood, an aristocracy, or the majority of the existing generation, in proportion as it is efficient and successful, it establishes a despotism over the mind, leading by natural tendency to one over the body. (*CW* xviii, 302 [v, 13])

It is plausible to suggest that Mill would regard attempts by parents, whether unwitting or intentional, to shape a clone's life according to that of the genetic donor's to be as despicable as the molding effects of a state education. The role of a decent education on Mill's view is to equip young individuals with the capacities to define, reflect on, and revise their own respective conceptions of the good, when they reach maturity. Were it necessarily the case that choosing a clone's genes denied cloned individuals the possibility of fashioning their own lives in critically reflective ways, Mill would doubtless find fault with this practice.

However, it is far from apparent that the autonomy objections (1) and (2) to cloning are either factually complete or sound. First, the mere fact that all of a child's genes are chosen in accordance with a parent's conception of the good seems different only in degree from the usual situation in which the decision by two parties to procreate defines the range of genes out of which a child can be created. Second, the motivation of would-be cloners presumably would, in practice, vary greatly – it certainly does in the case of parents who use sexual means to reproduce. Some individuals might want to access SCNT technology solely because they had no other way of conceiving a genetically related child. These parents might therefore be utterly unconcerned about who the genetic donor was above and beyond the desire that he/she bear a genetic relation to one of the nurturing parents. Others who sought to clone a child because they wanted a child who *looked* like X might not go on to hope or try to ensure that X's clone *behaved* like X. Others still might initially want a cloned child who had the same behavioral attributes as the genetic donor but might quickly become disabused of the idea that this could ever become reality as soon as the cloned child began to exhibit his own unique personality. Even if, to concede the point, a number of cloners really did want to produce a child who would be as close to X in all ways possible, and strove concertedly to realize this aim through their approaches to teaching and socializing their cloned children, while they might be guilty on Millian grounds of denying their child certain requisite conditions for autonomous development it does not follow from this that cloning should be disallowed. Mill regarded parents who denied an education to their offspring as morally blameworthy, and as legitimate targets of sanctions by the state. Although Mill recommended state intervention when children were denied proper conditions, he did not further suggest that they should never have come to exist.

Parental power is as susceptible of abuse as any other power, and is, as a matter of fact, constantly abused. If laws do not succeed in preventing parents from brutally ill-treating, and even from murdering their children, far less ought it to be presumed that the interests of children will never be sacrificed, in more common-place and less revolting ways, to the selfishness or ignorance of their parents. Whatever it can be clearly seen that parents ought to do or forbear for the interests of children, the law is warranted, if it is able, in compelling to be done and forborne, and is generally bound to do so.[47]

This passage and others of Mill's writings reviewed in preceding sections supply some grounds for state interference in parenting. Parents might justifiably be coerced into treating or teaching their children in certain ways. But this is quite distinct from the view that all individuals should be prevented from having offspring through certain means because a proportion of their offspring might lead sub-optimally autonomous lives. In addition, it merits emphasis that there are countless ways in which parents actively impede the autonomous development of their offspring. To single out cloning as if it could be the only or most serious fetter on autonomy is misleading.

V CLONING, SHARED VALUES, AND CUSTOMARY MORALITY

In the closing section of this chapter, I shall scrutinize the argument advanced by Leon Kass: to wit, that cloning is morally impermissible because it would undermine certain fundamental shared human values and threaten customary morality. Kass writes:

Finally, and perhaps most important, the practice of human cloning by nuclear transfer – like other anticipated forms of genetic engineering of the next

---

[47] John Stuart Mill, *Principles of Political Economy with Some of Their Applications to Social Philosophy*, Part I (1948), vol. II of *The Collected Works of John Stuart Mill*, ed. John M. Robson, introduction by V. W. Bladen (Toronto: University of Toronto Press; London: Routledge & Kegan Paul, 1965), 952 (Bk. V, 9).

generation – would enshrine and aggravate a profound and mischievous misunderstanding of the meaning of having children and of the parent–child relationship.
When a couple now chooses to procreate, the partners are saying yes to the
emergence of new life in its novelty, saying yes not only to having a child but
also, tacitly, to having whatever child this child turns out to be. In accepting our
finitude and opening ourselves to our replacement, we are tacitly confessing the
limits of our control. In this ubiquitous way of nature, embracing the future by
procreating means precisely that we are relinquishing our grip, in the very activity
of taking up our own share in what we hope will be the immortality of human life
and the human species.[48]

Mill was unambiguous about the worth of doing something because it was
the "custom."

But it is the privilege and proper condition of a human being, arrived at the
maturity of his faculties, to use and interpret experience in his own way. It is for
him to find out what part of recorded experience is properly applicable to his own
circumstances and character. The traditions and customs of other people are to a
certain extent, evidence of what their experience has taught them: presumptive
evidence, and as such, have a claim to his deference: but, in the first place, their
experience may be too narrow; or they may not have interpreted it rightly.
Secondly, their interpretation of experience may be correct, but unsuitable to
him. Customs are made for customary circumstances, and customary characters:
and his circumstances or his character may be uncustomary. Thirdly though the
customs be both good as customs, and suitable to him, yet to conform to custom,
merely *as* custom, does not educate or develop in him any of the qualities which are
the distinctive endowment of a human being. The human faculties of perception,
judgment, discriminative feeling, mental activity, and even moral preference, are
exercised only in making a choice. He who does anything because it is the custom,
makes no choice … He who lets the world, or his own portion of it, choose his plan
of life for him, has no need of any other faculty than the ape-like one of imitation.
(*CW* XVIII, 262 [III, 1])

I infer from the preceding passage that Mill's first rejoinder to Kass would be
that just because over the centuries humans have reproduced through
natural means, according to the vagaries of chance, it is not morally
demanded of them to continue choosing the same means of reproduction.
Customary methods of reproduction, in short, cannot be valued merely on
the grounds that they are the custom. Second, and relatedly, Mill's rationale
for introducing the liberty principle is to protect individuals against all those
who wish to force others to adopt their own meaning of what is most sacred
about human life.

---

[48] Kass, "The Wisdom of Repugnance," 24.

But Kass is pointing to something deeper than simply the facts that cloning is a non-customary way of begetting children, and introduces a different dynamic to parent–child relationships. SCNT would allow individuals to dictate quite fully the genetic complement of their offspring. This has striking implications for our shared morality, a point aptly articulated by Ronald Dworkin:

> My hypothesis is that genetic science has suddenly made us aware of the possibility of a similar though far greater pending moral dislocation [than did changes in deathbed medicine]. We dread the prospect of people designing other people because that possibility in itself shifts – much more dramatically than in those other examples – the chance/choice boundary that structures our values as a whole, and such a shift threatens, not to offend any of our present values, detached or derivative, but, on the contrary, to make a great part of these suddenly obsolete. Our physical being – the brain and body which furnishes [*sic*] each person's material substrate – has long been the absolute paradigm of what is both devastatingly important to us, and in its initial condition, beyond our power to alter and therefore beyond the scope of our responsibility, either individual or collective.[49]

The power that SCNT would bestow – detailed control over procreative outcomes – entails that an area of human activity which had always resided outside the sphere of moral responsibility would come to fall squarely within it. This possibility elicits quite different normative responses from Kass and from Dworkin respectively. Both recognize that SCNT, along with other technologies which might afford us more control over the sort of people who come to exist, would pose challenges to our shared morality. But, whereas Kass seeks a ban on cloning, Dworkin positively affirms the need for a reorientation of our moral parameters.[50] As for Mill, he would be untroubled by the prospect that advances in genetics, such as human cloning, might require that we reevaluate customary morality. For Mill, challenges to existing morals and practices which do not involve the violation of individuals' vital interests are potential spurs to human progress.

CONCLUSION

In this chapter, our inquiry into Mill's stance on human reproductive cloning has necessarily involved drawing many inferences from his writings

---

49 Ronald Dworkin, *Sovereign Virtue: The Theory and Practice of Equality* (Cambridge, MA: Harvard University Press, 2000), 444–5. I have argued elsewhere that Dworkin's claim that cloning confronts us with a moral sea change is overstated. See my "Morality and the New Genetics," in Justine Burley, ed., *Ronald Dworkin and His Critics* (Oxford: Blackwell, 2002), 170–92.
50 Dworkin, *Sovereign Virtue*, 445–6.

on other relevant topics. I have argued that Mill would have no objection to
human reproductive cloning "in principle." Mill would reason that whenever it could be reliably predicted that possible future people would have
lives that were not worth living – wretched, poverty-stricken, meager
existences in which there might also be no possibility for individual self-
creation or flourishing – measures should be taken to prevent them from
being brought into existence. This will not be feasible in all cases. It is,
however, feasible legally to curtail reproductive liberty in the case of assisted
reproduced technologies, if the risk of harm to possible people is significant.
In addition, I have argued that although creating the conditions for people
to live autonomous lives was one of Mill's chief intellectual preoccupations,
he would not regard the possibility that cloning might lead some parents to
impede the development of their children's capacities of critical reflection as
a sufficiently weighty reason to deny general access to cloning technology.
Finally, while cloning might very well alter our understanding of human
procreation as a whole and/or precipitate a shift in the parameters of our
moral views and discourse, this would not count, for Mill, as in any way a
reason to condemn its practice.

CHAPTER 10

John Stuart Mill, Ronald Dworkin, and paternalism

Robert Young

INTRODUCTION

In *On Liberty* Mill famously wrote that

> the sole end for which mankind are warranted, individually or collectively, in interfering with the liberty of action of any of their number, is self-protection. [Indeed] the only purpose for which power can be rightfully exercised over any member of a civilized community, against his will, is to prevent harm to others. His own good, either physical or moral, is not a sufficient warrant. He cannot rightfully be compelled to do or forbear because it will be better for him to do so, because it will make him happier, because, in the opinion of others, to do so would be wise, or even right. These are good reasons for remonstrating with him, or reasoning with him, or persuading him, but not for compelling him, or visiting him with any evil in case he do otherwise. (*CW* XVIII, 223–4 [1, 9])

Several aspects of Mill's account call for preliminary comment. First, even though he railed against interfering with the liberty of persons both for their physical good *and* for their moral good, it is Mill's denunciation of interferences of the former kind, rather than of the latter, that has made him a famed opponent of *paternalistic* interferences.[1] Second, Mill's characterization of paternalism as involving interference with the liberty of individuals by way of compulsion suggests that he was presupposing the use of physical force. However, it is also possible to treat people paternalistically by way of deception (e.g., through the withholding of information). Though there can be little doubt that Mill's predominant concern was with forms of paternalism requiring physical interference with liberty, he could, without inconsistency, have widened his perspective to include instances of paternalism like those involving deception, which, strictly, do not require interference with liberty. Both perspectives incorporate the idea of an affront to individual liberty, and so capture the central complaint of opponents of

---

[1] Interferences of the latter kind are helpfully analysed by Gerald Dworkin, "Moral Paternalism," *Law and Philosophy*, 24 (2005), 305–19.

paternalism. Third, his strictures about paternalism apply only to interferences with the liberty of *competent* agents, because he specifically exempted those in the care of others, *viz.*, children, adolescents, those whose "reflective faculties" are defective, and those in their "nonage" (*CW* XVIII, 224 [I, 10]).[2] A few contemporary writers have taken the view that the only form of paternalism worthy of the name is the sort that consists in overriding the wishes of competent agents for their own good (so-called "hard" or "strong" paternalism). But many consider, for example, that decisions made for the good of children, who have never been competent, or for those who once were competent but are so no longer, also constitute paternalism (so-called "soft" or "weak" paternalism).[3] Fourth, even though Mill focused on paternalistic *actions*, paternalistic goals may also, on occasion, be achieved by *refraining from acting*. Wealthy parents sometimes deliberately refrain from bequeathing their wealth to their children because they think it will be better for them to make their own way in life. It is plausible to claim that if *A* refrains from helping *B* with the intention of helping *B* to become more self-reliant, *A*'s refraining ought to be counted as paternalistic.[4] This fact leads directly to the fifth and final feature of Mill's characterization of paternalism on which I wish to offer a preliminary comment, namely that he emphasized both the motivation for, and the effects of, paternalism. Several reasons have already been given for modifying Mill's characterization of paternalism as involving actions that interfere with the liberty of individuals. There is reason, too, for thinking that Mill's account of the motive for paternalism requires modification.[5] In the famous passage cited in my opening paragraph, Mill seems to believe that paternalism arises out of a disagreement between *A* and *B* about what would be best for *A*. However, in acting paternalistically toward *B*, *A*'s motivation may be to promote what *B* wants, *viz.*, to be made better off (or, alternatively, not to be made worse off).

---

[2] The last mentioned are from "those backward states of society in which the race itself may be considered in its nonage" (i.e., in an immature stage of development).

[3] Tom Beauchamp, "Paternalism and Bio-Behavioral Control," *The Monist*, 60 (1976), 62–80, is one who contends that weak paternalism is "not paternalism in any interesting sense." The same sentiment is evident in Richard Arneson, "Mill versus Paternalism," *Ethics*, 90 (1980), 470–89, especially 471ff. (although it has to be added that he has recently outlined a markedly different view in "Joel Feinberg and the Justification of Hard Paternalism," *Legal Theory*, 11 (2005), 259–84). Joel Feinberg, who first drew the distinction between weak and strong paternalism in "Legal Paternalism," *Canadian Journal of Philosophy*, 1 (1971), 105–24, later came to concur with Beauchamp's view but, because of the potential for confusion, was prepared to say so only in a whisper. See Joel Feinberg, *The Moral Limits of the Criminal Law*, vol. III: *Harm to Self* (New York: Oxford University Press, 1986), 12–16.

[4] Seana Valentine Shiffrin "Paternalism, Unconscionability Doctrine, and Accommodation," *Philosophy & Public Affairs*, 29 (2000), 205–50, especially 213.

[5] Ibid., 215f.

If *A* believes that *B* will act contrary to what they have agreed would be in *B*'s best interests, and prevents *B* from so acting (say, because of *B*'s weakness of will), *A*'s behavior will be paternalistic. Thus, for example, a woman acts paternalistically if she hides her partner's money to prevent him from gambling even if he agrees with her that gambling is contrary to his best interests.

Given these preliminary points, I shall take *A* to behave paternalistically if, irrespective of whether *B* has competently reached a contrary judgment about how to promote or protect his own interests, *A* seeks to justify an action or an omission which is intended to affect *B* by claiming that it will make *B* better off, or protect *B* from harm. This brief statement encapsulates a broad understanding of paternalism even though much of the chapter will be concerned with the narrower notion of strong paternalism and with whether it may ever be justifiable. I will begin by briefly reviewing Mill's seminal discussion of the issue, before giving consideration to a prominent recent attempt by Ronald Dworkin to elaborate a similar opposition to strong paternalism,[6] albeit in a manner he thinks less vulnerable to criticism. I will argue that neither Mill's position nor that of Dworkin precludes the justifiability of at least some instances of strong paternalism.

MILL'S MAIN ARGUMENTS AGAINST PATERNALISM AND SOME CRITICAL COMMENTS ON THEM

Mill's opposition to paternalism stemmed fundamentally from his commitment to liberty as the means by which we may best develop our capacities (consistent, of course, with others enjoying similar liberty). He put forward a number of arguments that have been given different taxonomies by commentators.[7] I lay no claim to offering a definitive account of his arguments, merely an indicative one.

Mill argues against paternalism on, at least, the following four main grounds. First, because competent persons know their own interests better

---

[6] Ronald Dworkin, *Sovereign Virtue: The Theory and Practice of Equality* (Cambridge, MA: Harvard University Press, 2000). Dworkin distinguishes (217) between "volitional paternalism," which is aimed at helping an individual achieve what he already wants to achieve, and "critical paternalism," which is aimed at forcing an individual to lead a life that is in accord with his critical interests rather than with what he now values. I believe that Dworkin's rejection of critical paternalism can be likened to the rejection by many liberals of "strong paternalism."

[7] See, e.g., Gerald Dworkin, "Paternalism," *The Monist*, 56 (1972), 64–84, especially 70–6; Arneson, "Mill versus Paternalism," especially 476–81; and John Kleinig, *Paternalism* (Totowa, NJ: Rowman & Allanheld, 1984), 28ff.

than do others (especially governments[8]), their liberty should not be interfered with on the ground that others know better how to protect or promote
those interests (*CW* xviii, 277 [iv, 4]). Second, paternalistic interferences with
liberty are prone to error (especially when undertaken by governments)
because they rely on general presumptions of no direct relevance to any
particular person, and so are apt to be misapplied because of lack of acquaint-
ance with the specific circumstances of affected persons (*CW* xviii, 277 [iv,
4], 283 [iv, 12]). Third, paternalistic interferences fail to show respect for
individual liberty, which is vital to the treatment of individuals as equals (*CW*
xviii, 263 [iii, 4]). Fourth, since the exercise of liberty is instrumental to the
development of individual character, individuals ought to be allowed to make
their own mistakes in order to develop their particular characters (*CW* xviii,
283 [iv, 12]). I will review these arguments consecutively.

Mill's first line of reasoning relies on a questionable premise. Indeed, as I
shall shortly point out, Mill himself raised doubts about it in one of his
publications. However, this did not dissuade him from employing it to
argue that paternalism should be prohibited.

It is true that competent individuals are, in general, better placed than
others to know what is in their own best interests, if only because the good
for individuals is, in significant part, determined by their subjective preferences. This has particular significance when it is the state that proposes to
act paternalistically. In fact, Mill thought his position at its strongest in
relation to the paternalistic use of the law because

the interference of society to overrule [a person's] judgment and purposes in what
only regards himself, must be grounded on general presumptions; which may be
altogether wrong, and even if right, are as likely as not to be misapplied to
individual cases, by persons no better acquainted with the circumstances of such
cases than those are who look at them merely from without. (*CW* xviii, 277 [iv, 4])

These generalizations are supposed to bolster the claim that to compel
competent individuals to behave in ways that they do not judge to be in
their best interests will render them worse off; but they are open to
challenge. Since competent individuals do not always know what is in
their best interests, and, even when they do, they do not always act

---

[8] Douglas N. Husak, "Legal Paternalism," in Hugh LaFollette, ed., *The Oxford Handbook of Practical Ethics* (New York: Oxford University Press, 2003), 387–412, argues that the characterization of certain laws as "paternalistic" is highly problematic (390ff.). Nonetheless, he goes on to argue that despite it being more difficult to justify state paternalism than (non-legal) paternalism by individuals (395ff.), state paternalism may sometimes be justified on consequentialist grounds (401ff.). In *Overcriminalization: The Limits of the Criminal Law* (New York: Oxford University Press, 2008), Husak argues that the state should not, however, make use of the criminal law for paternalistic purposes.

accordingly, it is obvious that Mill's claims about our knowledge of and solicitude for our own good ought to be rejected.[9]

Furthermore, as previously mentioned, Mill acknowledged in another publication that such generalizations have their limitations. In an earlier discussion of the proper limits of government intervention in the economy (which continued to be included without revision in later editions), he stated similar views about the sovereignty of the individual, but noted that the above generalizations could "be admitted only with numerous abatements and exceptions."[10]

His second argument also ought to be rejected. In addition to the points made in the passage just cited, he claimed that "the strongest of all arguments against the interference of the public with purely personal conduct, is that when it does interfere, the odds are that it interferes wrongly, and in the wrong place" (*CW* XVIII, 283 [IV, 12]). This contention about the likely misapplication of paternalistic laws to individual cases lacks credibility, most particularly because Mill directed it against *all* (legal) paternalism. It fails to provide a convincing ground for opposing legislation, for example, for "cooling off" periods to afford consumers protection against making unwise purchases, or for compelling the use of safety equipment in industrial settings. It is simply not credible to suggest that laws like these involve interferences that are so seriously misplaced as to constitute an affront to individual liberty. Undoubtedly, it is possible for laws to be objectionably paternalistic in virtue of aiming to offer protection that is quite unwelcome. Thus, for example, proposals to use the law to compel pregnant women who are contemplating having an abortion to delay making their decision until they have attended a counseling session have met with this response. But this does not gainsay the point that legal paternalism is not always misguided in the way Mill nominated in his second argument. Furthermore, in relation to non-legal paternalism, his argument has little or no relevance. Hence, his second argument is no more compelling than his first.

The third ground for Mill's opposition to paternalism was its disrespect for the equal standing of competent individuals within society. Because the interests of each individual matter equally, compulsion is permissible as a means of securing the interests of individuals only when they are endangered by the conduct of others. Thus, there is no place for compulsion in

---

[9] See, e.g., H. L. A. Hart, *Law, Liberty and Morality* (Oxford: Oxford University Press; Stanford: Stanford University Press, 1963), 32f.

[10] John Stuart Mill, *Principles of Political Economy with Some of Their Applications to Social Philosophy*, Part II, vol. III of *The Collected Works of John Stuart Mill*, ed. J. M. Robson, introduction by V. W. Bladen (Toronto: University of Toronto Press; London: Routledge & Kegan Paul, 1965), 947 (Bk. V, x, 8).

that sphere of action "in which society, as distinguished from the individual, has, if any, only an indirect interest; comprehending all that portion of a person's life and conduct which affects only himself, or if it also affects others, only with their free, voluntary, and undeceived consent and participation" (*CW* xviii, 225 [I, 12]). If individuals are not to be robbed of their equal standing with others once they are "capable of being improved by free and equal discussion" (*CW* xviii, 224 [I, 10]), paternalism has to be prohibited. Without such a prohibition they would be at risk of having a conception of the good different from their own imposed upon them, which would signal that their self-determination had been usurped and that their equal standing was not respected.

There can be no doubt that this third argument captures what many critics of paternalism take to be the essence of why they find it offensive. Competent individuals do bridle when others treat them as though they are still in their nonage. But must paternalism involve such demeaning treatment? Consider (to give just two examples) the legal requirement for passengers on ships to be given training to prepare them for the extremely unlikely eventuality of having to abandon ship, and the legal mandating of fire drills for occupants of certain kinds of building. Even if paternalism is not the only motive for legal requirements like these, it surely is among the more significant of the reasons for their promulgation. Despite having, on occasion, been mildly resentful myself about the inconvenience involved, it is hard to take seriously the idea of passengers or occupants of buildings being demeaned by having to undertake these forms of compulsory training. In particular, I think it hard to take seriously any claim that having to undertake the training is offensive because it causes a diminution in the standing of the one who is required to undertake the training as compared with that of the legislators or instructors. I say this with full awareness of how remote the prospect is that the training will help to save the lives of those being trained (and, hence, be in their interests). In short, I am no more persuaded by Mill's third main argument against paternalism than by his two previous arguments.

Mill's fourth (and, perhaps, most important) argument is built on the idea that because value inheres in individuals being able to decide things for themselves (as a means to the development of their individuality), the loss in value that must result from paternalistic interferences with decision-making is sufficient to warrant their prohibition.[11] Since he seems to have thought

---

[11] He devotes chapter III of *On Liberty* almost entirely to furnishing a case for the instrumental value (or utility) of individual self-determination. See *CW* xviii, 260–75.

that the good for individuals consists in self-fulfillment, *and* that development of the capacities needed for decision-making is a key component of self-fulfillment, it is plain why, on his account, sovereignty in decision-making is instrumentally significant for the good of individuals.[12] Coupled with his first argument, which was supposed to show that no improvement in well-being could ever result from preempting or overriding an individual's decision-making (such decision-making being causally necessary for the individual's own good), the foundations for Mill's anti-paternalism might seem to have been firmly laid. However, even supposing that a significant cost is imposed on individuals when their decisions are forcibly preempted or overridden, it still does not follow that that cost will always exceed any benefit the individual obtains (e.g., the benefit obtained in being protected against harm). Mill's fourth argument is, therefore, indecisive regardless of whether it is harnessed together with his first argument.

Notwithstanding this, I will say a little more here (in order that I may draw upon it later) about the relationship Mill posited between self-fulfillment and the good for an individual. As mentioned, Mill seems to have thought that decision-making sovereignty is instrumental to the good for an individual. However, he recognized that it is possible, on occasion, to question whether an individual's decision is both free and informed, as in the following famous example:

If either a public officer or any one else saw a person attempting to cross a bridge which had been ascertained to be unsafe, and there were no time to warn him of his danger, they might seize him and turn him back, without any real infringement of his liberty; for liberty consists in doing what one desires, and he does not desire to fall into the river. (*CW* xviii, 294 [v, 5])

Because he acknowledged that there are such circumstances, it has seemed to many that Mill's account of the relationship between decision-making sovereignty and individual good is not as inflexible as has hitherto been suggested, and, instead, implies that only those who are both informed and free[13] are to be recognized as sovereign decision-makers. On this understanding, it is consistent with his position to employ weak paternalism when individuals are either inadequately informed or unfree.

---

[12] This argument is sometimes referred to as his "moral muscles argument" because of the analogy he draws with the building up of the "muscular powers." See *CW* xviii, 260–5 (iii, 1–6); Feinberg, *The Moral Limits of the Criminal Law*, vol. iii, 384.

[13] Mill's claim that "liberty consists in doing what one desires" is open to obvious objections, but a more plausible account could be substituted without significantly altering his stance.

However, Mill had more to say about the example, so the remainder of the passage cannot be ignored. He continued:

Nevertheless, when there is not a certainty, but only a danger of mischief, no one but the person himself can judge of the sufficiency of the motive which may prompt him to incur the risk: in this case, therefore, (unless he is a child, or delirious, or in some state of excitement or absorption incompatible with the full use of the reflecting faculty) he ought, I conceive, to be only warned of the danger; not forcibly prevented from exposing himself to it. (*CW* xviii, 294 [v, 5])

This suggests that Mill was prepared to modify his position on the sovereignty of the (competent) individual only when it was *certain* that an individual would behave in a manner contrary to his own good if not constrained. Accordingly, his concession to weak paternalism was quite limited. However, in the next section it will emerge that, in at least one circumstance, Mill was willing to break the nexus he claimed to exist between individual self-determination and the good, and, in consequence, to concede far more than weak paternalism.

TWO CRITICISMS OF THE INTERNAL CONSISTENCY OF MILL'S POSITION ON THE JUSTIFIABILITY OF PATERNALISM

It has been contended not only that Mill's specific arguments against paternalism are open to criticism, but that in proposing a blanket prohibition on paternalism he left himself open to a charge of holding inconsistent positions. Two main reasons have been offered for thinking there is an internal inconsistency between Mill's anti-paternalism and his other published views.

First, his anti-paternalism appears to be at odds with his commitment to utilitarianism.[14] Elsewhere he regards "utility as the ultimate appeal on all ethical questions," albeit this is immediately qualified when he adds that he means "utility in the largest sense, grounded on the permanent interests of man as a progressive being" (*CW* xviii, 224 [1, 11]). Since it is conceivable that instances of paternalism may be justified on utilitarian grounds, various critics have contended that Mill's anti-paternalist standpoint makes the protection of individual liberty, rather than utility, his supreme value. Second, as I hinted at the end of the preceding section, Mill allows that there is one circumstance in which a competent adult's right to be a

---

[14] See James Fitzjames Stephen, *Liberty, Equality, Fraternity* (1874), ed. R. J. White (Cambridge: Cambridge University Press, 1967), 86.

sovereign chooser should be challenged. He holds that society should not permit the enforcement of a contract for perpetual servitude, even if it has been entered into voluntarily (*CW* XVIII, 299 [v, 11]). As a result, he has been accused of inconsistency.[15]

Various of Mill's supporters have sought to defend him against the first objection by drawing attention to the key role that the protection and fostering of individual liberty played in his understanding of the good for an individual. Thus, they believe that Mill could consistently hold, first, that a competent individual's good consisted in his free pursuit of his preferred way of living, and, second, that any society wishing to maximize well-being (in accordance with the dictates of utilitarianism) ought to prohibit paternalism in order to protect the liberty of each individual to choose his own way of life and to live accordingly.[16] Though it can readily be granted that being free is an element in the good for an individual, it need not be granted (and I do not grant) that it is exhaustive of the good. An individual can, for example, quite legitimately trade some of his liberty for other goods like health, or can do so with an eye to ensuring he has more and better options in the future. So, it would seem that Mill and these supporters ultimately have to fall back on their insistence that the overriding of an individual's competent judgment by others will undermine that individual's status as a sovereign chooser. Of course, in the event that there is any doubt about an individual's competence at the time that a particular choice is made, it will, without inconsistency, be permissible to endorse a weak paternalist response.

In order to be in a better position to assess the defensibility of this claim about the sovereignty of competent decision-makers I turn to the second of the criticisms concerning the internal consistency of Mill's anti-paternalism. In discussing exceptions to the legal requirement to honor agreements voluntarily entered into, Mill notoriously wrote:

It is sometimes considered a sufficient reason for releasing [persons] from an engagement, that it is injurious to themselves. In this, and most other civilized countries, for example, an engagement by which a person should sell himself, or allow himself to be sold, as a slave, would be null and void; neither enforced by law nor by opinion. The ground for thus limiting his power of voluntarily disposing of his own lot in life, is apparent, and is very clearly seen in this extreme case. The

---

[15] Versions of these two arguments can be found in, e.g., Gerald Dworkin, "Paternalism," 70ff.; Arneson, "Mill versus Paternalism," 473f.; C. L. Ten, *Mill on Liberty* (Oxford: Clarendon Press, 1980), ch. 7; and Feinberg, *The Moral Limits of the Criminal Law*, vol. III, 75ff., 384.

[16] See, e.g., Rolf E. Sartorius, *Individual Conduct and Social Norms* (Encino and Belmont, CA: Dickenson, 1975), 155ff.; and Alan E. Fuchs, "Autonomy, Slavery, and Mill's Critique of Paternalism," *Ethical Theory and Moral Practice*, 4 (2001), 231–51, especially 233ff.

reason for not interfering, unless for the sake of others, with a person's voluntary acts, is consideration for his liberty. His voluntary choice is evidence that what he so chooses is desirable, or at the very least endurable, to him, and his good is on the whole best provided for by allowing him to take his own means of pursuing it. But by selling himself for a slave, he abdicates his liberty; he forgoes any future use of it beyond that single act. He therefore defeats, in his own case, the very purpose which is the justification of allowing him to dispose of himself. He is no longer free; but is thenceforth in a position which has no longer the presumption in its favour, that would be afforded by his voluntarily remaining in it. The principle of freedom cannot require that he should be free not to be free. It is not freedom, to be allowed to alienate his freedom. (*CW* xviii, 299f. [v, 11])

Mill's comments about voluntary enslavement have ruffled his supporters and been seized upon by certain of his critics. The former seek to play down what seems to be inconsistency, while the latter think that the inconsistency between Mill's discussion of voluntary slavery contracts and his usual strictures on the paternalistic treatment of those intending voluntarily to endanger their interests (provided they have been warned of the danger) should simply be acknowledged, *and* that, no matter the explanation for the inconsistency, its existence exposes how difficult it is to maintain a rationally justifiable blanket prohibition on paternalism.[17] So, even if, for the most part, the sovereignty of the individual rightfully holds sway, occasions will arise when protection or promotion of an individual's own good justifiably requires overruling his sovereignty (as, I believe, various examples have already illustrated). Hence, proposals for acting paternalistically, and instances of paternalism, including those involving strong paternalism, should be considered one by one to determine which, if any, are rationally justifiable. I will seek below to make good on these assertions. But it will help if I first consider several of the ways in which Mill's supporters have responded to the charge that he is inconsistent.

SOME RESPONSES TO THE CHARGE THAT MILL IS INCONSISTENT

Some supporters point to the cautious way Mill expresses himself in the passage quoted above and conclude that his opposition to paternalism was reserved for all bar extreme cases like that of a person selling himself into

---

[17] See Gerald Dworkin, "Paternalism"; Robert Young, "Autonomy and Paternalism," in Steven C. Patten, ed., *New Essays in Ethics and Public Policy, Canadian Journal of Philosophy*, sup. vol. 8 (1982), 47–66; Kleinig, *Paternalism*; Dan Brock, "Paternalism and Autonomy," *Ethics*, 98 (1988), 550–65; and Danny Scoccia, "Paternalism and Respect for Autonomy," *Ethics*, 100 (1990), 318–34.

perpetual slavery. For them, the language of prohibition used elsewhere by Mill is simply a rhetorical device and any picture of Mill's position on paternalism will be incomplete if it ignores his remarks about voluntary slavery contracts.[18] The complete picture tells a story of restricted opposition to paternalism. The trouble with any interpretation along these lines is that it can hardly be thought accurate to regard Mill as indulging in mere rhetoric in the passage cited at the very beginning of this chapter (or, indeed, in other passages with a similar drift that are to be found throughout the first chapter of *On Liberty*).

A second response has been to suggest that Mill should have reaffirmed his statements opposing paternalism and discarded his paternalistic objection to voluntary slavery contracts.[19] Arneson endeavors to back up this claim by suggesting that though Mill expressed warranted opposition to voluntary slavery contracts, he neglected to consider the possibility that there may be non-paternalistic rationales for outlawing them. At first glance this may seem a more reasonable way to account for Mill's contentions. Alas, however, given that Mill repeated his claim about the importance of disallowing voluntary slavery contracts without modification over a period of three decades, it beggars belief to think that he misidentified why he thought they should be disallowed.

A third, and quite influential, response has come from those supporters who believe that Mill's comments about perpetual slavery can be

---

[18] In support of such a view, there is the consideration that in his earlier work, *Principles of Political Economy*, in a section dealing with cases of contract in perpetuity, Mill wrote: "A second exception to the doctrine that individuals are the best judges of their own best interest, is when an individual attempts to decide irrevocably now, what will be best for his interest at some future and distant time. The presumption in favour of individual judgment is only legitimate, where the judgment is grounded on actual, and especially on present, personal experience; not where it is formed antecedently to experience, and not suffered to be reversed even after experience has condemned it. When persons have bound themselves by a contract, not simply to do some one thing, but to continue doing something for ever or for a prolonged period, without any power of revoking the engagement, the presumption which their perseverance in that course of conduct would otherwise raise in favour of its being advantageous to them, does not exist; and any such presumption which can be grounded on their having voluntarily entered into the contract, perhaps at an early age, and without any real knowledge of what they undertook, is commonly next to null. The practical maxim of leaving contracts free, is not applicable without great limitations in case of engagements in perpetuity; and the law should be extremely jealous of such engagements; should refuse its sanction to them, when the obligations they impose are such as the contracting party cannot be a competent judge of; if it ever does sanction them, it should take every possible security for their being contracted with foresight and deliberation; and in compensation for not permitting the parties themselves to revoke their engagement, should grant them a release from it, on a sufficient case being made out before an impartial authority" (*CW* III, 935f. [Bk. v, xi, 9]). This passage remained unaltered through six further editions, including the final edition published in 1871.

[19] Arneson, "Mill versus Paternalism," 473, 487.

accommodated by construing him as making a weak paternalist claim.[20] On this reading, Mill's opposition to perpetual slavery contracts is compatible with his opposition to paternalism because an individual who enters into such a contract deprives himself of the capacity to make revisions in the future concerning how he will live his life, and, since this is an essential element in Mill's concept of liberty, such an individual shows thereby that his choice is not fully voluntary. But if Mill's opposition to paternalism throughout the bulk of *On Liberty* simply reflects his opposition to strong paternalism, it is difficult to reconcile this with his emphasis on the *voluntariness* of the decision by an individual to sell himself into perpetual slavery. If he wished only to oppose strong paternalism he surely would have made it clear that he did not consider it possible for someone to enter into such a contract fully voluntarily. Still, it may be said, regardless of the consistency or otherwise of Mill's claims about paternalism, the justifiability of overriding the judgments of competent individuals about which goals are worthy of being pursued remains a key issue for those who value liberty.

With that in mind, I shall consider a significant recent attempt by Ronald Dworkin to reject the view that a person's life can be improved by forcing him to do something he does not value. Dworkin allows that what he labels "volitional paternalism" may be morally justifiable if it is sufficiently short term and limited in scope, but contends that "critical paternalism" can never be morally justifiable from a liberal perspective.

RONALD DWORKIN'S CRITIQUE OF PATERNALISM

For Dworkin, an individual's "volitional well-being is improved whenever he has or achieves something he wants,"[21] whereas "his critical well-being is improved only by his having or achieving those things that he should want, that is, achievements or experiences that it would make his life a worse one not to want."[22] Correspondingly, "volitional paternalism supposes that

---

[20] See, e.g., Feinberg, "Legal Paternalism"; John D. Hodson, "The Principle of Paternalism," *American Philosophical Quarterly*, 14 (1977) 61–9; Ten, *Mill on Liberty*; and Fuchs, "Autonomy, Slavery, and Mill's Critique of Paternalism," especially 241–50. In *The Moral Limits of the Criminal Law*, vol. III, especially chs. 17–22, Feinberg subjected this strategy to searching criticism. By the time he wrote the later work his strong conviction was that the competent have a "sovereign right of self-determination," and he no longer considered weak paternalism to be paternalism at all, but, as previously mentioned, was prepared only to whisper this for fear of causing confusion. However, he sought, in consequence, to identify implicit non-paternalistic rationales for apparently paternalistic interventions, including in relation to voluntary perpetual slavery. For a spirited defense of his approach see Heidi Malm, "Feinberg's Anti-paternalism and the Balancing Strategy," *Legal Theory*, 11 (2005), 193–212.
[21] See Ronald Dworkin, *Sovereign Virtue*, 216.   [22] Ibid.

coercion can sometimes help people achieve what they already want to
achieve, and is for that reason in their volitional interests. Critical paternalism supposes that coercion can sometimes provide people with lives that are
better than the lives they now think good and is therefore sometimes in their
critical interests."[23] Dworkin believes that it is a significant philosophical
issue whether the former view is to be preferred to the latter, because an
individual's life can be evaluated *either* by reference to whether it includes
the components that make a life a good life *or* by whether the individual
endorses the components that make up his life. Dworkin favors the latter
(which he dubs "the constitutive view")[24] on the ground that the former
("the additive view") is incapable of explaining "why a good life is distinctively valuable for or to the person whose life it is."[25] On the additive view,
whether a component is in someone's critical interests is separable from
whether it is endorsed, albeit it is possible to hold that the stronger the
degree of endorsement of a component the greater its value.[26] On the
constitutive view, by contrast, endorsement is a necessary condition of a
component's having value, so unless and until an individual endorses a
component it cannot contribute to making his life valuable for him.

   Such a view accords well with Mill's conception of individuality in *On
Liberty*; indeed, it is just the kind of view that he seems to have had in mind
on those occasions when he proposed a blanket prohibition on (strong)
paternalism. For the present, though, I want to draw attention to the close
fit between the constitutive view and Dworkin's preferred model of critical
value, his so-called "challenge model" (which he contrasts with an "impact

[23] Ibid., 217.
[24] His view in this respect is similar to that of Will Kymlicka, *Contemporary Political Philosophy: An Introduction* (Oxford: Oxford University Press, 1990), 203f., though Kymlicka is less concerned to oppose (state) paternalism than (state) *perfectionism*, namely, the idea that, in order to develop the qualities that will perfect our natures as human beings, the state should "promote goods that are worthy of promotion but whose value is not adequately recognised by the persons for whom they are goods," which is how Colin Macleod expresses the view on p. 135 of his "Agency, Goodness, and Endorsement: Why We Can't Be Forced to Flourish," *Imprints*, 7 (2003), 131–60. For a statement of Dworkin's opposition to state perfectionism see "Ronald Dworkin Replies," in Justine Burley (ed.), *Dworkin and His Critics* (Oxford: Blackwell, 2004), 357.
[25] Ronald Dworkin, *Sovereign Virtue*, 217.
[26] T. M. Wilkinson, "Dworkin on Paternalism and Well-Being," *Oxford Journal of Legal Studies*, 16 (1996), 433–44, distinguishes between a weak and a strong form of the additive view. The former is the view that the greater the degree of endorsement of an option the better it is, *other things being equal*, whereas the latter is the view that the greater the degree of endorsement of an option the better it is, *all things considered*. On the weak additive view, the less endorsed of two options can still be better, provided it has a sufficiently greater critical value; whereas, according to the strong view, "of equivalently endorsed options, the one with greater critical value contributes more to the success of a person's life" (437). The difference, as he sees it, between the constitutive view and the strong additive view is that only on the former is endorsement a necessary condition for a component's having value.

model"). The challenge model, whose focus is on meeting the challenge of living life well, is supposed to make more coherent sense of our ethical experience than the impact model, which holds that what matters is the difference a person's life makes to the world's objective value.

Dworkin believes that on the challenge model the connection between conviction and value is constitutive.[27] Once the constitutive view is accepted, critical paternalism can be rejected out of hand – an individual's life can be improved only with his endorsement. It cannot be improved by treating him paternalistically, unless "the paternalism is sufficiently short-term and limited so that it does not significantly constrict choice if the endorsement never comes."[28] (Dworkin thinks that, in contrast, critical paternalism, at the very least, makes sense on the impact model, even if its supporters are not required to approve of that model.) Because he is aware of the possibility of an endorsement being produced through manipulation (e.g., through chemical or electrical brainwashing, or out of fear), he adds that an individual's endorsement of a change in his life will be acceptable only if the mechanisms used to secure it do not weaken "his ability to consider the critical merits of the change in a reflective way."[29]

In order to see whether Dworkin's approach represents an improvement on Mill's arguments against the justifiability of strong paternalism it will be necessary to give close consideration to the key concept of "endorsement" and to the supporting arguments he offers for its use as a bulwark against strong paternalism.

The way in which Dworkin (and Kymlicka) appear to understand the concept of endorsement makes it less straightforward than they imply and leaves Dworkin's use of it open to objection. For them, endorsement seems to admit of no degrees – it is all or nothing. But it is easy to imagine circumstances in which an individual endorses several options that cannot be simultaneously realized.[30] Given both this and Dworkin's commitment to the constitutive view, wherein endorsement is a necessary condition for the realization of value, it appears to follow, as Wilkinson has pointed out,[31] that an individual's life could be improved by forcing him (paternalistically, if necessary) to take the critically most valuable among the various options

---

[27] Ronald Dworkin, *Sovereign Virtue*, 268; and "*Sovereign Virtue* Revisited," *Ethics*, 113 (2002), 106–43, especially 141f.

[28] "Ronald Dworkin Replies," 355 (which corrects a misprint in the rendition of this claim in *Sovereign Virtue*, 269).

[29] Ronald Dworkin, *Sovereign Virtue*, 218.

[30] Cf. Wilkinson, "Dworkin on Paternalism and Well-Being," 435; and Macleod, "Agency, Goodness, and Endorsement," 143f.

[31] Wilkinson, "Dworkin on Paternalism and Well-Being," 436.

he endorses. Furthermore, since Dworkin conceives of endorsement as all or nothing, he should consider that an option that is not taken up is one that is, strictly, no longer endorsed. If he does, then given that what is unendorsed is without value, it would appear that he must implausibly hold that an option that is initially endorsed, but is deposed by another option that is more strongly endorsed, has no intrinsic value for the agent. It is surely more plausible to believe that such an option is still regarded by the agent as having value, just not as great value as its replacement.[32]

Given the confines of this chapter, I will say no more about Dworkin's construal of the concept of endorsement, but will, instead, concentrate on how he argues against critical paternalism. In particular, I will focus on the way he links endorsement with integrity. He offers two related arguments for the link. According to the first, in the absence of endorsement a person's life will lack integrity and so will feel false:

If we accept the challenge model we can insist on the priority of ethical integrity in any judgments we make about how good someone's life is. Someone has achieved ethical integrity, we may say, when he lives out of the conviction that his life, in its central features, is an appropriate one, that no other life he might live would be a plainly better response to the parameters of his ethical situation rightly judged.[33]

He allows, of course, that an agent who lives in a manner that is faithful to his convictions can modify his convictions in light of advice from those well placed to give it, or in light of his own continuing reflection. But, from the third-person perspective, which he thinks is the crucial one for the issue of critical paternalism, we are precluded from requiring a competent individual to act contrary to his convictions once we give ethical integrity priority. It is permissible to debate with the individual about what would be in his best interests, but not to impose values that he does not endorse, for that would require him to live a life in which he would not be at peace with himself.[34]

The key point to notice about this argument is the contention that integrity is undermined by critical paternalism. As moral or ethical integrity is commonly understood, it involves holding steadfastly to a consistent set of moral values, standards, or principles that have been deliberately and successfully integrated into a person's sense of self. So, when Dworkin

---

[32] See Thomas Hurka, "Indirect Perfectionism: Kymlicka on Liberal Neutrality," *Journal of Political Philosophy*, 3 (1995), 36–57, who distinguishes a strong interpretation of endorsement from a weak interpretation, which sees it as only a necessary condition of the realization by an agent of the highest degree of value present in a valuable activity. This implies that an unendorsed activity may still have value for an agent.
[33] Ronald Dworkin, *Sovereign Virtue*, 270.   [34] Ibid., 271f.

writes that integrity "fails conspicuously when people are made to live, by the fiat of other people, in a way they regret and never endorse,"[35] what he says may, at first sight, seem undeniable. We do think that individuals suffer a loss of integrity when they fail to act in accordance with their convictions, including when third parties have induced them to act contrary to those convictions. But when a third party compels an individual to act in a way he does not endorse, we do not think that he has, as a result, failed to act with integrity. Even supposing that critical paternalism always gives rise to a moral problem, Dworkin has misidentified the problem in thinking it has to do with an individual suffering a loss of moral integrity.[36]

Integrity does require coherence, but it is question-begging to claim that critical paternalism must destroy the coherence of an individual's life. Suppose that one of the key ingredients in a professional fire-fighter's sense of self is his readiness to put his life on the line to save others in an emergency. Suppose further that such a fire-fighter expresses the desire to enter an inferno to rescue a bedridden occupant who cannot escape without assistance. Suppose, finally, that his commanding officer orders him not to enter the building because the risk to his life would be too great, and tells him that he will have him restrained if he makes an attempt. The commanding officer's behavior is properly describable as critically paternalistic, but it is not obvious that the fire-fighter must, in consequence, suffer a loss of personal (or professional) integrity, or a loss of coherence in his response to the challenge to live his life well just because he has to follow such an order. Examples of the state engaging in critical paternalism are less common, but they are to hand. Thus, for instance, ocean beaches may be closed to swimmers during shark alerts; professional fishing fleets can be prohibited from leaving port when extreme weather conditions are forecast; those wishing to engage in ocean racing of yachts cannot enter events without an EPIRB (an emergency position indicating radio beacon) on board; and in various countries employees are required to contribute to pension funds or superannuation schemes. In none of these cases, it seems to me, is there a loss of integrity or coherence for those who are compelled to conform.

Dworkin's second argument for a link between endorsement and integrity is that there is no good non-question-begging reason to think that people will lead better lives if they are made to choose between options

[35] Ibid., 271.
[36] Cf. Wilkinson, "Against Dworkin's Endorsement Constraint," *Utilitas*, 15 (2003), 175–93, especially 189, who registers a similar complaint.

others have decided would improve their lives. Critical paternalism "assumes an independent, transcendent picture of ethical value, and the challenge model rejects any such picture"[37] on the ground that it misrepresents the complex phenomenology of ethical judgment (which assigns a central constitutive role to reflective or intuitive conviction). It is a premise of this argument that others cannot know better than a competent individual what would be in his best interests (leaving aside interventions that are both temporary and non-invasive). This is a constitutive feature of the model of challenge and it is what is supposed to make critical paternalist attempts at restricting the options from among which individuals may choose (to prevent them making bad choices) self-defeating.

Is it not possible, however, for individuals to be seriously, even fatally, mistaken about the benefits to be had, or the harms to be suffered, as a result of the options they choose, despite others knowing about those benefits and harms? If an individual holds factually false beliefs about, for example, the suitability for consumption by him of a dose of the designer drug GBH (gammahydroxybutyrate),[38] but he endorses its consumption, should he still be permitted untrammeled access to the GBH?

Does Dworkin's model of challenge have anything helpful to say about such matters? Unfortunately, his own examples of how critical paternalism impacts on competent adults are highly contrived and, more significantly, are in a key respect very like Mill's example of contracts for perpetual servitude in that they concern decisions which impact on a life as a whole. One has to do with prohibiting an individual from pursuing his preferred vocation for life and the other with prohibiting expression of sexual orientation. He appears to think that other examples he canvasses can all be excluded from the category of critical paternalism on the ground that they would involve only temporary and non-invasive restrictions on people's behavior and so would prove not to constrict choice in the event that endorsement is never given. By contrast, the everyday examples of paternalism that I have given throughout this chapter have been advanced as examples of strong (or, critical) paternalism. I do not deny that some individuals may willingly embrace the restrictions involved in the examples. But there will also be others for whom being required to conform involves a significant constraint. Dworkin's test for determining whether an instance

---

[37] Ronald Dworkin, *Sovereign Virtue*, 274.
[38] The drug is sometimes known as "liquid ecstasy"; overdoses are common because the dosage needed to get a "high" differs very little from dosages that can cause severe irritability, hallucinations, blackouts, memory loss, seizures, comas, respiratory failures, and deaths.

of paternalism is to be regarded as objectionably critical is whether it involves overriding an individual's convictions rather than his will (and, as has already been indicated, he considers the connection between conviction and value to be constitutive).[39] Given the usual understanding of paternalism (*viz.*, the one that I have been working with in this chapter), this is mere stipulation.

CONCLUSION

Just as Mill sought in his more belligerent moments in chapter 1 of *On Liberty* to champion the sovereignty of the competent individual, Dworkin seeks to champion such an individual's moral integrity. Neither has put forward a decisive case. Mill inconsistently claimed that a competent individual should be prevented from entering into a contract to be a perpetual slave. Dworkin is more resolute in his commitment to individual liberty, but this comes at a cost, namely the cost of holding implausibly that an individual who is subject to critical paternalism is thereby stripped of his integrity (since the only options capable of promoting his well-being are those he endorses). This is so no matter how serious the bad consequences of an individual's actions may be for him, and no matter how mistaken he may be in his beliefs about those consequences, because to compel him to act against his convictions *necessarily* renders him even worse off.

Elsewhere I have argued that once an individual's occurrently autonomous choices (those choices made autonomously but which are in themselves of only incidental significance) are distinguished from his more important dispositionally autonomous choices (those choices made autonomously that have more global significance for his life), strong paternalism may sometimes justifiably be invoked to restrict the exercise of the former to protect future exercise of the latter.[40] My suggestion is that whether the autonomous behavior of a competent individual in a particular instance will seriously undermine his capacity in future to make autonomous choices must be taken into account in deciding the justifiability of a paternalistic intervention. Hence, whether paternalism is justifiable is not an all-or-nothing matter. The onus is always on those, whether individuals or the state, who propose to act paternalistically to shoulder the burden of proof for its being necessary, but, even when that can satisfactorily be done,

---

[39] Ronald Dworkin, *Sovereign Virtue*, 268.
[40] Robert Young, *Personal Autonomy: Beyond Negative and Positive Liberty* (London: Croom Helm, 1986), ch. 6.

paternalism should be subject to strict limits. There is space here only to mention the sorts of consideration relevant to the determination of those limits.[41] They include the following: the seriousness of the harm that will be suffered, or the benefit that will be forgone; how extensive any intervention needs to be; and, whether it is possible to intervene without reducing those who are treated paternalistically to a condition of dependence.

On many issues to do with paternalism there will be no disagreement between what I want to say and what Mill and Ronald Dworkin have said. Thus, for example, I share Mill's opposition to perpetual slavery contracts, and believe that in opposing them he was expressing a point quite like the one I have made. I also endorse Dworkin's views that a competent adult Jehovah's Witness should be allowed to refuse life-saving blood transfusions even though his refusal is tantamount to accepting death, and that a competent individual should be permitted access by law to medically assisted death,[42] because strong paternalistic interference in these matters requires overriding the dispositional autonomy of the individuals concerned (and this in turn explains why it would be unjustified). However, I part company from Mill and Dworkin in believing that the same explanation serves to justify more interventions than they seem willing to countenance (e.g., the enforcement of occupational health and safety requirements despite the objections of employees, and the issuing of orders by lifeguards requiring surfers to leave the surf when there is a shark in the near vicinity, despite protests by the surfers). I think that anyone who values liberty in its more important dispositional guise should do the same.

---

[41] See, e.g., Gerald Dworkin, "Paternalism," 82ff. and Jeffrie Murphy, "Incompetence and Paternalism," *Archiv für Rechts- und Sozialphilosophie*, 60 (1974), 465–86, especially 483ff.

[42] See Ronald Dworkin, *Life's Dominion: An Argument About Abortion, Euthanasia, and Individual Freedom* (New York: Alfred A. Knopf, 1993), chs. 7 and 8.

Bibliography

Appiah, Kwame Anthony. *The Ethics of Identity* (Princeton: Princeton University Press, 2005).

  "Identity, Authenticity, Survival: Multicultural Societies and Social Reproduction," in Amy Gutmann, ed., *Multiculturalism: Examining the Politics of Recognition* (Princeton: Princeton University Press, 1994), 149–67.

Archard, David. *The Ethics of Identity* (Princeton: Princeton University Press, 2005).

  "Freedom Not to Be Free: The Case of the Slavery Contract in J. S. Mill's *On Liberty*," *Philosophical Quarterly*, 40 (1990), 453–65.

Arneson, Richard J. "Joel Feinberg and the Justification of Hard Paternalism," *Legal Theory*, 11 (2005), 259–84.

  "Mill versus Paternalism," *Ethics*, 90 (1980), 470–89.

Baum, Bruce. *Rereading Power and Freedom in J. S. Mill* (Toronto: Toronto University Press, 2000).

Beauchamp, Tom. "Paternalism and Bio-Behavioral Control," *The Monist*, 60 (1976), 62–80.

Benatar, David. *Better Never to Have Been: The Harm of Coming into Existence* (Oxford: Oxford University Press, 2006).

  "Why It is Better Never to Come into Existence," *American Philosophical Quarterly*, 34.3 (1997), 345–55.

  "Why It is Better Never to Come into Existence," in David Benatar, ed., *Life, Death and Meaning* (Lanham, MD: Rowman & Littlefield, 2004), 155–68.

Benn, S. I. *A Theory of Freedom* (Cambridge: Cambridge University Press, 1988).

Bentham, Jeremy. *Constitutional Code*, in *The Works of Jeremy Bentham*, vol. IX, ed. J. Bowring (New York: Russell & Russell, 1962).

  Plan for Parliamentary Reform, in *The Works of Jeremy Bentham*, vol. III, ed. J. Bowring (New York: Russell & Russell, 1962).

Berger, Fred. *Happiness, Justice, and Freedom* (Los Angeles: University of California Press, 1984).

Bird, Colin. *An Introduction to Political Philosophy* (Cambridge: Cambridge University Press, 2006).

Bogen, James, and Farrell, Daniel. "Freedom and Happiness in Mill's Defence of Liberty," *Philosophical Quarterly*, 28 (1978), 325–38.

Boklage, C. "Survival Probability of Human Conceptions from Fertilization to Term," *International Journal of Fertility*, 35 (1990), 75–94.

Bosanquet, Bernard. "The Philosophical Theory of the State," in Bernard Bosanquet, *The Philosophical Theory of the State and Related Essays*, ed. Gerald F. Gaus and William Street (Indianapolis: St. Augustine Press, 2001), 1–293.

Brink, David. "Mill's Moral and Political Philosophy," in Edward N. Zalta, ed., *Stanford Encyclopedia of Philosophy* (2007).

"Millian Principles, Freedom of Expression, and Hate Speech," *Legal Theory*, 7 (2001), 119–57.

Brison, S. J. "The Autonomy Defence of Free Speech," *Ethics*, 108 (1998), 312–39.

Brock, Dan. "Paternalism and Autonomy," *Ethics*, 98 (1988), 550–65.

Brown, D. G. "Mill on Liberty and Morality," *Philosophical Review*, 81 (1972), 133–58.

Buchanan, Allen. "Social Moral Epistemology," *Social Philosophy & Policy*, 19.2 (2002), 126–52.

Buchanan, Allen, *et al.*, *From Chance to Choice* (Cambridge: Cambridge University Press, 2002).

Burley, Justine. "Exactly the Same but Different," *Nature*, 417 (2002), 224–5.

"Morality and the New Genetics," in Justine Burley, ed., *Ronald Dworkin and His Critics* (Oxford: Blackwell, 2002), 170–92.

Burley, Justine, and Harris, John. "Human Cloning and Child Welfare," *Journal of Medical Ethics*, 25 (1999), 108–13.

Callan, Eamonn. "Political Liberalism and Political Education," *Review of Politics*, 58.1 (1996), 5–33.

Caney, Simon. "Consequentialist Defenses of Liberal Neutrality," *The Philosophical Quarterly*, 41 (1991), 457–77.

Clayton, Matthew. "Individual Autonomy and Genetic Choice," in Justine Burley and John Harris, eds., *A Companion to Genethics* (Oxford: Blackwell, 2002), 191–205.

Crisp, Roger. *Mill and Utilitarianism* (London: Routledge & Kegan Paul, 1997).

"Database of Global Policies on Human Cloning and Germ-Line Engineering," available at www.glphr.org/genetic/genetic.htm.

Davis, Gordon, and Neufeld, Blain. "Political Liberalism, Civic Education, and Educational Choice," *Social Theory and Practice*, 33.1 (2007), 47–74.

Devlin, Patrick. *The Enforcement of Morals* (London: Oxford University Press, 1965).

Donner, Wendy. "Is Cultural Membership a Good? Kymlica and Ignatieff on the Virtues and Perils of Belonging," in William Aiken and John Haldane, eds., *Philosophy and Its Public Role: Essays in Ethics, Politics, Society and Culture*, St. Andrews Studies in Philosophy and Public Affairs (Exeter: Imprint Academic, 2004), 84–101.

"John Stuart Mill on Education and Democracy," in Nadia Urbinati and Alex Zakaras, eds., *J. S. Mill's Political Thought: A Bicentennial Re-Assessment* (Cambridge: Cambridge University Press, 2007), 250–76.

"John Stuart Mill's Liberal Feminism," *Philosophical Studies*, 69 (1993), 155–66.

The Liberal Self: John Stuart Mill's Moral and Political Philosophy (Ithaca: Cornell University Press, 1991).

"Mill's Theory of Value," in Henry West, ed., *The Blackwell Guide to Mill's Utilitarianism* (Oxford: Blackwell, 2005), 117–83.

"Mill's Utilitarianism," in John Skorupski, ed., *The Cambridge Companion to Mill* (Cambridge: Cambridge University Press, 1998), 255–92.

Donner, Wendy, and Fumerton, Richard. *Mill* (Oxford: Wiley-Blackwell, 2009).

Dworkin, Gerald. "Is More Choice Better than Less?," in Gerald Dworkin, *The Theory and Practice of Autonomy* (Cambridge and New York: Cambridge University Press, 1988), 62–81.

"Moral Paternalism," *Law and Philosophy*, 24 (2005), 305–19.

"Paternalism," *The Monist*, 56 (1972), 64–84.

Dworkin, Ronald. *Life's Dominion: An Argument about Abortion, Euthanasia, and Individual Freedom* (New York: Alfred A. Knopf, 1993).

"Ronald Dworkin Replies," in Justine Burley, ed., *Dworkin and His Critics* (Oxford: Blackwell, 2004), 362–6.

Sovereign Virtue: The Theory and Practice of Equality (Cambridge, MA: Harvard University Press, 2000).

"*Sovereign Virtue* Revisited," *Ethics*, 113 (2002), 106–43.

Dyzenhaus, David. "John Stuart Mill and the Harm of Pornography," *Ethics*, 102 (1992), 534–51.

Feinberg, Joel. "The Child's Right to an Open Future," in J. Howie, ed., *Ethical Principles and Social Policy* (Carbondale: Southern Illinois University Press, 1983), 97–122.

"Legal Paternalism," *Canadian Journal of Philosophy*, 1 (1971), 105–24.

The Moral Limits of the Criminal Law, 4 vols. (New York: Oxford University Press, 1984–90).

Freeman, Samuel, ed., *The Cambridge Companion to Rawls* (Cambridge: Cambridge University Press, 2003).

Friedman, Marilyn. "Feminism and Modern Friendship: Dislocating the Community," in Shlomo Avineri and Avner de-Shalit, eds., *Communitarianism and Individualism* (Oxford: Oxford University Press, 1992), 101–19.

Fuchs, Alan E. "Autonomy, Slavery, and Mill's Critique of Paternalism," *Ethical Theory and Moral Practice*, 4 (2001), 231–51.

"Mill's Theory of Morally Correct Action," in Henry West, ed., *The Blackwell Guide to Mill's Utilitarianism* (Oxford: Blackwell, 2005), 139–58.

Gaus, Gerald F. *Justificatory Liberalism* (New York: Oxford University Press, 1996).

"Liberal Neutrality: A Radical and Compelling Principle," in George Klosko and Steven Wall, eds., *Perfectionism and Neutrality* (Lanham: Rowman & Littlefield, 2003), 137–65.

Modern Liberal Theory of Man (London: Croom-Helm, 1983).

"The Moral Necessity of Liberal Neutrality," in Thomas Christiano and John Christman, eds., *Contemporary Debates in Political Philosophy* (Oxford: Blackwell, forthcoming).

Political Theory and Political Concepts (Boulder, CO: Westview, 2000).

Social Philosophy (Armonk, NY: M. E. Sharpe, 1999).

George, Robert P. *Making Men Moral: Civil Liberties and Public Morality* (Oxford: Oxford University Press, 1993).

Glover, Jonathan. *Choosing Children* (Oxford: Oxford University Press, 2006).

Gray, John. "John S. Mill, Traditional and Revisionist Interpretations," *Literature of Liberty*, 2 (1979), 7–37.

    Mill's On Liberty: *A Defence* (London: Routledge & Kegan Paul, 1983).

    Two Faces of Liberalism (Cambridge: Polity Press, 2000).

Green, Leslie. "Internal Minorities and Their Rights," in Will Kymlicka, ed., *The Rights of Minority Cultures* (Oxford: Oxford University Press, 1995), 257–72.

Green, T. H. "Lecture on 'Liberal Legislation' and Freedom of Contract," in Paul Harris and John Morrow, eds., *Lectures on the Principles of Political Obligation and Other Writings* (Cambridge: Cambridge University Press, 1986), 194–212.

Gutmann, Amy. "Civic Education and Social Diversity," *Ethics*, 105.3 (1995), 557–79.

Harris, John. "Clones, Genes, and Human Rights," in Justine Burley, ed., *The Genetic Revolution and Human Rights* (New York: Oxford University Press, 1999), 61–94.

    On Cloning (London: Routledge & Kegan Paul, 2004).

    "Procreative Beneficence: Why We Should Select the Best Children," *Bioethics*, 15 (2001), 413–26.

Harris, John, and Savulescu, Julian. "The Creation Lottery: Final Lessons from Natural Reproduction: Why Those Who Accept Natural Reproduction Should Accept Cloning and Other Frankenstein Reproductive Technologies," *Cambridge Quarterly of Healthcare Ethics*, 13 (2004), 90–5.

Hart, H. L. A. *Law, Liberty and Morality* (Oxford: Oxford University Press; Stanford: Stanford University Press, 1963).

Hodson, John D. "The Principle of Paternalism," *American Philosophical Quarterly*, 14 (1977), 61–9.

Hoffman, Eva. *The Secret* (London: Secker & Warburg, 2001).

Holm, Søren. "A Life in the Shadow: One Reason Why We Should Not Clone Humans," *Cambridge Quarterly of Healthcare Ethics*, 7.2 (1998), 160–2.

Hurka, Thomas. "Indirect Perfectionism: Kymlicka on Liberal Neutrality," *Journal of Political Philosophy*, 3 (1995), 36–57.

Husak, Douglas N. "Legal Paternalism," in Hugh LaFollette, ed., *The Oxford Handbook of Practical Ethics* (New York: Oxford University Press, 2003), 387–412.

Jacobsen, Daniel. "Mill on Liberty, Speech, and the Free Society," *Philosophy & Public Affairs*, 29 (2000), 276–309.

Jaenisch, Rudolf. "Human Cloning – The Science and Ethics of Nuclear Transplantation," *New England Journal of Medicine*, 351.27 (2004), 2787–91.

Javitt, Gail H., Suthers, Kristen, and Hudson, Kathy. "Cloning: A Policy Analysis," Genetics and Public Policy Center (rev. June 2006), available at www.DNApolicy.org.

Kass, Leon. "The Wisdom of Repugnance," *The New Republic*, June 2, 1997, 17–26.

Kleinig, John. *Paternalism* (Totowa, NJ: Rowman & Allanheld, 1984).

Kubler-Ross, Elisabeth. *The Wheel of Life: A Memoir of Living and Dying* (New York: Scribner, 1997).

Kymlicka, Will. *Contemporary Political Philosophy: An Introduction* (Oxford: Oxford University Press, 1990; 2nd edn. 2002).

"Liberal Individualism and Liberal Neutrality," *Ethics*, 99.3 (1989), 833–905.

Liberalism, Community, and Culture (Oxford: Clarendon Press, 1989).

Multicultural Citizenship: A Liberal Theory of Minority Rights (Oxford: Clarendon Press, 1995).

Politics in the Vernacular: Nationalism, Multiculturalism, and Citizenship (Oxford: Oxford University Press, 2001).

Larmore, Charles. *Patterns of Moral Complexity* (Cambridge: Cambridge University Press, 1987).

"Political Liberalism," in Charles Larmore, *The Morals of Modernity* (Cambridge: Cambridge University Press, 1996), 121–51.

Leridon, H. *Human Fertility: The Basic Components* (Chicago: Chicago University Press, 1977).

Locke, John. *Second Treatise of Government* (1690), ed. C. B. Macpherson (Indianapolis: Hackett Publishing, 1980).

Lyons, David. "Liberty and Harm to Others," reprinted in Lyons, *Rights, Welfare, and Mill's Moral Theory* (New York: Oxford University Press, 1994), 89–108.

Macedo, Stephen. *Diversity and Distrust: Civic Education in a Multicultural Democracy* (Cambridge, MA: Harvard University Press, 2000).

MacIntyre, Alasdair. *After Virtue* (Notre Dame: University of Notre Dame Press, 1981).

Macleod, Colin. "Agency, Goodness, and Endorsement: Why We Can't Be Forced to Flourish," *Imprints*, 7 (2003), 131–60.

McLuhan, Marshall. *Understanding Media: The Extensions of Man*, ed. L. H. Lapham (Cambridge, MA: MIT Press, 1994).

Malm, Heidi. "Feinberg's Anti-paternalism and the Balancing Strategy," *Legal Theory*, 11 (2005), 193–212.

Mill, James. "Essay on Government" (1824), in Jack Lively and John Rees, eds., *Utilitarian Logic and Politics* (Oxford: Clarendon Press, 1978), 53–95.

Mill, John Stuart, *Auguste Comte and Positivism* (1865), in *The Collected Works of John Stuart Mill*, gen. ed. John M. Robson, vol. x: *Essays on Ethics, Religion and Society* (Toronto: University of Toronto Press; London: Routledge & Kegan Paul, 1969), 261–368.

Autobiography (1873), in *The Collected Works of John Stuart Mill*, vol. i: *Autobiography and Literary Essays*, ed. John M. Robson and Jack Stillinger, introduction by Lord Robbins (Toronto: University of Toronto Press; London: Routledge & Kegan Paul, 1981), 1–290.

The Collected Works of John Stuart Mill, 33 vols., gen. ed. John M. Robson (Toronto: University of Toronto Press; London: Routledge & Kegan Paul, 1963–91).

Considerations on Representative Government (1861), in *The Collected Works of John Stuart Mill*, vol. xix: *Essays on Politics and Society*, Part II, ed. John M.

Robson, introduction by Alexander Brady (Toronto: University of Toronto Press; London: Routledge & Kegan Paul, 1977), 371–577.

The Later Letters of John Stuart Mill (1849–1873), vols. XIV–XVII of *The Collected Works of John Stuart Mill,* ed. Francis E. Mineka and Dwight N. Lindley (Toronto: University of Toronto Press; London: Routledge & Kegan Paul, 1972).

Nature (1874), in *The Collected Works of John Stuart Mill,* vol. X: *Essays on Ethics, Religion, and Society,* ed. John M. Robson, introduction by F. E. L. Priestley (Toronto: University of Toronto Press; London: Routledge & Kegan Paul, 1985), 373–402.

On Liberty (1859), in *The Collected Works of John Stuart Mill,* vol. XVIII: *Essays on Politics and Society,* Part I, ed. John M. Robson, introduction by Alexander Brady (Toronto: University of Toronto Press; London: Routledge & Kegan Paul, 1977), 213–310.

Principles of Political Economy with Some of Their Applications to Social Philosophy, Part II (1848), vol. III of *The Collected Works of John Stuart Mill,* ed. John M. Robson, introduction by V. W. Bladen (Toronto: University of Toronto Press; London: Routledge & Kegan Paul, 1965).

"Sedgwick's Discourse" (1835), in *The Collected Works of John Stuart Mill,* vol. X: *Essays on Ethics, Religion and Society,* ed. John M. Robson (Toronto: University of Toronto Press; London: Routledge & Kegan Paul, 1969), 31–74.

The Subjection of Women (1869), in *The Collected Works of John Stuart Mill,* vol. XXI: *Essays on Equality, Law, and Education,* ed. John M. Robson, introduction by Stefan Collini (Toronto: University of Toronto Press; London: Routledge & Kegan Paul, 1984), 259–340.

A System of Logic Ratiocinative and Inductive (1843; 8th edn. 1871), vols. VII–VIII of *The Collected Works of John Stuart Mill,* ed. John M. Robson, introduction by R. F. McRae (Toronto: University of Toronto Press; London: Routledge & Kegan Paul, 1973).

Utilitarianism (1861), in *The Collected Works of John Stuart Mill,* vol. X: *Essays on Ethics, Religion and Society,* ed. John M. Robson (Toronto: University of Toronto Press; London: Routledge & Kegan Paul, 1969), 203–59.

"Theism" (1874), in *The Collected Works of John Stuart Mill,* vol. X: *Essays on Ethics, Religion and Society,* ed. John M. Robson (Toronto: University of Toronto Press; London: Routledge & Kegan Paul, 1969), 429–89.

Murphy, Jeffrie. "Incompetence and Paternalism," *Archiv für Rechts- und Sozialphilosophie,* 60 (1974), 465–86.

Nagel, Thomas. "Rawls and Liberalism," in Samuel Freeman, ed., *The Cambridge Companion to Rawls* (Cambridge: Cambridge University Press, 2003), 62–85.

Narveson, Jan. *The Libertarian Idea* (Calgary: Broadview Press, 2001).

Nozick, Robert. *Anarchy, State, and Utopia* (New York: Basic Books, 1974).

Nussbaum, Martha C. *Hiding from Humanity: Disgust, Shame, and the Law* (Princeton: Princeton University Press, 2004).

"Little C," in Martha C. Nussbaum and C. R. Sunstein, eds., *Clones and Clones: Facts and Fantasies about Human Cloning* (New York: Norton, 1998), 338–46.

Okin, Susan Moller. *Justice, Gender, and the Family* (New York: Basic Books, 1989).

   Is Multiculturalism Bad for Women? (Princeton: Princeton University Press, 1999).

   "Whose Traditions? Which Understandings?," in Susan Moller Okin, *Justice, Gender, and the Family* (New York: Basic Books, 1989), 41–73.

O'Neill, Onora. *Autonomy and Trust in Bioethics* (Cambridge: Cambridge University Press, 2002).

O'Rourke, K. C. *John Stuart Mill and Freedom of Expression: The Genesis of a Theory* (London: Routledge, 2001).

Peffer, Rodney. *Marxism, Morality, and Social Justice* (Princeton: Princeton University Press, 1989).

Pendlebury, Michael. "In Defense of Moderate Neutralism," *Journal of Social Philosophy*, 33.3 (2002), 360–76.

Pettit, Philip. *Republicanism: A Theory of Freedom and Government* (Oxford: Clarendon Press, 1997).

   A Theory of Freedom: From the Psychology to the Politics of Agency (Oxford: Oxford University Press, 2001).

Pogge, Thomas. *John Rawls: His Life and Theory of Justice* (New York: Oxford University Press, 2007).

Rawls, John. *Collected Papers*, ed. Samuel Freeman (Cambridge, MA: Harvard University Press, 1999).

   "The Domain of the Political and Overlapping Consensus," in *Collected Papers*, ed. Samuel Freeman (Cambridge, MA: Harvard University Press, 1999), 473–96.

   "The Idea of Public Reason Revisited," in *Collected Papers*, ed. Samuel Freeman (Cambridge, MA: Harvard University Press, 1999), 573–615.

   Justice as Fairness, ed. Erin Kelly (Cambridge, MA: Harvard University Press, 2001).

   Political Liberalism (New York: Columbia University Press, 1993).

   A Theory of Justice (Cambridge MA: Harvard University Press, 1971; rev. edn. 1999).

Raz, Joseph. *The Morality of Freedom* (Oxford: Clarendon Press, 1986).

Riley, Jonathan. "Introduction" to John Stuart Mill, *Principles of Political Economy, and Chapters on Socialism* (Oxford: Oxford University Press, 1998), vii–xlvii.

   Liberal Utilitarianism (Cambridge: Cambridge University Press, 1988).

   Mill on Liberty (London: Routledge, 1998).

   "Mill: *On Liberty*," in J. Shand, ed., *Central Works of Philosophy* (Chesham: Acumen, 2005), vol. III, 127–57.

   "Mill's Doctrine of Freedom of Expression," *Utilitas*, 17 (2005), 147–79.

   "Mill's Neo-Athenian Model of Liberal Democracy," in N. Urbinati, and A. Zakaras, eds., *J. S. Mill's Political Thought: A Bicentennial Reassessment* (New York: Cambridge University Press, 2007).

   Mill's Radical Liberalism (London: Routledge, forthcoming).

   "Utilitarian Liberalism: Between Gray and Mill," *Critical Review of International Social and Political Philosophy*, 9 (2006), 117–35.

Robertson, John. *Children of Choice: Freedom and the Reproductive Technologies* (Princeton: Princeton University Press, 1994).

Rosenblum, Nancy L. *Another Liberalism: Romanticism and the Reconstruction of Liberal Thought* (Cambridge: Cambridge University Press, 1987).

Rousseau, Jean-Jacques. "The Social Contract" (1762), in *The Basic Political Writings*, tr. Donald A. Cress (Indianapolis: Hackett Publishing, 1987), 139–227.

Rudisill, John Patrick. "The Neutrality of the State and its Justification in Rawls and Mill," *Auslegung*, 23 (2000), 153–68.

Sartorius, Rolf E. *Individual Contact and Social Norms* (Encina and Belmont, CA: Dickenson, 1975).

Scanlon, T. M. "A Theory of Freedom of Expression," *Philosophy & Public Affairs*, 1 (1972), 204–26.

Schwartz, Pedro. *The New Political Economy of J. S. Mill* (London: Weidenfeld & Nicholson, 1972).

Scoccia, Danny. "Paternalism and Respect for Autonomy," *Ethics*, 100 (1990), 318–34.

Sen, Amartya. "Two Confusions, and Counting," *The Globe and Mail*, August 23, 2006,

Sher, George. *Beyond Neutrality: Perfectionism and Politics* (Cambridge: Cambridge University Press, 1997).

Shiffrin, Seana Valentine. "Paternalism, Unconscionability Doctrine, and Accommodation," *Philosophy & Public Affairs*, 29 (2000), 205–50.

"Wrongful Life, Procreative Responsibility, and the Significance of Harm," *Legal Theory*, 5 (1999), 117–48.

Skinner, Quentin. "The Idea of Negative Liberty," in Richard Rorty, J. B. Schneewind, and Quentin Skinner, eds., *Philosophy of History: Essays on the Historiography of Philosophy* (Cambridge: Cambridge University Press, 1984), 193–221.

Liberty Before Liberalism (Cambridge: Cambridge University Press, 1998).

"The Paradoxes of Political Liberty," in David Miller, ed., *Liberty* (Oxford: Oxford University Press, 1991), 183–205.

Skorupski, John, *Why Read Mill Today?* (London: Routledge, 2006).

Solan, Lawrence M. "Private Language, Public Laws: The Central Role of Legislative Intent in Statutory Interpretation," *Georgetown Law Journal*, 93.2 (2005), 427–85.

Steiner, Hillel. *An Essay on Rights* (Oxford: Blackwell, 1994).

Stephen, James Fitzjames. *Liberty, Equality, Fraternity* (1874), ed. R. J. White (Cambridge: Cambridge University Press, 1967).

Strum, P. *When the Nazis Came to Skokie: Freedom for Speech We Hate* (Lawrence: University Press of Kansas, 1999).

Sumner, L. W. *The Hateful and the Obscene: Studies in the Limits of Free Expression* (Toronto: University of Toronto Press, 2004).

Taylor, Charles. "Atomism," in Shlomo Avineri and Avner de-Shalit, eds., *Communitarianism and Individualism* (Oxford: Oxford University Press, 1992), 29–50.

The Ethics of Authenticity (Cambridge, MA: Harvard University Press, 1991).

"The Politics of Recognition," in Amy Gutmann, ed., *Multiculturalism: Examining the Politics of Recognition* (Princeton: Princeton University Press, 1994), 25–73.

Taylor, Robert. S. "Rawls's Defense of the Priority of Liberty: A Kantian Reconstruction," *Philosophy & Public Affairs*, 31.3 (2003), 246–71.

Ten, C. L. *Mill on Liberty* (Oxford: Clarendon Press, 1980).

    Was Mill a Liberal? (Singapore: Marshall Cavendish Academic, 2004).

Thoreau, Henry David. "Walden; or, Life in the Woods" (1854), in Robert F. Sayre, ed., *A Week on the Concord and Merrimack Rivers; Walden, or, Life in the Woods; The Maine Woods; Cape Cod* (New York: Library of America, 1985), 321–587.

Urbinati, Nadia. *Mill on Democracy: From the Athenian Polis to Representative Government* (Chicago: University of Chicago Press, 2002).

Urbinati, Nadia, and Zakaras, Alex. *J. S. Mill's Political Thought: A Bicentennial Reassessment* (Cambridge: Cambridge University Press, 2007).

Viroli, Maurizio. *Republicanism*, tr. Antony Shugaar (New York: Hill & Wang, 2002).

Waldron, Jeremy. "Cultural Responsibility and Civic Responsibility," in Will Kymlicka and Wayne Norman, eds., *Citizenship in Diverse Societies* (Oxford: Oxford University Press, 2000), 155–74.

    "Legislation and Moral Neutrality," in Jeremy Waldron, *Liberal Rights* (Cambridge: Cambridge University Press, 1993), 149–67.

    "Mill on the Contagious Diseases Acts," in Nadia Urbinati and Alex Zakaras, eds., *J. S. Mill's Political Thought: A Bicentennial Reassessment* (Cambridge: Cambridge University Press, 2007), 11–42.

    "One Law for All: The Logic of Cultural Accommodation," *Washington and Lee Law Review*, 59 (2003), 3–34.

Walzer, Michael. "Mill's 'A Few Words on Non-Intervention' – A Commentary," in Nadia Urbinati and Alex Zakaras, eds., *J. S. Mill's Political Thought: A Bicentennial Reassessment* (Cambridge: Cambridge University Press, 2007), 347–56.

West, Henry, ed. *The Blackwell Guide to Mill's Utilitarianism* (Oxford: Blackwell, 2005).

Wilkinson, T. M. "Against Dworkin's Endorsement Constraint," *Utilitas*, 15 (2003), 175–93.

    "Dworkin on Paternalism and Well-Being," *Oxford Journal of Legal Studies*, 16 (1996), 433–44.

Wilmut, Ian. "The Age of Biological Control," in Justine Burley, ed., *The Genetic Revolution and Human Rights* (Oxford: Oxford University Press, 1999), 19–28.

Wilson, Woodrow. *Message to Congress*, 63rd Congress, 2nd Session, Senate Doc. No. 566 (Washington, 1914).

Wolff, Robert Paul. *The Poverty of Liberalism* (Boston: Beacon Press, 1968).

Young, Robert. "Autonomy and Paternalism," in Steven C. Patten, ed., *New Essays in Ethics and Public Policy, Canadian Journal of Philosophy*, sup. vol. 8 (1982), 47–66.

    Personal Autonomy: Beyond Negative and Positive Liberty (London: Croom-Helm, 1986).

Index